Microsoft Windows PowerShell Step by Step

Ed Wilson

PUBLISHED BY
Microsoft Press
A Division of Microsoft Corporation
One Microsoft Way
Redmond, Washington 98052-6399

Copyright © 2007 by Ed Wilson

All rights reserved. No part of the contents of this book may be reproduced or transmitted in any form or by any means without the written permission of the publisher.

Library of Congress Control Number: 2007924649

Printed and bound in the United States of America.

1 2 3 4 5 6 7 8 9   QWT   2 1 0 9 8 7

Distributed in Canada by H.B. Fenn and Company Ltd.

A CIP catalogue record for this book is available from the British Library.

Microsoft Press books are available through booksellers and distributors worldwide. For further information about international editions, contact your local Microsoft Corporation office or contact Microsoft Press International directly at fax (425) 936-7329. Visit our Web site at www.microsoft.com/mspress. Send comments to mspinput@microsoft.com.

Microsoft, Microsoft Press, Active Accessibility, Active Desktop, Active Directory, ActiveMovie, ActiveStore, ActiveSync, ActiveX, Age of Mythology, Authenticode, BackOffice, BizTalk, ClearType, DataTips, Developer Studio, Direct3D, DirectAnimation, DirectDraw, DirectInput, DirectMusic, DirectPlay, DirectShow, DirectSound, DirectX, Excel, FrontPage, IntelliMouse, IntelliSense, Internet Explorer, J/Direct, Jscript, Liquid Motion, MSDN, MS-DOS, Outlook, PivotChart, PivotTable, PowerPoint, Rushmore, SQL Server, Visual Basic, Visual C++, Visual FoxPro, Visual InterDev, Visual J++, Visual SourceSafe, Visual Studio, Win32, Win32s, Windows, Windows NT, Windows PowerShell, Windows Server, and Windows Vista are either registered trademarks or trademarks of Microsoft Corporation in the United States and/or other countries. Other product and company names mentioned herein may be the trademarks of their respective owners.

The example companies, organizations, products, domain names, e-mail addresses, logos, people, places, and events depicted herein are fictitious. No association with any real company, organization, product, domain name, e-mail address, logo, person, place, or event is intended or should be inferred.

This book expresses the author's views and opinions. The information contained in this book is provided without any express, statutory, or implied warranties. Neither the authors, Microsoft Corporation, nor its resellers, or distributors will be held liable for any damages caused or alleged to be caused either directly or indirectly by this book.

Acquisitions Editor: Martin DelRe
Developmental and Project Editor: Maureen Zimmerman
Editorial Production: P.M. Gordon Associates
Technical Reviewer: Bob Hogan; technical review services provided by Content Master, a member of CM Group, Ltd.

Body Part No. X13-68391

To Teresa: my friend, my helper, and my muse.

Contents at a Glance

Table of Contents

What do you think of this book? We want to hear from you!

Microsoft is interested in hearing your feedback so we can continually improve our books and learning resources for you. To participate in a brief online survey, please visit:

www.microsoft.com/learning/booksurvey/

Acknowledgments

Books of this length, or for that matter, even very short books, do not happen automatically—nor do they arrive in a vacuum. If the book being contemplated is about software that is not even released . . . dude, you are going to need some help. One of the cool things about writing more than a dozen books is that, through the years, I have developed a stable of friends (nice for a guy named Mr. Ed), loved ones, technical mentors, and coworkers who have all taken an interest in the writing process and have wanted to help out.

The number-one person . . . well, actually, there are several number-one persons that need thanking. The one I had *better* thank first is my wife, Teresa. This poor girl, an accountant by training, has become the de facto scripting expert in her company. Why, you may ask? Other than the fact that she is married to me and sees me walking around aimlessly from time to time, she has had the privilege of reading four books on scripting—not once, but many times. What about this book on Windows PowerShell? Well, she has read it at least three times. Of course, I would not dare say that if you find problems, it is her fault! No way!

There are several other number one-persons I need to thank. My agent, Claudette Moore of the Moore Literary Agency, for instance, needs thanking. If not for her efforts, my book never would have been published by Microsoft Press. She is also a good person to talk to when I need encouragement.

Another number-one person to thank is Martin DelRe, my acquisitions editor at MSPress. This guy is awesome! I love talking to him. He is such a believer in the power and message of scripting that he has devoted a sizable portion of his titles to scripting. It is very rare to deal with an acquisitions editor who is as knowledgeable about scripting, networking, and the like as is Martin. The best compliment I have ever received from an editor came from him. He said, "Your book looks good. I think I will take it home and read it this weekend." My best friend didn't even say that!

The other number-one person I need to think is Maureen Zimmerman. She worked so hard to keep the book on track, and I was in 14 different countries last year while writing the book. There were time zone issues, VPN issues, language barriers—language barriers, did I say? Yes. Not between me and Maureen, but between me and the keyboard in the concierge lounge in Vienna, or Munich, or London, or Sydney, or this place. . . . Do you know how hard it is to find the @ key while trying to use American input on a German keyboard? I ended up opening Notepad and typing every key on the silly thing until I found it . . . then I cut and pasted it. Hey, better than getting locked out of your e-mail.

This book had some awesome assistance from other people as well. First among them is Jit Banerjie, a consultant for Microsoft in Australia. Technically, I am his mentor. But I always learn more when talking to him than I think he ever learns from me. Whenever I would get stuck trying to figure out something in Windows PowerShell, I would type a quick e-mail to him . . . "Hey Jit! Help! I need to figure out how to do. . . . " Sometimes it worked. Other times, well, he is on the other side of the world from me most of the time . . . unless I happen to be in Canberra, then I just show up at his door step looking hungry (his wife is a great cook).

Then there is the PowerShell Community Extension project. One of the awesome things that the Microsoft Windows PowerShell team did was to make PowerShell extensible. There is a guy named Keith Hill who is working with this project. He gave me permission (along with some of his other cohorts) to include the PSCX version 2.0 on the CD with this book. This is *awesome!* Interestingly enough, one of my other tech reviewers (on my first VBScript book) was Alex Angelopoulos, and wouldn't you know it, he is working with the PSCX guys on extending Windows PowerShell. This is very cool. Then there were Oisin Grehan, Matt Hamilton, jachymko, Reinhard Lehrbaum, and Mark Maier, all of whom worked on this project, and without their permission, I would not have been able to include PSCX on the CD. If you ever see one of them, say thanks.

Bill Mell, MCSE, and Terry Lawson, MCSE, reviewed the labs for the book. They have been working with me since my book on Netmon many years ago.

I need to thank Dr. Tobias Weltner for allowing me to include the free version of his PowerShell IDE in my book. Every time I go to Germany, someone in one of my classes will ask me: "Do you know Dr. Weltner?" Now I can say, "Sure, he let me use his PowerShell IDE in my book!"

Then there is Ivan Giugni, the product manager for Power Gadgets. He was good enough to make sure I got the latest build of Power Gadgets for the book. Do you want to produce some impressive-looking output from Windows PowerShell? You need to use Power Gadgets. The scripting guys love Power Gadgets. The Windows PowerShell team love Power Gadgets—because they are cool.

I also need to thank Alexander Riedel from Sapien for allowing me to include a demo version of Primal Script 4.1 with my book. Primal Script has always been an awesome script editor, and now with support for Windows PowerShell, it is even better.

I need to thank the Microsoft Scripting Guys: Greg Stemp, Dean Tsaltas, and Peter Costantini for allowing me to include their VBScript to Windows PowerShell conversion guide as Appendix C. This is an awesome document and represents hundreds of hours of work. I included it in my book because I wanted to always have it close by. Okay, you are looking at me strangely. You mean you don't always carry a copy of a scripting book around with you? Hmmmmm.

One other person I need to thank is Ben Pearce, who is a supportability engineer for Microsoft in the United Kingdom. He created the Cheat Sheet V1.0, which I have included in the supplemental resources folder on the CD. This is a beautiful cheat sheet, which I have printed out, laminated, and posted next to my computer in my office at home. I think you will like it as well.

About This Book

The launching of Microsoft Windows PowerShell marks a significant event in the world of Windows scripting. No longer must network administrators contend with the legacy of arcane commands "simply because they were in Visual Basic"; rather, they can leverage the power of the Microsoft .NET Framework in a clean and organized fashion.

As the author of three books on Windows scripting and as a consultant for Microsoft, I am in constant contact with people who have been using VBScript to manage their environments. I am often asked, "Is there an easier way to do this?" Until now, the answer has been, "Unfortunately, no." That has all changed!

With the release of Microsoft Exchange Server 2007, there is a new scripting language on the market—Windows PowerShell. This book seeks to unravel the mysteries of and misconceptions about this powerful and elegant scripting language.

Windows PowerShell is being released with Microsoft Exchange Server 2007. It is also a release to the Web product and can be downloaded and installed on Windows Server 2003 SP1, Windows XP SP2, and Windows Vista. Many Microsoft customers currently running those versions of the operating system will consider installing Windows PowerShell because of its ease of use.

The Microsoft Exchange Server 2007 administrator tools are built on Windows PowerShell, so Exchange administrators will be among the first to explore and use PowerShell, but other network administrators can certainly also benefit from PowerShell.

Accessing Security objects, working with the registry, and leveraging the power of the .NET Framework all have been either difficult or impossible to do from a VBScript. Windows PowerShell makes these tasks much simpler.

A Practical Approach to Scripting

Microsoft Windows PowerShell Step by Step equips readers with the tools to automate setup, deployment, and management of Windows machines. In addition, it provides readers with an understanding of commandlets (or, in this guide, *cmdlets*). This should lead readers into an awareness of the basics of programming through modeling of fundamental techniques.

The approach I take to teaching readers how to use Windows PowerShell to automate their Windows servers and workstations is similar to the approach I used in my previous three VBScript books. The reader will learn by using the language. In addition, concepts are presented—not in a dry, academic fashion, but in a dynamic and living manner. When a concept is needed to accomplish something, then it is presented. If a topic is not useful for automating network management, then it is not brought forward.

Is This Book for Me?

Microsoft Windows PowerShell Step by Step is aimed at several audiences, including the following:

- **Windows networking consultants** Anyone desiring to standardize and automate the installation and configuration of networking components

- **Windows network administrators** Anyone desiring to automate the day-to-day management of Windows networks

- **Windows Help Desk staff** Anyone desiring to verify configuration of remotely connected desktops

- **Microsoft Certified Systems Engineers (MCSEs) and Microsoft Certified Trainers (MCTs)** Although not a strategic core competency within the Microsoft Certified Professional (MCP) program, several questions about Windows PowerShell are on the Exchange 2007 exams.

- **General technical staff** Anyone desiring to collect information; configure settings on Windows Server 2003 SP1, Windows XP SP2, or Windows Vista; or implement management by scripting

- **Power users** Anyone wishing to obtain maximum power and configurability of Windows Server 2003 SP1, Windows XP SP2, or Windows Vista either at home or in an unmanaged desktop workplace environment

Outline of This Book

This book is divided into nine chapters, each covering a major facet of Windows PowerShell. The following sections describe these parts:

Chapter 1, "Overview of Windows PowerShell" Okay, so you've decided you need to learn Windows PowerShell—but where do you begin? Start here in Chapter 1! In this chapter, I talk about the difference between Windows PowerShell and the VBScript. There are actually times when you will use both in the same script.

Chapter 2, "Using Windows PowerShell Cmdlets" This chapter presents an overview of some of the more useful cmdlets included with the basic installation of Windows PowerShell.

Chapter 3, "Leveraging PowerShell Providers" Windows PowerShell provides a consistent way to access information external to the shell environment. To do this, it uses providers. This chapter shows how to leverage the PowerShell providers.

Chapter 4, "Using PowerShell Scripts" The ability to perform so many actions from inside Windows PowerShell in an interactive fashion may have some thinking there is no need to write scripts. For many network administrators, one-line PowerShell commands will indeed solve many routine problems. These commands can become extremely powerful when they are combined into batch files and perhaps called from a login script. However, there are some very good reasons to write Windows PowerShell scripts. We examine them as we move into this chapter.

Chapter 5, "Using WMI"   Windows Management Instrumentation (WMI) is foundational management technology in the Windows world. To use WMI in Windows PowerShell, you need a good understanding of WMI.

Chapter 6, "Querying WMI"   Nearly everything you want to do with WMI begins with a query. In this chapter, we look at some of the different ways to query WMI and work with the classes to produce useful management scripts.

Chapter 7, "Working with Active Directory"   Network management in the Windows world begins and ends with Active Directory. In this chapter, we look at some of the different ways to work with Active Directory.

Chapter 8, "Leveraging the Power of ADO"   ActiveX Data Objects (ADO) is the pervasive data access strategy used in the Windows world. In this chapter, we look at using ADO to query Active Directory.

Chapter 9, "Managing Exchange 2007"   In Exchange 2007, everything that can done using the Graphical User Interface can also be done using PowerShell. This is because the Exchange 2007 admin tool is built using PowerShell. In this chapter, we look at how we can leverage PowerShell to simplify user management, Exchange configuration, and administration and as a tool for troubleshooting some of the common issues confronting the enterprise Exchange administrator.

The appendices in this book are not the normal "never read" stuff—indeed, you will find yourself referring again and again to these three crucial documents. Appendix A provides a listing of the cmdlets installed with Windows PowerShell that you can refer to when you find yourself stuck for ideas. Appendix B shows you the relationship between the cmdlet naming convention and the commands. For example, did you know there are four *Add* commands? This kind of linkage can greatly speed the learning process. Appendix C helps you make the transition from VBScript to Windows PowerShell. The Microsoft Scripting Guys—Greg Stemp, Dean Tsaltas, and Peter Costantini—gave me permission to print this here. It represents hundreds of hours of work in finding "new ways" to do "old things." I wanted to put this in my book for a selfish reason: I used it nearly every day, so I wanted to make sure it was close by.

- Appendix A, "Cmdlets Installed with Windows PowerShell"
- Appendix B, "Cmdlet Naming"
- Appendix C, "Translating VBScript to Windows PowerShell"

Finding Your Best Starting Point

This book will help you add essential skills for using Windows PowerShell to automate your Windows environment. You can use this book if you are new to scripting, new to programming, or switching from another scripting language. The following table will assist you in picking the best starting point in the book.

If You Are	Follow These Steps
New to programming	Install the practice files as described in the section "Installing the Scripts on Your Computer" later in this introduction.
	Learn the basic skills for using Windows PowerShell by working through Chapters 1 to 4 in order.
New to Windows PowerShell	Install the practice files as described in the section "Installing the Scripts on Your Computer" later in this introduction.
	Skim through Chapter 1, making sure you pay attention to the section on creating objects.
	Skim Chapters 2 and 3.
	Complete Chapters 4 to 6 in order.
Experienced with Windows Power-Shell but interested in using WMI	Install the practice files as described in the section "Installing the Scripts on Your Computer" later in this introduction.
	Read Chapter 4, paying attention to the *Get-WMIObject* cmdlet.
	Work through Chapters 5 and 6.

About the Companion CD

The CD accompanying this book contains additional information and software components, including the following files:

- **Scripts**   The scripts folder contains starter scripts, same-text files, and completed solutions for each of the 40 procedures. It also contains the 18 step-by-step exercises included in this book as well as all the one-line commands illustrated in each chapter. For instance, in Chapter 1, we talk about launching Notepad and obtaining information about the newly created process. All the commands covering that topic are found in the text file \My Documents\Microsoft Press\PowerShellSBS\Scripts\Ch01\ ConfirmingExecutionOfCommandlets.txt.

- **eBook**   You can view an electronic version of this book using Adobe Acrobat Reader. For more information, see the Readme.txt file included in the root folder of the Companion CD.

- **Tools**   On the CD are Scriptomatic files, including Tweakomatic and EzADScriptomatic; selected WMI tools, including WMI Code Creator; and information about Microsoft Windows Script Technologies. You can link to an evaluation copy of Primal Script, a fully functional copy of PowerShell IDE, an evaluation copy of Power Gadgets, and a fully functional copy of the Windows PowerShell communition extensions project.

- **Supplemental Material**   In the supplemental folder, you can find several Excel spreadsheets that detail information about the various WMI providers and performing privileged operations in WMI scripts. There is also an Excel spreadsheet that lists all the Exchange 2007 cmdlets. As an added bonus, there is a Windows Powershell cheat sheet that outlines syntax for some common commands.

Installing the Scripts on Your Computer

Follow these steps to install the scripts on your computer so that you can use them with the procedures and exercises in the book.

1. Remove the companion CD from the package inside this book and insert it into your CD-ROM drive.

2. Review the end user license agreement. If you accept the terms, select Accept and then click Next.

3. Click Scripts.

4. Follow the instructions that appear.

Uninstalling the Scripts

Follow these instructions to remove the practice files from your computer.

1. In Control Panel, open Add Or Remove Programs.

2. From the list of Currently Installed Programs, select Microsoft Windows PowerShell Step by Step.

3. Click Remove.

4. Follow the instructions that appear to remove the scripts.

System Requirements

- Minimum 233 MHz in the Intel Pentium/Celeron family or the AMD k6/Atholon/Duron family

- 64 MB memory

- 1.5 GB available hard disk space

- Display monitor capable of 800 × 600 resolution or higher

- CD-ROM drive or DVD drive

- Microsoft Mouse or compatible pointing device

- Windows Server 2003 SP1, Windows XP SP2, or Windows Vista

- Microsoft .NET Framework 2.0

- Microsoft Office Excel or Excel Viewer

Technical Support

Every effort has been made to ensure the accuracy of this book and the contents of the companion CD-ROM. Microsoft Press provides corrections for books through the World Wide Web at *http://www.microsoft.com/learning/support/default.mspx.*

To connect directly with the Microsoft Press Knowledge Base and enter a query regarding a question or an issue that you might have, go to *http://www.microsoft.com/mspress/support/search.aspx.*

If you have comments, questions, or ideas regarding this book or the companion CD-ROM, please send them to Microsoft Press using either of the following methods:

E-mail:

mspinput@microsoft.com

Postal Mail:

Microsoft Press
Attn: Editor, *Microsoft Windows PowerShell Step by Step*
One Microsoft Way
Redmond, WA 98052

Please note that product support is not offered through the preceding addresses.

Chapter 1
Overview of Windows PowerShell

After completing this chapter, you will be able to:

■ Understand basic use and capabilities of Microsoft Windows PowerShell

■ Install Windows PowerShell

■ Use basic command-line utilities inside Windows PowerShell

■ Use Windows PowerShell help

■ Run basic Windows PowerShell cmdlets

■ Get help on basic Windows PowerShell cmdlets

■ Configure Windows PowerShell to run scripts

The release of Windows PowerShell marks a significant advance for the Windows network administrator. Combining the power of a full-fledged scripting language, with access to command-line utilities, Windows Management Instrumentation (WMI), and even VBScript, PowerShell provides both the power and ease of use that have been missing from the Windows platform since the beginning of time. All the scripts mentioned in this chapter can be found in the corresponding scripts folder on the CD.

Understanding Windows PowerShell

Perhaps the biggest obstacle for a Windows network administrator in migrating to Windows PowerShell is understanding what the PowerShell actually is. In some respects, it is like a replacement for the venerable CMD (command) shell. As shown here, after the Windows PowerShell is launched, you can use *cd* to change the working directory, and then use *dir* to produce a directory listing in exactly the same way you would perform these tasks from the CMD shell.

```
Windows PowerShell
Copyright (C) 2006 Microsoft Corporation. All rights reserved.

PS C:\Documents and Settings\edwilson> cd c:\
PS C:\> dir

    Directory: Microsoft.PowerShell.Core\FileSystem::C:\

Mode                LastWriteTime     Length Name
----                -------------     ------ ----
d----          7/2/2006  12:14 PM            audioBOOK
d----          1/13/2006  9:34 AM            bt
d----         11/4/2006   2:57 AM            Documents and Settings
```

```
d----        2/6/2006   2:49 PM            DsoFile
d----        9/5/2006  11:30 AM            fso
d----       7/21/2006   3:08 AM            fso2
d----      11/15/2006   9:57 AM            OutlookMail
d-r--      11/20/2006   4:44 PM            Program Files
d----       7/16/2005  11:52 AM            RAS
d----       1/30/2006   9:30 AM            smartPhone
d----       11/1/2006  11:35 PM            Temp
d----       8/31/2006   6:48 AM            Utils
d----       1/30/2006   9:10 AM            vb05sbs
d----      11/21/2006   5:36 PM            WINDOWS
-a---       7/16/2005  10:39 AM         0  AUTOEXEC.BAT
-a---       11/7/2006   1:09 PM      3988  bar.emf
--r-s       8/27/2006   6:37 PM       211  boot.ini
-a---       7/16/2005  10:39 AM         0  CONFIG.SYS
-a---       8/16/2006  11:42 AM        60  MASK.txt
-a---        4/5/2006   3:09 AM       288  MRED1.log
-a---       9/28/2006  11:20 PM     16384  mySheet.xls
-a---       9/19/2006   4:28 AM      2974  new.txt
-a---      11/15/2006   2:08 PM      6662  notepad
-a---       9/19/2006   4:23 AM      4887  old.txt
-a---        6/3/2006  11:11 AM       102  Platform.ini

PS C:\>
```

You can also combine "traditional" CMD interpreter commands with some of the newer utilities such as *fsutil*. This is shown here:

```
PS C:\> md c:\test

    Directory: Microsoft.PowerShell.Core\FileSystem::C:\

Mode                LastWriteTime     Length Name
----                -------------     ------ ----
d----        11/23/2006  11:42 AM            test

PS C:\> cd c:\test
PS C:\test> fsutil file createNew c:\test\myNewFile.txt 1000
File c:\test\myNewFile.txt is created
PS C:\test> dir

    Directory: Microsoft.PowerShell.Core\FileSystem::C:\test

Mode                LastWriteTime     Length Name
----                -------------     ------ ----
-a---        11/23/2006  11:43 AM       1000 myNewFile.txt

PS C:\test> del *.txt
PS C:\test> cd c:\
PS C:\> rd c:\test
PS C:\>
```

We have been using Windows PowerShell in an interactive manner. This is one of the primary uses of PowerShell and is accomplished by opening a PowerShell prompt and typing commands. The commands can be entered one at a time, or they can be grouped together like a batch file. We will look at this later because you need more information to understand it.

Using Cmdlets

In addition to using traditional programs and commands from the CMD.exe command interpreter, we can also use the commandlets (cmdlets) that are built into PowerShell. Cmdlets are name-created by the Windows PowerShell team to describe the commands that are built into PowerShell. They are like executable programs, but they take advantage of the facilities built into Windows PowerShell, and therefore are easy to write. They are not scripts, which are uncompiled code, because they are built using the services of a special .NET Framework namespace. Windows PowerShell comes with more than 120 cmdlets that are designed to assist the network administrator or consultant to leverage the power of PowerShell without having to learn the PowerShell scripting language. These cmdlets are documented in Appendix A. In general, the cmdlets follow a standard naming convention such as *Get-Help, Get-EventLog*, or *Get-Process*. The *get* cmdlets display information about the item that is specified on the right side of the dash. The *set* cmdlets are used to modify or to set information about the item on the right side of the dash. An example of a *set* cmdlet is *Set-Service*, which can be used to change the startmode of a service. An explanation of this naming convention is seen in Appendix B.

Installing Windows PowerShell

It is unfortunate that Windows PowerShell is not installed by default on any of the current Windows operating systems, including Windows Vista. It is installed with Exchange Server 2007 because Exchange leverages Windows PowerShell for management. This is a tremendous advantage to Exchange admins because it means that everything that can be done through the Exchange Admin tool can also be done from a PowerShell script or cmdlet.

Windows PowerShell can be installed on Windows XP SP2, Windows Server 2003 SP1, and Windows Vista. Windows PowerShell requires Microsoft .NET Framework 2.0 (or greater) and will generate the error shown in Figure 1-1 if this level of the .NET Framework is not installed.

Figure 1-1   A Setup error is generated if .NET Framework 2.0 is not present

To prevent frustration during the installation, it makes sense to use a script that checks for the operating system (OS), service pack level, and .NET Framework 2.0. A sample script that will check for the prerequisites is DetectPowerShellRequirements.vbs, which follows.

DetectPowerShellRequirements.vbs

```
strComputer = "."
wmiNS = "\root\cimv2"
wmiQuery = "Select name from win32_Product where name like '%.NET Framework 2.0%'"
wmiQuery1 = "Select * from win32_OperatingSystem"

WScript.Echo "Retrieving settings on " & _ CreateObject("wscript.network").computername
    & " this will take some time ..."
Set objWMIService = GetObject("winmgmts:\\" & strComputer & wmiNS)
Set colItems = objWMIService.ExecQuery(wmiQuery)
Set colItems1= objWMIService.ExecQuery(wmiQuery1,,RtnImmedFwdOnly)

If colItems.count <>1 Then
    WScript.Echo ".NET Framework 2.0 is required for PowerShell"
    Else
    WScript.Echo ".NET Framework 2.0 detected"
End If

For Each objItem1 In colItems1
    osVER= objItem1.version
    osSP= objItem1.ServicePackMajorVersion
Next

Select Case osVER
Case "5.1.2600"
    If osSP < 2 Then
        WScript.Echo "Service Pack 2 is required on Windows XP"
    Else
        WScript.Echo "Service Pack",osSP,"detected on",osVER
    End If
Case "5. 2.3790"
    If osSP <1 Then
        WScript.Echo "Service Pack 1 is required on Windows Server 2003"
    Else
        WScript.Echo "Service Pack",osSP,"detected on",osVER
    End if
Case "XXX"
    WScript.Echo "No service pack is required on Windows Vista"
Case Else
    WScript.Echo "Windows PowerShell does not install on Windows version " & osVER
End Select
```

Deploying Windows PowerShell

After Windows PowerShell is downloaded from *http://www.Microsoft.com/downloads*, you can deploy Windows PowerShell to your enterprise by using any of the standard methods you currently use. A few of the methods some customers have used to accomplish Windows PowerShell deployment are listed next.

1. Create a Microsoft Systems Management Server (SMS) package and advertise it to the appropriate Organizational Unit (OU) or collection.

2. Create a Group Policy Object (GPO) in Active Directory (AD) and link it to the appropriate OU.

If you are not deploying to an entire enterprise, perhaps the easiest way to install Windows Powershell is to simply double-click the executable and step through the wizard.

> **Note**   To use a command line utility in Windows PowerShell, launch Windows PowerShell by using *Start | Run | PowerShell*. At the PowerShell prompt, type in the command to run.

Using Command Line Utilities

As mentioned earlier, command-line utilities can be used directly within Windows PowerShell. The advantages of using command-line utilities in Windows PowerShell, as opposed to simply running them in the CMD interpreter, are the Windows PowerShell pipelining and formatting features. Additionally, if you have batch files or CMD files that already utilize existing command-line utilities, they can easily be modified to run within the Windows PowerShell environment. This command is in the RunningIpconfigCommands.txt file.

Running *ipconfig* commands

1. Start the Windows PowerShell by using *Start | Run | Windows PowerShell*. The PowerShell prompt will open by default at the root of your Documents And Settings.

2. Enter the command *ipconfig /all*. This is shown here:

    ```
    PS C:\> ipconfig /all
    ```

3. Pipe the result of *ipconfig /all* to a text file. This is illustrated here:

    ```
    PS C:\> ipconfig /all >ipconfig.txt
    ```

4. Use Notepad to view the contents of the text file. This is shown here:

    ```
    PS C:\> notepad ipconfig.txt
    ```

Typing a single command into Windows PowerShell is useful, but at times you may need more than one command to provide troubleshooting information, or configuration details to assist with setup issues or performance problems. This is where Windows PowerShell really shines. In the past, one would have to either write a batch file or type the commands manually.

> **Note**   Netdiag.exe referenced in the TroubleShoot.bat file is not part of the standard Windows install, but is a resource kit utility that can be downloaded from *http://www.microsoft.com/downloads*.

This is seen in the TroubleShoot.bat script that follows.

TroubleShoot.bat

```
ipconfig /all >C:\tshoot.txt
route print >>C:\tshoot.txt
netdiag /q >>C:\tshoot.txt
net statistics workstation >>C:\tshoot.txt
```

Of course, if you typed the commands manually, then you had to wait for each command to complete before entering the subsequent command. In that case, it was always possible to lose your place in the command sequence, or to have to wait for the result of each command. The Windows PowerShell eliminates this problem. You can now enter multiple commands on a single line, and then leave the computer or perform other tasks while the computer produces the output. No batch file needs to be written to achieve this capability.

> **Tip**   Use multiple commands on a single Windows PowerShell line. Type each complete command, and then use a semicolon to separate each command.

The use of this procedure is seen in the Running multiple commands procedure. The command used in the procedure are in the RunningMultipleCommands.txt file.

Running multiple commands

1. Start the Windows PowerShell by using *Start | Run | Windows PowerShell*. The Power-Shell prompt will open by default at the root of your Documents And Settings.

2. Enter the *ipconfig /all* command. Pipe the output to a text file called Tshoot.txt by using the redirection arrow (>). This is the result:

    ```
    ipconfig /all >tshoot.txt
    ```

3. On the same line, use a semicolon to separate the *ipconfig /all* command from the *route print* command. Append the output from the command to a text file called Tshoot.txt by using the redirect and append arrow (>>). The command to this point is shown as follows:

    ```
    ipconfig /all >tshoot.txt; route print >>tshoot.txt
    ```

4. On the same line, use a semicolon to separate the *route print* command from the *netdiag /q* command. Append the output from the command to a text file called Tshoot.txt by using the redirect and append arrow. The command to this point is shown here:

    ```
    ipconfig /all >tshoot.txt; route print >>tshoot.txt; netdiag /q >>tshoot
    .txt
    ```

5. On the same line, use a semicolon to separate the *netdiag /q* command from the *net statistics workstation* command. Append the output from the command to a text file called Tshoot.txt by using the redirect and append arrow. The completed command looks like the following:

```
ipconfig /all >tshoot.txt; route print >>tshoot.txt; netdiag /q >>tshoot
.txt; net statistics workstation >>tshoot.txt
```

Security Issues with Windows PowerShell

As with any tool as versatile as Windows PowerShell, there are bound to be some security concerns. Security, however, was one of the design goals in the development of Windows PowerShell.

When you launch Windows PowerShell, it opens in your Documents And Settings folder; this ensures you are in a directory where you will have permission to perform certain actions and activities. This is far safer than opening at the root of the drive, or even opening in system root.

To change to a directory, you cannot automatically go up to the next level; you must explicitly name the destination of the change directory operation.

The running of scripts is disabled by default and can be easily managed through group policy.

Controlling Execution of PowerShell Cmdlets

Have you ever opened a CMD interpreter prompt, typed in a command, and pressed Enter so that you could see what it does? What if that command happened to be *Format C:\?* Are you sure you want to format your C drive? In this section, we will look at some arguments that can be supplied to cmdlets that allow you to control the way they execute. Although not all cmdlets support these arguments, most of those included with Windows PowerShell do. The three arguments we can use to control execution are -whatif, -confirm, and suspend. Suspend is not really an argument that is supplied to a cmdlet, but rather is an action you can take at a confirmation prompt, and is therefore another method of controlling execution.

> **Note**   To use -whatif in a Windows PowerShell prompt, enter the cmdlet. Type the -whatif parameter after the cmdlet.

Most of the Windows PowerShell cmdlets support a "prototype" mode that can be entered using the -whatif parameter. The implementation of -whatif can be decided on by the person developing the cmdlet; however, it is the recommendation of the Windows PowerShell team that developers implement -whatif. The use of the -whatif argument is seen in the procedure below. The commands used in the procedure are in the UsingWhatif.txt file.

Using -whatif to prototype a command

1. Start the Windows PowerShell by using *Start | Run | Windows PowerShell*. The Power-Shell prompt will open by default at the root of your Documents And Settings.

2. Start an instance of Notepad.exe. Do this by typing **notepad** and pressing the Enter key. This is shown here:

```
notepad
```

3. Identify the Notepad process you just started by using the *Get-Process* cmdlet. Type enough of the process name to identify it, and then use a wild card asterisk (*) to avoid typing the entire name of the process. This is shown as follows:

```
get-process note*
```

4. Examine the output from the *Get-Process* cmdlet, and identify the process ID. The output on my machine is shown here. Please note that in all likelihood, the process ID used by your instance of Notepad.exe will be different from the one on my machine.

```
Handles  NPM(K)    PM(K)      WS(K) VM(M)   CPU(s)      Id ProcessName
-------  ------    -----      ----- -----   ------      -- -----------
     39       2      944        400    29     0.05    1056 notepad
```

5. Use -whatif to see what would happen if you used *Stop-Process* to stop the process ID you obtained in step 4. This process ID will be found under the Id column in your output. Use the -id parameter to identify the Notepad.exe process. The command is as follows:

```
stop-process -id 1056 -whatif
```

6. Examine the output from the command. It tells you that the command will stop the Notepad process with the process ID that you used in your command.

```
What if: Performing operation "Stop-Process" on Target "notepad (1056)"
```

> **Tip**   To confirm the execution of a cmdlet, launch Windows PowerShell by using *Start | Run | Windows PowerShell*. At the Windows PowerShell prompt, supply the -whatif argument to the cmdlet.

Confirming Commands

As we saw in the previous section, we can use -whatif to prototype a cmdlet in Windows Pow-erShell. This is useful for seeing what a command would do; however, if we want to be prompted before the execution of the command, we can use the -confirm argument. The commands used in the Confirming the execution of cmdlets procedure are listed in the ConfirmingExecutionOfCmdlets.txt file.

Confirming the execution of cmdlets

1. Start the Windows PowerShell by using *Start | Run | Windows PowerShell*. The Power-Shell prompt will open by default at the root of your Documents And Settings.

2. Start an instance of Notepad.exe. Do this by typing **notepad** and pressing the Enter key. This is shown here:

```
notepad
```

3. Identify the Notepad process you just started by using the *Get-Process* cmdlet. Type enough of the process name to identify it, and then use a wild card asterisk (*) to avoid typing the entire name of the process. This is illustrated here:

```
get-process note*
```

4. Examine the output from the *Get-Process* cmdlet, and identify the process ID. The output on my machine is shown here. Please note that in all likelihood, the process ID used by your instance of Notepad.exe will be different from the one on my machine.

```
Handles  NPM(K)    PM(K)     WS(K) VM(M)    CPU(s)      Id ProcessName
-------  ------    -----     ----- -----    ------      -- -----------
     39       2      944       400    29      0.05    1768 notepad
```

5. Use the -confirm argument to force a prompt when using the *Stop-Process* cmdlet to stop the Notepad process identified by the *get-process note** command. This is shown here:

```
stop-process -id 1768 -confirm
```

6. The *Stop-Process* cmdlet, when used with the -confirm argument, displays the following confirmation prompt:

```
Confirm
Are you sure you want to perform this action?
Performing operation "Stop-Process" on Target "notepad (1768)".
[Y] Yes  [A] Yes to All  [N] No  [L] No to All  [S] Suspend  [?] Help
(default is "Y"):
```

7. Type **y** and press Enter. The Notepad.exe process ends. The Windows PowerShell prompt returns to the default ready for new commands, as shown here:

```
PS C:\>
```

Tip   To suspend cmdlet confirmation, at the confirmation prompt from the cmdlet, type **s** and press Enter

Suspending Confirmation of Cmdlets

The ability to prompt for confirmation of the execution of a cmdlet is extremely useful and at times may be vital to assisting in maintaining a high level of system uptime. There are times when you have typed in a long command and then remember that you need to do something else first. For such eventualities, you can tell the confirmation you would like to suspend execution of the command. The commands used for suspending execution of a cmdlet are in the SuspendConfirmationOfCmdlets.txt file.

Suspending execution of a cmdlet

1. Start the Windows PowerShell by using *Start | Run | Windows PowerShell*. The PowerShell prompt will open by default at the root of your Documents And Settings.

2. Start an instance of Notepad.exe. Do this by typing **notepad** and pressing the Enter key. This is shown here:

   ```
   notepad
   ```

3. Identify the Notepad process you just started by using the *Get-Process* cmdlet. Type enough of the process name to identify it, and then use a wild card asterisk (*) to avoid typing the entire name of the process. This is shown here:

   ```
   get-process note*
   ```

4. Examine the output from the *Get-Process* cmdlet, and identify the process ID. The output on my machine is seen below. Please note that in all likelihood, the process ID used by our instance of Notepad.exe will be different from the one on my machine.

   ```
   Handles  NPM(K)    PM(K)     WS(K) VM(M)   CPU(s)     Id ProcessName
   -------  ------    -----     ----- -----   ------     -- -----------
        39       2      944       400    29     0.05   3576 notepad
   ```

5. Use the -confirm argument to force a prompt when using the *Stop-Process* cmdlet to stop the Notepad process identified by the *Get-Process Note** command. This is illustrated here:

   ```
   stop-process -id 3576 -confirm
   ```

6. The *Stop-Process* cmdlet, when used with the -confirm argument, displays the following confirmation prompt:

   ```
   Confirm
   Are you sure you want to perform this action?
   Performing operation "Stop-Process" on Target "notepad (3576)".
   [Y] Yes  [A] Yes to All  [N] No  [L] No to All  [S] Suspend  [?] Help
   (default is "Y"):
   ```

7. To suspend execution of the *Stop-Process* cmdlet, enter **s**. A triple arrow prompt will appear, as follows:

   ```
   PS C:\>>>
   ```

8. Obtain a list of all the running processes that begin with the letter n. Use the *Get-Process* cmdlet to do this. The syntax is as follows:

```
get-process n*
```

9. On my machine, two processes appear. The Notepad process we launched earlier, and another process. This is shown here:

```
Handles  NPM(K)    PM(K)      WS(K) VM(M)   CPU(s)     Id ProcessName
-------  ------    -----      ----- -----   ------     -- -----------
     39       2      944        400    29     0.05   3576 notepad
     75       2     1776       2708    23     0.09    632 nvsvc32
```

10. Return to the previous confirmation prompt by typing **exit**. This is shown here:

```
exit
```

11. Once again, the confirmation prompt appears as follows:

```
Confirm
Are you sure you want to perform this action?
Performing operation "Stop-Process" on Target "notepad (3576)".
[Y] Yes  [A] Yes to All  [N] No  [L] No to All  [S] Suspend  [?] Help
(default is "Y"):
```

12. Type **y** and press Enter to stop the Notepad process. There is no further confirmation. The prompt will now display the default Windows PowerShell PS>, as shown here:

```
PS C:\>
```

Working with Windows PowerShell

Windows PowerShell can be used as a replacement for the CMD interpreter. Its many built-in cmdlets allow for large number of activities. These cmdlets can be used in a stand-alone fashion, or they can be run together as a group.

Accessing Windows PowerShell

After Windows PowerShell is installed, it becomes available for immediate use. However, using the Windows flag key on the keyboard and pressing the letter **r** to bring up a *run* command prompt, or "mousing around" and and using *Start | Run | Windows PowerShell* all the time, becomes somewhat less helpful. I created a shortcut to Windows PowerShell and placed that shortcut on my desktop. For me, and the way I work, this is ideal. This was so useful, as a matter of fact, that I wrote a script to do this. This script can be called through a logon script to automatically deploy the shortcut on the desktop. The script is called CreateShortCut-ToPowerShell.vbs, and is as follows:

CreateShortCutToPowerShell.vbs

```
Option Explicit
Dim objshell
Dim strDesktop
Dim objshortcut
Dim strProg
strProg = "powershell.exe"

Set objshell=CreateObject("WScript.Shell")
strDesktop = objshell.SpecialFolders("desktop")
set objShortcut = objshell.CreateShortcut(strDesktop & "\powershell.lnk")
objshortcut.TargetPath = strProg
objshortcut.WindowStyle = 1
objshortcut.Description = funfix(strProg)
objshortcut.WorkingDirectory = "C:\"
objshortcut.IconLocation= strProg
objshortcut.Hotkey = "CTRL+SHIFT+P"
objshortcut.Save

Function funfix(strin)
funfix = InStrRev(strin,".")
funfix = Mid(strin,1,funfix)
End function
```

Configuring Windows PowerShell

Many items can be configured for Windows PowerShell. These items can be stored in a Psconsole file. To export the Console configuration file, use the *Export-Console* cmdlet, as shown here:

```
PS C:\> Export-Console myconsole
```

The Psconsole file is saved in the current directory by default and has an extension of pscl. The Psconsole file is saved in an xml format. A generic console file is shown here:

```
<?xml version="1.0" encoding="utf-8"?>
<PSConsoleFile ConsoleSchemaVersion="1.0">
  <PSVersion>1.0</PSVersion>
  <PSSnapIns />
</PSConsoleFile>
```

Controlling PowerShell launch options

1. Launch Windows PowerShell without the banner by using the -nologo argument. This is shown here:

   ```
   PowerShell -nologo
   ```

2. Launch a specific version of Windows PowerShell by using the -version argument. This is shown here:

   ```
   PowerShell -version 1
   ```

3. Launch Windows PowerShell using a specific configuration file by specifying the -psconsolefile argument. This is shown here:

```
PowerShell -psconsolefile myconsole.psc1
```

4. Launch Windows PowerShell, execute a specific command, and then exit by using the -command argument. The command itself must be prefixed by the ampersand sign (&) and enclosed in curly brackets. This is shown here:

```
powershell -command "& {get-process}"
```

Supplying Options for Cmdlets

One of the useful features of Windows PowerShell is the standardization of the syntax in working with cmdlets. This vastly simplifies the learning of the new shell and language. Table 1-1 lists the common parameters. Keep in mind that all cmdlets will not implement these parameters. However, if these parameters are used, they will be interpreted in the same manner for all cmdlets because it is the Windows PowerShell engine itself that interprets the parameter.

Table 1-1   Common Parameters

Parameter	Meaning
-whatif	Tells the cmdlet to not execute but to tell you what would happen if the cmdlet were to run
-confirm	Tells the cmdlet to prompt before executing the command
-verbose	Instructs the cmdlet to provide a higher level of detail than a cmdlet not using the verbose parameter
-debug	Instructs the cmdlet to provide debugging information
-ErrorAction	Instructs the cmdlet to perform a certain action when an error occurs. Allowed actions are: continue, stop, silentlyContinue, and inquire.
-ErrorVariable	Instructs the cmdlet to use a specific variable to hold error information. This is in addition to the standard $error variable.
-Outvariable	Instructs the cmdlet to use a specific variable to hold the output information
-OutBuffer	Instructs the cmdlet to hold a certain number of objects before calling the next cmdlet in the pipeline

Note   To get help on any cmdlet, use the *Get-Help cmdletname* cmdlet.

Working with the Help Options

Windows PowerShell has a high level of discoverability; that is, to learn how to use Power-Shell, you can simply use PowerShell. Online help serves an important role in assisting in this discoverability. The help system in Windows PowerShell can be entered by several methods. To learn about using Windows PowerShell, use the *Get-Help* cmdlet as follows:

```
get-help get-help
```

This command prints out help about the *Get-Help* cmdlet. The output from this cmdlet is illustrated here:

```
NAME
    Get-Help

SYNOPSIS
    Displays information about Windows PowerShell cmdlets and concepts

SYNTAX
    Get-Help [[-name] <string>] [-component <string[]>] [-functionality <string
    []>] [-role <string[]>] [-category <string[]>] [-full] [<CommonParameters>]

    Get-Help [[-name] <string>] [-component <string[]>] [-functionality <string
    []>] [-role <string[]>] [-category <string[]>] [-detailed] [<CommonParamete
    rs>]

    Get-Help [[-name] <string>] [-component <string[]>] [-functionality <string
    []>] [-role <string[]>] [-category <string[]>] [-examples] [<CommonParamete
    rs>]

    Get-Help [[-name] <string>] [-component <string[]>] [-functionality <string
    []>] [-role <string[]>] [-category <string[]>] [-parameter <string>] [<Comm
    onParameters>]

DETAILED DESCRIPTION
    The Get-Help cmdlet displays information about Windows PowerShell cmdlets a
    nd concepts. You can also use "Help {<cmdlet name> | <topic-name>" or "<cmd
    let-name> /?". "Help" displays the help topics one page at a time. The "/?"
     displays help for cmdlets on a single page.

RELATED LINKS
    Get-Command
    Get-PSDrive
    Get-Member

REMARKS
    For more information, type: "get-help Get-Help -detailed".
    For technical information, type: "get-help Get-Help -full".
```

The good thing about online help with the Windows PowerShell is that it not only displays help about commands, which you would expect, but also has three levels of display: normal, detailed, and full. Additionally, you can obtain help about concepts in Windows PowerShell.

This last feature is equivalent to having an online instruction manual. To retrieve a listing of all the conceptual help articles, use the *Get-Help about** command as follows:

```
get-help about*
```

Suppose you do not remember the exact name of the cmdlet you wish to use, but you remember it was a *get* cmdlet? You can use a wild card, such as an asterisk (*), to obtain the name of the cmdlet. This is shown here:

```
get-help get*
```

This technique of using a wild card operator can be extended further. If you remember that the cmdlet was a *get* cmdlet, and that it started with the letter p, you can use the following syntax to retrieve the desired cmdlet:

```
get-help get-p*
```

Suppose, however, that you know the exact name of the cmdlet, but you cannot exactly remember the syntax. For this scenario, you can use the -examples argument. For example, for the *Get-PSDrive* cmdlet, you would use *Get-Help* with the -examples argument, as follows:

```
get-help get-psdrive -examples
```

To see help displayed one page at a time, you can use the help function, which displays the help output text through the more function. This is useful if you want to avoid scrolling up and down to see the help output. This formatted output is shown in Figure 1-2.

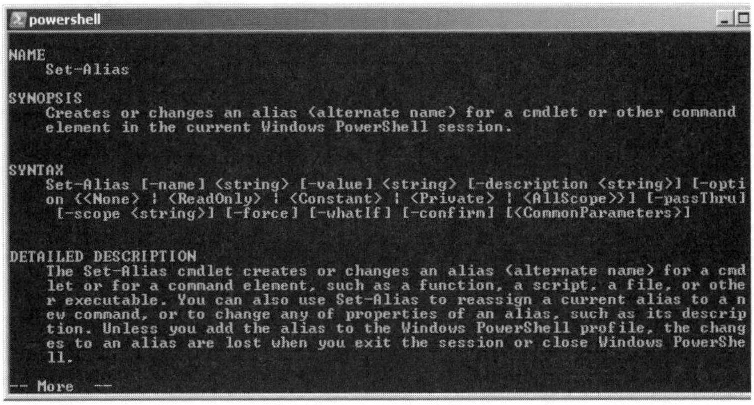

Figure 1-2   Using help to display information one page at a time

Getting tired of typing *Get-Help* all the time? After all, it is eight characters long, and one of them is a dash. The solution is to create an alias to the *Get-Help* cmdlet. The commands used for this are in the CreateAliasToGet-Help.txt file. An alias is a shortcut key stroke combination that will launch a program or cmdlet when typed. In the creating an alias for the *Get-Help* cmdlet procedure, we will assign the *Get-Help* cmdlet to the gh key combination.

> **Note**   To create an alias for a cmdlet, confirm there is not already an alias to the cmdlet by using *Get-Alias*. Use *Set-Alias* to assign the cmdlet to a unique key stroke combination.

Creating an alias for the *Get-Help* cmdlet

1. Start Windows PowerShell by using *Start | Run | Windows PowerShell*. The PowerShell prompt will open by default at the root of your Documents And Settings.

2. Retrieve an alphabetic listing of all currently defined aliases, and inspect the list for one assigned to either the *Get-Help* cmdlet or the key stroke combination gh. The command to do this is as follows:

    ```
    get-alias |sort
    ```

3. After you have determined that there is no alias for the *Get-Help* cmdlet, and that none is assigned to the gh key stroke combination, review the syntax for the *Set-Alias* cmdlet. Use the -full argument to the *Get-Help* cmdlet. This is shown here:

    ```
    get-help set-alias -full
    ```

4. Use the *Set-Alias* cmdlet to assign the gh key stroke combination to the *Get-Help* cmdlet. To do this, use the following command:

    ```
    set-alias gh get-help
    ```

Exploring Commands: Step-by-Step Exercises

In this exercise, we explore the use of command-line utilities in Windows PowerShell. You will see that it is as easy to use command-line utilities in the Windows PowerShell as in the CMD interpreter; however, by using such commands in the Windows PowerShell, you gain access to new levels of functionality.

1. Start Windows PowerShell by using *Start | Run | Windows PowerShell*. The PowerShell prompt will open by default at the root of your Documents And Settings.

2. Change to the C:\ root directory by typing **cd C:** inside the PowerShell prompt:

    ```
    Cd c:\
    ```

3. Obtain a listing of all the files in the C:\ root directory by using the *dir* command:

    ```
    dir
    ```

4. Create a directory off the C:\ root directory by using the *md* command:

    ```
    Md mytest
    ```

5. Obtain a listing of all files and folders off the root that begin with the letter m:

    ```
    Dir m*
    ```

6. Change the working directory to the PowerShell working directory. You can do this by using the *Set-Location* command as follows:

```
Set-location $pshome
```

7. Obtain a listing of memory counters related to the available bytes by using the *typeperf* command. This command is shown here:

```
typeperf "\memory\available bytes"
```

8. After a few counters have been displayed in the PowerShell window, use the *ctrl-c* command to break the listing.

9. Display the current boot configuration by using the *bootcfg* command:

```
Bootcfg
```

10. Change the working directory back to the C:\Mytest directory you created earlier:

```
set-location c:\mytest
```

11. Create a file named Mytestfile.txt in the C:\Mytest directory. Use the *fsutil* utility, and make the file 1,000 bytes in size. To do this, use the following command:

```
fsutil file createnew mytestfile.txt 1000
```

12. Obtain a "directory listing" of all the files in the C:\Mytest directory by using the *Get-ChildItem* cmdlet. This is shown here:

```
get-childitem
```

13. Print out the current date by using the *Get-Date* cmdlet. This is shown here:

```
get-date
```

14. Clear the screen by using the *cls* command. This is shown here:

```
cls
```

15. Print out a listing of all the cmdlets built into Windows PowerShell. To do this, use the *Get-Command* cmdlet. This is shown here:

```
get-command
```

16. Use the *Get-Command* cmdlet to get the *Get-Alias* cmdlet. To do this, use the -name argument while supplying *Get-Alias* as the value for the argument. This is shown here:

```
get-command -name get-alias
```

17. This concludes the step-by-step exercise. Exit the Windows PowerShell by typing **exit** and pressing Enter.

One Step Further: Obtaining Help

In this exercise, we use various help options to obtain assistance with various cmdlets.

1. Start Windows PowerShell by using *Start | Run | Windows PowerShell*. The PowerShell prompt will open by default at the root of your Documents And Settings.

2. Use the *Get-Help* cmdlet to obtain help about the *Get-Help* cmdlet. Use the command *Get-Help Get-Help* as follows:

   ```
   get-help get-help
   ```

3. To obtain detailed help about the *Get-Help* cmdlet, use the -detailed argument as follows:

   ```
   get-help get-help -detailed
   ```

4. To retrieve technical information about the *Get-Help* cmdlet, use the -full argument. This is shown here:

   ```
   get-help get-help -full
   ```

5. If you only want to obtain a listing of examples of command usage, use the -examples argument as follows:

   ```
   get-help get-help -examples
   ```

6. Obtain a listing of all the informational help topics by using the *Get-Help* cmdlet and the about noun with the asterisk (*) wild card operator. The code to do this is shown here:

   ```
   get-help about*
   ```

7. Obtain a listing of all the help topics related to *get* cmdlets. To do this, use the *Get-Help* cmdlet, and specify the word "get" followed by the wild card operator as follows:

   ```
   get-help get*
   ```

8. Obtain a listing of all the help topics related to *set* cmdlets. To do this, use the *Get-Help* cmdlet followed by the "set" verb followed by the asterisk wild card. This is shown here:

   ```
   get-help set*
   ```

9. This concludes the one step further exercise. Exit the Windows PowerShell by typing **exit** and pressing Enter.

Chapter 1 Quick Reference

To	Do This
Use an external command-line utility	Type the name of the command-line utility while inside Windows PowerShell
Use multiple external command-line utilities sequentially	Separate each command-line utility with a semicolon on a single Windows PowerShell line
Obtain a list of running processes	Use the *Get-Process* cmdlet
Stop a process	Use the *Stop-Process* cmdlet and specify either the name or the process ID as an argument
Model the effect of a cmdlet before actually performing the requested action	Use the -whatif argument
Instruct Windows PowerShell to startup, run a cmdlet, and then exit	Use the *PowerShell* command while prefixing the cmdlet with the ampersand sign and enclosing the name of the cmdlet in curly brackets
Prompt for confirmation before stopping a process	Use the *Stop-Process* cmdlet while specifying the -confirm argument

Using Windows PowerShell Cmdlets

After completing this chapter, you will be able to:

- Understand the basic use of Microsoft Windows PowerShell cmdlets
- Use *Get-Command* to retrieve a listing of cmdlets
- Configure search options
- Configure output parameters
- Use *Get-Member*
- Use *New-Object*

The inclusion of a large amount of cmdlets in Windows PowerShell makes it immediately useful to network administrators and others who need to perform various maintenance and administrative tasks on their Windows servers and desktop systems. In this chapter, we review several of the more useful cmdlets as a means of highlighting the power and flexibility of Windows PowerShell. However, the real benefit of this chapter is the methodology we use' to discover the use of the various cmdlets. All the scripts mentioned in this chapter can be found in the corresponding scripts folder on the CD.

Understanding the Basics of Cmdlets

In Chapter 1, Overview of Windows PowerShell, we learned about using the various help utilities available that demonstrate how to use cmdlets. We looked at a couple of cmdlets that are helpful in finding out what commands are available and how to obtain information about them. In this section, we describe some additional ways to use cmdlets in Windows PowerShell.

 Tip Typing long cmdlet names can be somewhat tedious. To simplify this process, type enough of the cmdlet name to uniquely distinguish it, and then press the Tab key on the keyboard. What is the result? *Tab Completion* completes the cmdlet name for you. This also works with argument names and other things you are entering. Feel free to experiment with this great time-saving technique. You may never have to type **get-command** again!

Because the cmdlets return objects instead of "string values," we can obtain additional information about the returned objects. The additional information would not be available to us if we were working with just string data. To do this, we can use the pipe character (|) to take information from one cmdlet and feed it to another cmdlet. This may seem complicated, but it is actually quite simple and, by the end of this chapter, will seem quite natural. At the most basic level, consider obtaining a directory listing; after you have the directory listing, perhaps you would like to format the way it is displayed—as a table or a list. As you can see, these are two separate operations: obtaining the directory listing, and formatting the list. The second task will take place on the right side of the pipe.

Using the *Get-ChildItem* Cmdlet

In Chapter 1, we used the *dir* command to obtain a listing of all the files in a directory. This works because there is an alias built into Windows PowerShell that assigns the *Get-ChildItem* cmdlet to the letter combination *dir*.

> **Just the Steps   Obtaining a directory listing** In a Windows PowerShell prompt, enter the *Get-ChildItem* cmdlet followed by the directory to list. Example:
>
> ```
> get-childitem C:\
> ```

In Windows PowerShell, there actually is no cmdlet called *dir*, nor does it actually use the *dir* command. The alias *dir* is associated with the *Get-ChildItem* cmdlet. This is why the output from *dir* is different in Windows PowerShell than in the CMD.exe interpreter. The alias *dir* is used when we use the *Get-Alias* cmdlet to resolve the association, as follows:

```
PS C:\> get-alias dir

CommandType     Name                    Definition
-----------     ----                    ----------
Alias           dir                     Get-ChildItem
```

If you use the *Get-ChildItem* cmdlet to obtain the directory listing, it will obtain a listing the same as *dir* because *dir* is simply an alias for *Get-ChildItem*. This is shown here:

```
PS C:\> get-childitem C:\

    Directory: Microsoft.PowerShell.Core\FileSystem::C:\

Mode                LastWriteTime     Length Name
----                -------------     ------ ----
d----          7/2/2006   3:14 PM            audioBOOK
d----         11/4/2006   4:57 AM            Documents and Settings
d----          2/6/2006   4:49 PM            DsoFile
d----          9/5/2006   2:30 PM            fso
d----         11/30/2006  2:08 PM            fso1
d----          7/21/2006  6:08 AM            fso2
d----         12/2/2005   5:41 AM            German
d----          9/24/2006  1:54 AM            music
d----         12/10/2006  6:54 AM            mytest
d----         12/13/2006  8:30 AM            OutlookMail
```

```
d-r--        11/20/2006    6:44 PM              Program Files
d----         7/16/2005    2:52 PM              RAS
d----         1/30/2006   11:30 AM              smartPhone
d----         11/2/2006    1:35 AM              Temp
d----         8/31/2006    9:48 AM              Utils
d----         1/30/2006   11:10 AM              vb05sbs
d----         12/5/2006    8:01 AM              WINDOWS
-a---         12/8/2006    7:24 PM      22950   a.txt
-a---         12/5/2006    8:48 AM      23902   alias.txt
-a---         7/16/2005    1:39 PM          0   AUTOEXEC.BAT
-a---         11/7/2006    3:09 PM       3988   bar.emf
--r-s         8/27/2006    9:37 PM        211   boot.ini
-a---         12/3/2006    7:36 AM      21228   cmdlets.txt
-a---        12/13/2006    9:44 AM     273612   commandHelp.txt
-a---        12/10/2006    7:34 AM      21228   commands.txt
-a---         7/16/2005    1:39 PM          0   CONFIG.SYS
-a---         12/7/2006    3:14 PM       8261   mySheet.xls
-a---         12/7/2006    5:29 PM       2960   NetDiag.log
-a---         12/5/2006    8:29 AM      16386   notepad
-a---          6/3/2006    2:11 PM        102   Platform.ini
-a---         12/7/2006    5:29 PM      10670   tshoot.txt
-a---         12/4/2006    9:09 PM      52124   VistaResKitScripts.txt
```

If you were to use *Get-Help* and then *dir*, you would receive the same output as if you were to use *Get-Help Get-ChildItem*. In Windows PowerShell, the two can be used in exactly the same fashion.

> **Just the Steps**   Formatting a directory listing using *Format-List* In a Windows Power-Shell prompt, enter the *Get-ChildItem* cmdlet followed by the directory to list followed by the pipe character and the *Format-List* cmdlet. Example:
>
> ```
> get-childitem C:\ | format-list
> ```

Formatting output with the *Format-List* cmdlet

1. Start Windows PowerShell by using *Start | Run | Windows PowerShell*. The PowerShell prompt will open by default at the root of your Documents And Settings.

2. Use the *Get-ChildItem* cmdlet to obtain a directory listing of the C:\ directory.

   ```
   get-childItem C:\
   ```

3. Use the *Format-List* cmdlet to arrange the output of *Get-ChildItem*.

   ```
   get-childitem |format-list
   ```

4. Use the -property argument of the *Format-List* cmdlet to retrieve only a listing of the name of each file in the root.

   ```
   get-childitem C:\ | format-list -property name
   ```

5. Use the property argument of the *Format-List* cmdlet to retrieve only a listing of the name and length of each file in the root.

   ```
   get-childitem C:\ | format-list -property name, length
   ```

Using the *Format-Wide* Cmdlet

In the same way that we use the *Format-List* cmdlet to produce an output in a list, we can use the *Format-Wide* cmdlet to produce a more compact output.

> **Just the Steps**   **Formatting a directory listing using *Format-Wide*** In a Windows Power-Shell prompt, enter the *Get-ChildItem* cmdlet followed by the directory to list followed by the pipe character and the *Format-Wide* cmdlet. Example:
>
> ```
> get-childitem C:\ | format-wide
> ```

Formatting output with the *Format-Wide* cmdlet

1. Start Windows PowerShell by using *Start | Run | Windows PowerShell*. The PowerShell prompt will open by default at the root of your Documents And Settings.

2. Use the *Get-ChildItem* cmdlet to obtain a directory listing of the C:\Windows directory.

    ```
    get-childitem C:\Windows
    ```

3. Use the -recursive argument to cause the *Get-ChildItem* cmdlet to walk through a nested directory structure, including only .txt files in the output.

    ```
    get-childitem C:\Windows -recurse -include *.txt
    ```

4. A partial output from the command is shown here:

    ```
        Directory: Microsoft.PowerShell.Core\FileSystem::C:\Windows\Driver Cache

    Mode                LastWriteTime     Length Name
    ----                -------------     ------ ----
    -a---        11/26/2004   6:29 AM      13512 yk51x86.txt


        Directory: Microsoft.PowerShell.Core\FileSystem::C:\Windows\Help\Tours\mmTo
        ur

    Mode                LastWriteTime     Length Name
    ----                -------------     ------ ----
    -a---          8/4/2004   8:00 AM        807 intro.txt
    -a---          8/4/2004   8:00 AM        407 nav.txt
    -a---          8/4/2004   8:00 AM        747 segment1.txt
    -a---          8/4/2004   8:00 AM        772 segment2.txt
    -a---          8/4/2004   8:00 AM        717 segment3.txt
    -a---          8/4/2004   8:00 AM        633 segment4.txt
    -a---          8/4/2004   8:00 AM        799 segment5.txt
    ```

5. Use the *Format-Wide* cmdlet to adjust the output from the *Get-ChildItem* cmdlet. Use the -columns argument and supply a parameter of 3 to it. This is shown here:

    ```
    get-childitem C:\Windows -recurse -include *.txt |format-wide -column 3
    ```

6. Once this command is run, you will see an output similar to this:

```
Directory: Microsoft.PowerShell.Core\FileSystem::C:\Windows\Driver Cache

yk51x86.txt

    Directory: Microsoft.PowerShell.Core\FileSystem::C:\Windows\Help\Tours\mmTo
    ur

intro.txt                nav.txt                  segment1.txt
segment2.txt             segment3.txt             segment4.txt
segment5.txt

    Directory: Microsoft.PowerShell.Core\FileSystem::C:\Windows\Microsoft.NET\F
    ramework\v1.1.4322\1033

SetupENU1.txt            SetupENU2.txt

    Directory: Microsoft.PowerShell.Core\FileSystem::C:\Windows\Microsoft.NET\F
    ramework\v2.0.50727\Microsoft .NET Framework 2.0

eula.1025.txt            eula.1028.txt            eula.1029.txt
eula.1030.txt            eula.1031.txt            eula.1032.txt
eula.1033.txt            eula.1035.txt            eula.1036.txt
eula.1037.txt            eula.1038.txt            eula.1040.txt
eula.1041.txt            eula.1042.txt            eula.1043.txt
eula.1044.txt            eula.1045.txt            eula.1046.txt
eula.1049.txt            eula.1053.txt            eula.1055.txt
eula.2052.txt            eula.2070.txt            eula.3076.txt
eula.3082.txt
```

7. Use the *Format-Wide* cmdlet to adjust the output from the *Get-ChildItem* cmdlet. Use the property argument to specify the name property, and group the outputs by size. The command shown here appears on two lines; however, when typed into Windows PowerShell, it is a single command and needs to be on the same line:

```
get-childitem C:\Windows -recurse -include *.txt |format-wide -property
name -groupby length -column 3
```

8. A partial output is shown here. Note that although three columns were specified, if there are not three files of the same length, only one column will be used:

```
    Length: 13512

yk51x86.txt

    Length: 807

intro.txt

    Length: 407

nav.txt

    Length: 747

segment1.txt
```

> **Just the Steps** **Formatting a directory listing using *Format-Table*** In a Windows Power-
> Shell prompt, enter the *Get-ChildItem* cmdlet followed by the directory to list followed by the
> pipe character and the *Format-Table* cmdlet. Example:
>
> ```
> get-childitem C:\ | format-table
> ```

Formatting output with the *Format-Table* cmdlet

1. Start the Windows PowerShell by using *Start | Run | Windows PowerShell*. The Power-Shell prompt will open by default at the root of your Documents And Settings.

2. Use the *Get-ChildItem* cmdlet to obtain a directory listing of the C:\Windows directory

   ```
   get-childitem C:\Windows
   ```

3. Use the -recursive argument to cause the *Get-ChildItem* cmdlet to walk through a nested directory structure, include only .txt files in the output.

   ```
   get-childitem C:\Windows -recurse -include *.txt
   ```

4. Use the *Format-Table* cmdlet to adjust the output from the *Get-ChildItem* cmdlet. This is shown here:

   ```
   get-childitem C:\Windows -recurse -include *.txt |format-table
   ```

5. The command results in the creation of a table, as follows:

```
    Directory: Microsoft.PowerShell.Core\FileSystem::C:\Windows\Driver Cache

Mode              LastWriteTime     Length Name
----              -------------     ------ ----
-a---       11/26/2004   6:29 AM     13512 yk51x86.txt


    Directory: Microsoft.PowerShell.Core\FileSystem::C:\Windows\Help\Tours\mmTo
    ur

Mode              LastWriteTime     Length Name
----              -------------     ------ ----
-a---        8/4/2004   8:00 AM       807 intro.txt
-a---        8/4/2004   8:00 AM       407 nav.txt
-a---        8/4/2004   8:00 AM       747 segment1.txt
-a---        8/4/2004   8:00 AM       772 segment2.txt
-a---        8/4/2004   8:00 AM       717 segment3.txt
-a---        8/4/2004   8:00 AM       633 segment4.txt
-a---        8/4/2004   8:00 AM       799 segment5.txt


    Directory: Microsoft.PowerShell.Core\FileSystem::C:\Windows\Microsoft.NET\F
    ramework\v1.1.4322\1033

 Mode              LastWriteTime     Length Name
 ----              -------------     ------ ----
 -a---        3/6/2002   2:36 PM        38 SetupENU1.txt
 -a---        3/6/2002   2:36 PM        38 SetupENU2.txt
```

6. Use the -property argument of the *Format-Table* cmdlet and choose the name, length, and last-write-time properties. This is shown here:

```
get-childitem C:\Windows -recurse -include *.txt |format-table -property
name, length, lastwritetime
```

7. This command results in producing a table with the name, length, and last write time as column headers. A sample of this output is shown here:

```
Name                                          Length LastWriteTime
----                                          ------ -------------
yk51x86.txt                                    13512 11/26/2004 6:29:00 AM
intro.txt                                        807 8/4/2004 8:00:00 AM
nav.txt                                          407 8/4/2004 8:00:00 AM
segment1.txt                                     747 8/4/2004 8:00:00 AM
segment2.txt                                     772 8/4/2004 8:00:00 AM
segment3.txt                                     717 8/4/2004 8:00:00 AM
segment4.txt                                     633 8/4/2004 8:00:00 AM
```

Leveraging the Power of *Get-Command*

Using the *Get-Command* cmdlet, you can obtain a listing of all the cmdlets installed on the Windows PowerShell, but there is much more that can be done using this extremely versatile cmdlet. One such method of using the *Get-Command* cmdlet is to use wild card characters. This is shown in the following procedure:

> **Just the Steps**   **Searching for cmdlets using wild card characters** In a Windows Power-Shell prompt, enter the *Get-Command* cmdlet followed by a wild card character. Example:
>
> ```
> get-command *
> ```

Finding commands by using the *Get-Command* cmdlet

1. Start Windows PowerShell by using *Start | Run | Windows PowerShell*. The PowerShell prompt will open by default at the root of your Documents And Settings.

2. Use an alias to refer to the *Get-Command* cmdlet. To find the correct alias, use the *Get-Alias* cmdlet as follows:

```
get-alias g*
```

3. This command produces a listing of all the aliases defined that begin with the letter g. An example of the output of this command is shown here:

```
CommandType     Name                          Definition
-----------     ----                          ----------
Alias           gal                           Get-Alias
Alias           gc                            Get-Content
Alias           gci                           Get-ChildItem
Alias           gcm                           Get-Command
Alias           gdr                           Get-PSDrive
```

```
Alias           ghy                           Get-History
Alias           gi                            Get-Item
Alias           gl                            Get-Location
Alias           gm                            Get-Member
Alias           gp                            Get-ItemProperty
Alias           gps                           Get-Process
Alias           group                         Group-Object
Alias           gsv                           Get-Service
Alias           gsnp                          Get-PSSnapin
Alias           gu                            Get-Unique
Alias           gv                            Get-Variable
Alias           gwmi                          Get-WmiObject
Alias           gh                            Get-Help
```

4. Using the *gcm* alias, use the *Get-Command* cmdlet to return the *Get-Command* cmdlet. This is shown here:

```
gcm get-command
```

5. This command returns the *Get-Command* cmdlet. The output is shown here:

```
CommandType     Name                          Definition
-----------     ----                          ----------
Cmdlet          Get-Command                   Get-Command [[-ArgumentList]...
```

6. Using the *gcm* alias to get the *Get-Command* cmdlet, pipe the output to the *Format-List* cmdlet. Use the wild card asterisk (*) to obtain a listing of all the properties of the *Get-Command* cmdlet. This is shown here:

```
gcm get-command |format-list *
```

7. This command will return all the properties from the *Get-Command* cmdlet. The output is shown here:

```
DLL               : C:\WINDOWS\assembly\GAC_MSIL\System.Management.Automation\1.
                    0.0.0__31bf3856ad364e35\System.Management.Automation.dll
Verb              : Get
Noun              : Command
HelpFile          : System.Management.Automation.dll-Help.xml
PSSnapIn          : Microsoft.PowerShell.Core
ImplementingType  : Microsoft.PowerShell.Commands.GetCommandCommand
ParameterSets     : {CmdletSet, AllCommandSet}
Definition        : Get-Command [[-ArgumentList] <Object[]>] [-Verb <String[]>]
                    [-Noun <String[]>] [-PSSnapin <String[]>] [-TotalCount <Int3
                    2>] [-Syntax] [-Verbose] [-Debug] [-ErrorAction <ActionPrefe
                    rence>] [-ErrorVariable <String>] [-OutVariable <String>] [-
                    OutBuffer <Int32>]
                    Get-Command [[-Name] <String[]>] [[-ArgumentList] <Object[]>
                    ] [-CommandType <CommandTypes>] [-TotalCount <Int32>] [-Synt
                    ax] [-Verbose] [-Debug] [-ErrorAction <ActionPreference>] [-
                    ErrorVariable <String>] [-OutVariable <String>] [-OutBuffer
                    <Int32>]

Name              : Get-Command
CommandType       : Cmdlet
```

8. Using the *gcm* alias and the *Get-Command* cmdlet, pipe the output to the *Format-List* cmdlet. Use the -property argument, and specify the definition property of the *Get-Command* cmdlet. Rather than retyping the entire command, use the up arrow on your keyboard to retrieve the previous *gcm Get-Command | Format-List ** command. Use the Backspace key to remove the asterisk and then simply add -property definition to your command. This is shown here:

```
gcm get-command | format-list -property definition
```

9. This command only returns the property definition for the *Get-Command* cmdlet. The returned definition is shown here:

```
Definition : Get-Command [[-ArgumentList] <Object[]>] [-Verb <String[]>] [-Noun
             <String[]>] [-PSSnapin <String[]>] [-TotalCount <Int32>] [-Syntax
             ] [-Verbose] [-Debug] [-ErrorAction <ActionPreference>] [-ErrorVar
             iable <String>] [-OutVariable <String>] [-OutBuffer <Int32>]
             Get-Command [[-Name] <String[]>] [[-ArgumentList] <Object[]>] [-Co
             mmandType <CommandTypes>] [-TotalCount <Int32>] [-Syntax] [-Verbos
             e] [-Debug] [-ErrorAction <ActionPreference>] [-ErrorVariable <Str
             ing>] [-OutVariable <String>] [-OutBuffer <Int32>]
```

10. Because objects are returned from cmdlets instead of simply string data, we can also retrieve the definition of the *Get-Command* cmdlet by directly using the definition property. This is done by putting the expression inside parentheses, and using a "dotted notation," as shown here:

```
(gcm get-command).definition
```

11. The definition returned from the previous command is virtually identical to the one returned by using *Format-List* cmdlet.

12. Use the *gcm* alias and specify the -verb argument. Use *se** for the verb. This is shown here:

```
gcm -verb se*
```

13. The previous command returns a listing of all the cmdlets that contain a verb beginning with se. The result is as follows:

CommandType	Name	Definition
Cmdlet	Select-Object	Select-Object [[-Property] <...
Cmdlet	Select-String	Select-String [-Pattern] <St...
Cmdlet	Set-Acl	Set-Acl [-Path] <String[]> [...
Cmdlet	Set-Alias	Set-Alias [-Name] <String> [...
Cmdlet	Set-AuthenticodeSignature	Set-AuthenticodeSignature [-...
Cmdlet	Set-Content	Set-Content [-Path] <String[...
Cmdlet	Set-Date	Set-Date [-Date] <DateTime> ...
Cmdlet	Set-ExecutionPolicy	Set-ExecutionPolicy [-Execut...
Cmdlet	Set-Item	Set-Item [-Path] <String[]> ...
Cmdlet	Set-ItemProperty	Set-ItemProperty [-Path] <St...
Cmdlet	Set-Location	Set-Location [[-Path] <Strin...
Cmdlet	Set-PSDebug	Set-PSDebug [-Trace <Int32>]...
Cmdlet	Set-Service	Set-Service [-Name] <String>...
Cmdlet	Set-TraceSource	Set-TraceSource [-Name] <Str...
Cmdlet	Set-Variable	Set-Variable [-Name] <String...

14.   Use the *gcm* alias and specify the -noun argument. Use *o** for the noun. This is shown here:

```
gcm -noun o*
```

15.   The previous command will return all the cmdlets that contain a noun that begins with the letter o. This result is as follows:

```
CommandType      Name                        Definition
-----------      ----                        ----------
Cmdlet           Compare-Object              Compare-Object [-ReferenceOb...
Cmdlet           ForEach-Object              ForEach-Object [-Process] <S...
Cmdlet           Group-Object                Group-Object [[-Property] <O...
Cmdlet           Measure-Object              Measure-Object [[-Property] ...
Cmdlet           New-Object                  New-Object [-TypeName] <Stri...
Cmdlet           Select-Object               Select-Object [[-Property] <...
Cmdlet           Sort-Object                 Sort-Object [[-Property] <Ob...
Cmdlet           Tee-Object                  Tee-Object [-FilePath] <Stri...
Cmdlet           Where-Object                Where-Object [-FilterScript]...
Cmdlet           Write-Output                Write-Output [-InputObject] ...
```

16.   Retrieve only the syntax of the *Get-Command* cmdlet by specifying the -syntax argument. Use the *gcm* alias to do this, as shown here:

```
gcm -syntax get-command
```

17.   The syntax of the *Get-Command* cmdlet is returned by the previous command. The output is as follows:

```
Get-Command [[-ArgumentList] <Object[]>] [-Verb <String[]>] [-Noun <String[]>]
[-PSSnapin <String[]>] [-TotalCount <Int32>] [-Syntax] [-Verbose] [-Debug] [-Er
rorAction <ActionPreference>] [-ErrorVariable <String>] [-OutVariable <String>]
[-OutBuffer <Int32>]
Get-Command [[-Name] <String[]>] [[-ArgumentList] <Object[]>] [-CommandType <Co
mmandTypes>] [-TotalCount <Int32>] [-Syntax] [-Verbose] [-Debug] [-ErrorAction
<ActionPreference>] [-ErrorVariable <String>] [-OutVariable <String>] [-OutBuff
er <Int32>]
```

18.   Try to use only aliases to repeat the *Get-Command* syntax command to retrieve the syntax of the *Get-Command* cmdlet. This is shown here:

```
gcm -syntax gcm
```

19.   The result of this command is the not the nice syntax description of the previous command. The rather disappointing result is as follows:

```
Get-Command
```

20.   This concludes the procedure for finding commands by using the *Get-Command* cmdlet.

Quick Check

Q.   **To retrieve a definition of the *Get-Command* cmdlet, using the dotted notation, what command would you use?**

A.   *(gcm get-command).definition*

Using the *Get-Member* Cmdlet

The *Get-Member* cmdlet retrieves information about the members of objects. Although this may not seem very exciting, remember that because everything returned from a cmdlet is an object, we can use the *Get-Member* cmdlet to examine the methods and properties of objects. When the *Get-Member* cmdlet is used with *Get-ChildItem* on the filesystem, it returns a listing of all the methods and properties available to work with the filesystem object.

Objects, Properties, and Methods

One of the more interesting features of Windows PowerShell is that cmdlets return objects. An object is a thing that gives us the ability to either describe something or do something. If we are not going to describe or do something, then there is no reason to create the object. Depending on the circumstances, we may be more interested in the methods, or the properties. As an example, let's consider rental cars. I travel a great deal in my role as a consultant at Microsoft, and I often need to obtain a rental car.

When I get to the airport, I go to the rental car counter, and I use the *New-Object* cmdlet to create the rentalCAR object. When I use this cmdlet, I am only interest in the methods available from the rentalCAR object. I will need to use the DriveDowntheRoad method, the StopAtaRedLight method, and perhaps the PlayNiceMusic method. I am not, however, interested in the properties of the rentalCAR object.

At home, I have a cute little sports car. It has exactly the same methods as the rentalCAR object, but I created the sportsCAR object primarily because of its properties. It is green and has alloy rims, a convertible top, and a 3.5-liter engine. Interestingly enough, it has exactly the same methods as the rentalCAR object. It also has the DriveDowntheRoad method, the StopAtaRedLight method, and the PlayNiceMusic method, but the deciding factor in creating the sportsCAR object was the properties, not the methods.

Just the Steps   **Using the *Get-Member* cmdlet to examine properties and methods** In a Windows PowerShell prompt, enter the *Get-ChildItem* cmdlet followed by the path to a folder and pipe it to the *Get-Member* cmdlet. Example:

```
get-childitem C:\ | get-member
```

Using the *Get-Member* cmdlet

1. Start Windows PowerShell by using *Start | Run | Windows PowerShell*. The PowerShell prompt will open by default at the root of your Documents And Settings.

2. Use an alias to refer to the *Get-Alias* cmdlet. To find the correct alias, use the *Get-Alias* cmdlet as follows:

   ```
   get-alias g*
   ```

3. After you have retrieved the alias for the *Get-Alias* cmdlet, use it to find the alias for the *Get-Member* cmdlet. One way to do this is to use the following command, simply using *gal* in place of the *Get-Alias* name you used in the previous command:

   ```
   gal g*
   ```

4. The listing of aliases defined that begin with the letter g appears as a result of the previous command. The output is shown here:

   ```
   CommandType      Name                  Definition
   -----------      ----                  ----------
   Alias            gal                   Get-Alias
   Alias            gc                    Get-Content
   Alias            gci                   Get-ChildItem
   Alias            gcm                   Get-Command
   Alias            gdr                   Get-PSDrive
   Alias            ghy                   Get-History
   Alias            gi                    Get-Item
   Alias            gl                    Get-Location
   Alias            gm                    Get-Member
   Alias            gp                    Get-ItemProperty
   Alias            gps                   Get-Process
   Alias            group                 Group-Object
   Alias            gsv                   Get-Service
   Alias            gsnp                  Get-PSSnapin
   Alias            gu                    Get-Unique
   Alias            gv                    Get-Variable
   Alias            gwmi                  Get-WmiObject
   Alias            gh                    Get-Help
   ```

5. Use the *gal* alias to obtain a listing of all aliases that begin with the letter g. Pipe the results to the *Sort-Object* cmdlet, and sort on the property attribute called *definition*. This is shown here:

   ```
   gal g* |sort-object -property definition
   ```

6. The listings of cmdlets that begin with the letter g are now sorted, and the results of the command are as follows:

   ```
   CommandType      Name                  Definition
   -----------      ----                  ----------
   Alias            gal                   Get-Alias
   Alias            gci                   Get-ChildItem
   Alias            gcm                   Get-Command
   Alias            gc                    Get-Content
   Alias            gh                    Get-Help
   ```

Alias	ghy	Get-History
Alias	gi	Get-Item
Alias	gp	Get-ItemProperty
Alias	gl	Get-Location
Alias	gm	Get-Member
Alias	gps	Get-Process
Alias	gdr	Get-PSDrive
Alias	gsnp	Get-PSSnapin
Alias	gsv	Get-Service
Alias	gu	Get-Unique
Alias	gv	Get-Variable
Alias	gwmi	Get-WmiObject
Alias	group	Group-Object

7. Use the alias for the *Get-ChildItem* cmdlet and pipe the output to the alias for the *Get-Member* cmdlet. This is shown here:

```
gci | gm
```

8. To only see properties available for the *Get-ChildItem* cmdlet, use the membertype argument and supply a value of property. Use *Tab Completion* this time, rather than the *gci | gm* alias. This is shown here:

```
get-childitem | get-member -membertype property
```

9. The output from this command is shown here:

```
    TypeName: System.IO.DirectoryInfo

Name                 MemberType Definition
----                 ---------- ----------
Attributes           Property   System.IO.FileAttributes Attributes {get;set;}
CreationTime         Property   System.DateTime CreationTime {get;set;}
CreationTimeUtc      Property   System.DateTime CreationTimeUtc {get;set;}
Exists               Property   System.Boolean Exists {get;}
Extension            Property   System.String Extension {get;}
FullName             Property   System.String FullName {get;}
LastAccessTime       Property   System.DateTime LastAccessTime {get;set;}
LastAccessTimeUtc    Property   System.DateTime LastAccessTimeUtc {get;set;}
LastWriteTime        Property   System.DateTime LastWriteTime {get;set;}
LastWriteTimeUtc     Property   System.DateTime LastWriteTimeUtc {get;set;}
Name                 Property   System.String Name {get;}
Parent               Property   System.IO.DirectoryInfo Parent {get;}
Root                 Property   System.IO.DirectoryInfo Root {get;}

    TypeName: System.IO.FileInfo

Name                 MemberType Definition
----                 ---------- ----------
Attributes           Property   System.IO.FileAttributes Attributes {get;set;}
CreationTime         Property   System.DateTime CreationTime {get;set;}
CreationTimeUtc      Property   System.DateTime CreationTimeUtc {get;set;}
Directory            Property   System.IO.DirectoryInfo Directory {get;}
DirectoryName        Property   System.String DirectoryName {get;}
```

```
Exists           Property   System.Boolean Exists {get;}
Extension        Property   System.String Extension {get;}
FullName         Property   System.String FullName {get;}
IsReadOnly       Property   System.Boolean IsReadOnly {get;set;}
LastAccessTime   Property   System.DateTime LastAccessTime {get;set;}
LastAccessTimeUtc Property  System.DateTime LastAccessTimeUtc {get;set;}
LastWriteTime    Property   System.DateTime LastWriteTime {get;set;}
LastWriteTimeUtc Property   System.DateTime LastWriteTimeUtc {get;set;}
Length           Property   System.Int64 Length {get;}
Name             Property   System.String Name {get;}
```

10. Use the membertype argument of the *Get-Member* cmdlet to view the methods available from the object returned by the *Get-ChildItem* cmdlet. To do this, supply a value of method to the membertype argument, as follows:

```
get-childitem | get-member -membertype method
```

11. The output from the previous list returns all the methods defined for the *Get-ChildItem* cmdlet. This output is shown here:

```
TypeName: System.IO.DirectoryInfo

Name                        MemberType  Definition
----                        ----------  ----------
Create                      Method      System.Void Create(), System.Void Creat...
CreateObjRef                Method      System.Runtime.Remoting.ObjRef CreateOb...
CreateSubdirectory          Method      System.IO.DirectoryInfo CreateSubdirect...
Delete                      Method      System.Void Delete(), System.Void Delet...
Equals                      Method      System.Boolean Equals(Object obj)
GetAccessControl            Method      System.Security.AccessControl.Directory...
GetDirectories              Method      System.IO.DirectoryInfo[] GetDirectorie...
GetFiles                    Method      System.IO.FileInfo[] GetFiles(String se...
GetFileSystemInfos          Method      System.IO.FileSystemInfo[] GetFileSyste...
GetHashCode                 Method      System.Int32 GetHashCode()
GetLifetimeService          Method      System.Object GetLifetimeService()
GetObjectData               Method      System.Void GetObjectData(Serialization...
GetType                     Method      System.Type GetType()
get_Attributes              Method      System.IO.FileAttributes get_Attributes()
get_CreationTime            Method      System.DateTime get_CreationTime()
get_CreationTimeUtc         Method      System.DateTime get_CreationTimeUtc()
get_Exists                  Method      System.Boolean get_Exists()
get_Extension               Method      System.String get_Extension()
get_FullName                Method      System.String get_FullName()
get_LastAccessTime          Method      System.DateTime get_LastAccessTime()
get_LastAccessTimeUtc       Method      System.DateTime get_LastAccessTimeUtc()
get_LastWriteTime           Method      System.DateTime get_LastWriteTime()
get_LastWriteTimeUtc        Method      System.DateTime get_LastWriteTimeUtc()
get_Name                    Method      System.String get_Name()
get_Parent                  Method      System.IO.DirectoryInfo get_Parent()
get_Root                    Method      System.IO.DirectoryInfo get_Root()
InitializeLifetimeService   Method      System.Object InitializeLifetimeService()
MoveTo                      Method      System.Void MoveTo(String destDirName)
Refresh                     Method      System.Void Refresh()
SetAccessControl            Method      System.Void SetAccessControl(DirectoryS...
```

```
set_Attributes            Method      System.Void set_Attributes(FileAttribut...
set_CreationTime          Method      System.Void set_CreationTime(DateTime v...
set_CreationTimeUtc       Method      System.Void set_CreationTimeUtc(DateTim...
set_LastAccessTime        Method      System.Void set_LastAccessTime(DateTime...
set_LastAccessTimeUtc     Method      System.Void set_LastAccessTimeUtc(DateT...
set_LastWriteTime         Method      System.Void set_LastWriteTime(DateTime ...
set_LastWriteTimeUtc      Method      System.Void set_LastWriteTimeUtc(DateTi...
ToString                  Method      System.String ToString()
```

12. Use the up arrow key to retrieve the previous *Get-ChildItem | Get-Member -MemberType* method command, and change the value method to *m** to use a wild card to retrieve the methods. The output will be exactly the same as the previous listing of members because the only membertype beginning with the letter m on the *Get-ChildItem* cmdlet is the *MemberType* method. The command is as follows:

```
get-childitem | get-member -membertype m*
```

13. Use the -inputobject argument to the *Get-Member* cmdlet to retrieve member definitions of each property or method in the list. The command to do this is as follows:

```
get-member -inputobject get-childitem
```

14. The output from the previous command is shown here:

```
PS C:\> get-member -inputobject get-childitem


    TypeName: System.String

Name              MemberType      Definition
----              ----------      ----------
Clone             Method          System.Object Clone()
CompareTo         Method          System.Int32 CompareTo(Object value),...
Contains          Method          System.Boolean Contains(String value)
CopyTo            Method          System.Void CopyTo(Int32 sourceIndex,...
EndsWith          Method          System.Boolean EndsWith(String value)...
Equals            Method          System.Boolean Equals(Object obj), Sy...
GetEnumerator     Method          System.CharEnumerator GetEnumerator()
GetHashCode       Method          System.Int32 GetHashCode()
GetType           Method          System.Type GetType()
GetTypeCode       Method          System.TypeCode GetTypeCode()
get_Chars         Method          System.Char get_Chars(Int32 index)
get_Length        Method          System.Int32 get_Length()
IndexOf           Method          System.Int32 IndexOf(Char value, Int3...
IndexOfAny        Method          System.Int32 IndexOfAny(Char[] anyOf,...
Insert            Method          System.String Insert(Int32 startIndex...
IsNormalized      Method          System.Boolean IsNormalized(), System...
LastIndexOf       Method          System.Int32 LastIndexOf(Char value, ...
LastIndexOfAny    Method          System.Int32 LastIndexOfAny(Char[] an...
Normalize         Method          System.String Normalize(), System.Str...
PadLeft           Method          System.String PadLeft(Int32 totalWidt...
PadRight          Method          System.String PadRight(Int32 totalWid...
Remove            Method          System.String Remove(Int32 startIndex...
Replace           Method          System.String Replace(Char oldChar, C...
Split             Method          System.String[] Split(Params Char[] s...
StartsWith        Method          System.Boolean StartsWith(String valu...
```

```
Substring          Method              System.String Substring(Int32 startIn...
ToCharArray        Method              System.Char[] ToCharArray(), System.C...
ToLower            Method              System.String ToLower(), System.Strin...
ToLowerInvariant   Method              System.String ToLowerInvariant()
ToString           Method              System.String ToString(), System.Stri...
ToUpper            Method              System.String ToUpper(), System.Strin...
ToUpperInvariant   Method              System.String ToUpperInvariant()
Trim               Method              System.String Trim(Params Char[] trim...
TrimEnd            Method              System.String TrimEnd(Params Char[] t...
TrimStart          Method              System.String TrimStart(Params Char[]...
Chars              ParameterizedProperty System.Char Chars(Int32 index) {get;}
Length             Property            System.Int32 Length {get;}
```

15. This concludes the procedure for using the *Get-Member* cmdlet.

Quick Check

Q. **To retrieve a listing of aliases beginning with the letter g that is sorted on the definition property, what command would you use?**

A.   *gal g* | sort-object -property definition*

Using the *New-Object* Cmdlet

The use of objects in Windows PowerShell provides many exciting opportunities to do things that are not "built into" the PowerShell. You may recall from using VBScript that there is an object called the wshShell object. If you are not familiar with this object, a drawing of the object model is shown in Figure 2-1.

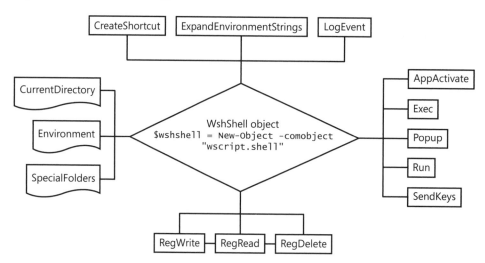

Figure 2-1   The VBScript wshShell object contributes many easy-to-use methods and properties for the network administrator

Just the Steps   To create a new instance of the wshShell object, use the *New-Object* cmdlet while specifying the -comobject argument and supplying the program ID of "wscript.shell". Hold the object created in a variable. Example:

```
$wshShell = new-object -comobject "wscript.shell":
```

After the object has been created and stored in a variable, you can directly use any of the methods that are provided by the object. This is shown in the two lines of code that follow:

```
$wshShell = new-object -comobject "wscript.shell"
$wshShell.run("calc.exe")
```

In the previous code, we use the *New-Object* cmdlet to create an instance of the wshShell object. We then use the run method to launch Calculator. After the object is created and stored in the variable, you can use *Tab Completion* to suggest the names of the methods contained in the object. This is shown in Figure 2-2.

```
powershell                                           _ □ ×
Windows PowerShell
Copyright (C) 2006 Microsoft Corporation. All rights reserved.

PS C:\> $wshShell = New-Object -comobject "wscript.shell"
PS C:\> $wshShell.Run(_
```

Figure 2-2   Tab Completion enumerates methods provided by the object

Creating the wshShell object

1. Start the Windows PowerShell by using *Start | Run | Windows PowerShell*. The PowerShell prompt will open by default at the root of your Documents And Settings.

2. Create an instance of the wshShell object by using the *New-Object* cmdlet. Supply the comobject argument to the cmdlet, and specify the program ID for the wshShell object, which is "wscript.shell". Hold the object that is returned into a variable called *$wshShell*. The code to do this is as follows:

```
$wshShell = new-object -comobject "wscript.shell"
```

3. Launch an instance of Calculator by using the run method from the wshShell object. Use *Tab Completion* to avoid having to type the entire name of the method. To use the method, begin the line with the variable you used to hold the wshShell object, followed by a period and the name of the method. Then supply the name of the program to run inside parentheses and quotes, as shown here:

    ```
    $wshShell.run("Calc.exe")
    ```

4. Use the ExpandEnvironmentStrings method to print out the path to the Windows directory. It is stored in an environmental variable called *%windir%*. The *Tab Completion* feature of Windows PowerShell is useful for this method name. The environment variable must be contained in quotation marks, as shown here:

    ```
    $wshShell.ExpandEnvironmentStrings("%windir%")
    ```

5. This command reveals the full path to the Windows directory on your machine. On my computer, the output looks like the following:

    ```
    C:\WINDOWS
    ```

Creating a PowerShell Profile

As you create various aliases and functions, you may decide you like a particular key stroke combination and wish you could use your definition without always having to create it.

> **Tip**   I recommend reviewing the listing of all the aliases defined within Windows PowerShell before creating very many new aliases. The reason is that it will be easy, early on, to create duplicate settings (with slight variations).

Of course, you could create your own script that would perform your configuration if you remembered to run it; however, what if you wish to have a more standardized method of working with your profile? To do this, you need to create a custom profile that will hold your settings. The really useful feature of creating a Windows PowerShell profile is that after the profile is created, it loads automatically when PowerShell is launched. The steps for creating a Windows PowerShell profile are listed here:

Just the Steps   Creating a Windows PowerShell profile

1. In a Windows PowerShell prompt, determine whether a profile exists by using the following command:

   ```
   test-path $profile
   ```

2. If tests-profile returns false, create a new profile file by using the following command:

   ```
   new-item -path $profile -itemtype file -force
   ```

3. Open the profile file in Notepad by using the following command:

   ```
   notepad $profile
   ```

4. Add the following toNotepad:

   A useful alias such as *gh* for *Get-Help*. This is shown here:

   ```
   Set-alias gh get-help
   ```

   A useful function to the profile such as one to open the profile in Notepad to allow for ease of editing the profile. This is shown here:

   ```
   function pro {notepad $profile}
   ```

5. When done editing, save the profile. Click Save As from the File menu, and ensure that you choose ALL Files in the dialog box to avoid saving the profile with a .txt extension. This is shown in Figure 2-3.

Figure 2-3   Ensure that Windows PowerShell can read the profile by saving it with the *All Files* option, under Save As Type, in Notepad

> **Just the Steps**   **Finding all aliases for a particular object** If you know the name of an
> object and you would like to retrieve all aliases for that object, you can use the *Get-Alias*
> cmdlet to retrieve the list of all aliases. Then you need to pipe the results to the *Where-Object*
> cmdlet and specify the value for the definition property. An example of doing this for the
> *Get-ChildItem* cmdlet is as follows:
>
> ```
> gal | where-object {$_.definition -match "get-childitem"}
> ```

Working with Cmdlets: Step-by-Step Exercises

In this exercise, we explore the use of the *Get-ChildItem* and *Get-Member* cmdlets in Windows
PowerShell. You will see that it is easy to use these cmdlets to automate routine administrative
tasks. We also continue to experiment with the pipelining feature of Windows PowerShell.

1. Start Windows PowerShell by using *Start | Run | Windows PowerShell.* The PowerShell
   prompt will open by default at the root of your Documents And Settings.

2. Use the *Get-Alias* cmdlet to retrieve a listing of all the aliases defined on the computer.
   Pipe this output to a *Where-Object* cmdlet. Specify a match argument against the definition property that matches the name of the *Get-ChildItem* cmdlet. The code is as follows:

   ```
   gal | where-object {$_.definition -match "get-childitem"}
   ```

3. The results from the previous command show three aliases defined for the *Get-ChildItem*
   cmdlet, as shown here:

   ```
   CommandType     Name                         Definition
   -----------     ----                         ----------
   Alias           gci                          Get-ChildItem
   Alias           ls                           Get-ChildItem
   Alias           dir                          Get-ChildItem
   ```

4. Using the *gci* alias for the *Get-ChildItem* cmdlet, obtain a listing of files and folders contained in the root directory. This is shown here:

   ```
   gci
   ```

5. To identify large files more quickly, pipe the output to a *Where-Object* cmdlet, and specify
   the gt argument with a value of 1,000 to evaluate the length property. This is shown here:

   ```
   gci | where-object {$_.length -gt 1000}
   ```

6. To remove the cluttered data from your Windows PowerShell window, use *cls* to clear the
   screen. This is shown here:

   ```
   cls
   ```

7. Use the *Get-Alias* cmdlet to resolve the cmdlet to which the *cls* alias points. You can use
   the *gal* alias to avoid typing **get-alias** if you wish. This is shown here:

   ```
   gal cls
   ```

8. Use the *Get-Alias* cmdlet to resolve the cmdlet to which the *mred* alias points. This is shown here:

```
gal mred
```

9. It is likely that no *mred* alias is defined on your machine. In this case, you will see the following error message:

```
Get-Alias : Cannot find alias because alias 'mred' does not exist.
At line:1 char:4
+ gal <<<< mred
```

10. Use the *Clear-Host* cmdlet to clear the screen. This is shown here:

```
clear-host
```

11. Use the *Get-Member* cmdlet to retrieve a list of properties and methods from the *Get-ChildItem* cmdlet. This is shown here:

```
get-childitem | get-member -membertype property
```

12. The output from the above command is shown here. Examine the output, and identify a property that could be used with a *Where-Object* cmdlet to find the date that files have been modified.

```
Name               MemberType Definition
----               ---------- ----------
Attributes         Property   System.IO.FileAttributes Attributes {get;set;}
CreationTime       Property   System.DateTime CreationTime {get;set;}
CreationTimeUtc    Property   System.DateTime CreationTimeUtc {get;set;}
Directory          Property   System.IO.DirectoryInfo Directory {get;}
DirectoryName      Property   System.String DirectoryName {get;}
Exists             Property   System.Boolean Exists {get;}
Extension          Property   System.String Extension {get;}
FullName           Property   System.String FullName {get;}
IsReadOnly         Property   System.Boolean IsReadOnly {get;set;}
LastAccessTime     Property   System.DateTime LastAccessTime {get;set;}
LastAccessTimeUtc  Property   System.DateTime LastAccessTimeUtc {get;set;}
LastWriteTime      Property   System.DateTime LastWriteTime {get;set;}
LastWriteTimeUtc   Property   System.DateTime LastWriteTimeUtc {get;set;}
Length             Property   System.Int64 Length {get;}
Name               Property   System.String Name {get;}
```

13. Use the *Where-Object* cmdlet and choose the LastWriteTime property. This is shown here:

```
get-childitem | where-object {$_.LastWriteTime}
```

14. Use the up arrow and bring the previous command back up onto the command line. Now specify the gt argument and choose a recent date from your previous list of files, so you can ensure the query will return a result. My command looks like the following:

```
get-childitem | where-object {$_.LastWriteTime -gt "12/25/2006"}
```

15. Use the up arrow and retrieve the last command. Now direct the *Get-ChildItem* cmdlet to a specific folder on your hard drive, such as C:\fso, which may have been created in the

step-by-step exercise from Chapter 1. You can, of course, use any folder that exists on your machine. This command will look like the following:

```
get-childitem "C:\fso"| where-object {$_.LastWriteTime -gt "12/25/2006"}
```

16. Once again, use the up arrow and retrieve the last command. Add the recurse argument to the *Get-ChildItem* cmdlet. If your previous folder was not nested, then you may want to change to a different folder. You can, of course, use your Windows folder, which is rather deeply nested. I used my VBScript workshop folder, and the command is shown here (keep in mind that this command has wrapped and should be interpreted as a single line):

```
get-childitem -recurse "d:\vbsworkshop"| where-object
{$_.LastWriteTime -gt "12/25/2006" }
```

17. This concludes this step-by-step exercise. Completed commands for this exercise are in the StepByStep.txt file.

One Step Further: Working with *New-Object*

In this exercise, we create a couple of objects.

1. Start Windows PowerShell by using *Start | Run | Windows PowerShell*. The PowerShell prompt will open by default at the root of your Documents And Settings.

2. Create an instance of the wshNetwork object by using the *New-Object* cmdlet. Use the comobject argument, and give it the program ID for the wshNetwork object, which is "wscript.network". Store the results in a variable called *$wshnetwork*. The code looks like the following:

```
$wshnetwork = new-object -comobject "wscript.network"
```

3. Use the EnumPrinterConnections method from the wshNetwork object to print out a list of printer connections that are defined on your local computer. To do this, use the wshNetwork object that is contained in the *$wshnetwork* variable. The command for this is as follows:

```
$wshnetwork.EnumPrinterConnections()
```

4. Use the EnumNetworkDrives method from the wshNetwork object to print out a list of network connections that are defined on your local computer. To do this, use the wshNetwork object that is contained in the *$wshnetwork* variable. The command for this is as follows:

```
$wshnetwork.EnumNetworkDrives()
```

5. Use the up arrow twice and retrieve the *$wshnetwork.EnumPrinterConnections()* command. Use the *$colPrinters* variable to hold the collection of printers that is returned by the command. The code looks as follows:

```
$colPrinters = $wshnetwork.EnumPrinterConnections()
```

6. Use the up arrow and retrieve the *$wshnetwork.EnumNetworkDrives()* command. Use the Home key to move the insertion point to the beginning of the line. Modify the command so that it holds the collection of drives returned by the command into a variable called *$colDrives*. This is shown here:

```
$colDrives = $wshnetwork.EnumNetworkDrives()
```

7. Use the *$userName* variable to hold the name that is returned by querying the username property from the wshNetwork object. This is shown here:

```
$userName = $wshnetwork.UserName
```

8. Use the *$userDomain* variable to hold the name that is returned by querying the User-Domain property from the wshNetwork object. This is shown here:

```
$userDomain = $wshnetwork.UserDomain
```

9. Use the *$computerName* variable to hold the name that is returned by querying the User-Domain property from the wshNetwork object. This is shown here:

```
$computerName = $wshnetwork.ComputerName
```

10. Create an instance of the wshShell object by using the *New-Object* cmdlet. Use the comobject argument and give it the program ID for the wshShell object, which is "wscript.shell". Store the results in a variable called *$wshShell*. The code for this follows:

```
$wshShell = new-object -comobject "wscript.shell"
```

11. Use the Popup method from the wshShell object to produce a popup box that displays the domain name, user name, and computer name. The code for this follows:

```
$wshShell.Popup($userDomain+"\$userName $computerName")
```

12. Use the Popup method from the wshShell object to produce a popup box that displays the collection of printers held in the *$colPrinters* variable. The code looks as follows:

```
$wshShell.Popup($colPrinters)
```

13. Use the Popup method from the wshShell object to produce a popup box that displays the collection of drives held in the *$colDrives* variable. The code is as follows:

```
$wshShell.Popup($colDrives)
```

14. This concludes this one step further exercise. Completed commands for this exercise are in the OneStepFurther.txt file.

Chapter 2 Quick Reference

To	Do This
Produce a list of all the files in a folder	Use the *Get-ChildItem* cmdlet and supply a value for the folder
Produce a list of all the files in a folder and in the sub-folders	Use the *Get-ChildItem* cmdlet, supply a value for the folder, and specify the recurse argument
Produce a wide output of the results of a previous cmdlet	Use the appropriate cmdlet and pipe the resulting object to the *Format-Wide* cmdlet
Produce a listing of all the methods available from the *Get-ChildItem* cmdlet	Use the cmdlet and pipe the results into the *Get-Member* cmdlet. Use the -membertype argument and supply the Noun method
Produce a popup box	Create an instance of the wshShell object by using the *New-Object* cmdlet. Use the Popup method
Retrieve the currently logged-on user name	Create an instance of the wshNetwork object by using the *New-Object* cmdlet. Query the username property
Retrieve a listing of all currently mapped drives	Create an instance of the wshNetwork object by using the *New-Object* cmdlet. Use the EnumNetworkDrives method

Chapter 3

Leveraging PowerShell Providers

After completing this chapter, you will be able to:

- Understand the role of providers in Windows PowerShell

- Use the *Get-PSProvider* cmdlet

- Use the *Get-PSDrive* cmdlet

- Use the *Get-Item* cmdlet

- Use the *Set-Location* cmdlet

- Use the file system model to access data from each of the built-in providers

Windows PowerShell provides a consistent way to access information external to the shell environment. To do this, it uses providers. These providers are actually .NET programs that hide all the ugly details to provide an easy way to access information. The beautiful thing about the way the provider model works is that all the different sources of information are accessed in exactly the same manner. This chapter demonstrates how to leverage the Power-Shell providers. All the scripts mentioned in this chapter can be found in the corresponding scripts folder on the CD.

Identifying the Providers

By identifying the providers installed with Windows PowerShell, we can begin to understand the capabilities intrinsic to a default installation. Providers expose information contained in different data stores by using a drive and file system analogy. An example of this is obtaining a listing of registry keys—to do this, you would connect to the registry "drive" and use the *Get-ChildItem* cmdlet, which is exactly the same method you would use to obtain a listing of files on the hard drive. The only difference is the specific name associated with each drive. Providers can be created by anyone familiar with Windows .NET programming. When a new provider is created, it is called a *snap-in*. A snap-in is a dynamic link library (*dll*) file that must be installed into Windows PowerShell. After a snap-in has been installed, it cannot be un-installed—however, the snap-in can be removed from the current Windows PowerShell console.

Just the Steps   To obtain a listing of all the providers, use the *Get-PSProvider* cmdlet. Example: get-psprovider. This command produces the following list on a default installation of the Windows PowerShell:

```
Name               Capabilities              Drives
----               ------------              ------
Alias              ShouldProcess             {Alias}
Environment        ShouldProcess             {Env}
FileSystem         Filter, ShouldProcess     {C, D, E, F...}
Function           ShouldProcess             {Function}
Registry           ShouldProcess             {HKLM, HKCU}
Variable           ShouldProcess             {Variable}
Certificate        ShouldProcess             {cert}
```

Understanding the Alias Provider

In Chapter 1, Overview of Windows PowerShell, we presented the various *Help* utilities available that show how to use cmdlets. The alias provider provides easy-to-use access to all aliases defined in Windows PowerShell. To work with the aliases on your machine, use the *Set-Location* cmdlet and specify the Alias:\ drive. You can then use the same cmdlets you would use to work with the file system.

Tip   With the alias provider, you can use a *Where-Object* cmdlet and filter to search for an alias by name or description.

Working with the alias provider

1. Open Windows PowerShell.

2. Obtain a listing of all the providers by using the *Get-PSProvider* cmdlet. This is shown here:

   ```
   Get-PSProvider
   ```

3. The PSDrive associated with the alias provider is called Alias. This is seen in the listing produced by the *Get-PSProvider* cmdlet. Use the *Set-Location* cmdlet to change to the Alias drive. Use the *sl* alias to reduce typing. This command is shown here:

   ```
   sl alias:\
   ```

4. Use the *Get-ChildItem* cmdlet to produce a listing of all the aliases that are defined on the system. To reduce typing, use the alias *gci* in place of *Get-ChildItem*. This is shown here:

   ```
   GCI
   ```

5. Use a *Where-Object* cmdlet filter to reduce the amount of information that is returned by using the *Get-ChildItem* cmdlet. Produce a listing of all the aliases that begin with the letter s. This is shown here:

   ```
   GCI | Where-Object {$_.name -like "s*"}
   ```

6. To identify other properties that could be used in the filter, pipeline the results of the *Get-ChildItem* cmdlet into the *Get-Member* cmdlet. This is shown here:

```
Get-ChildItem |Get-Member
```

7. Press the up arrow twice, and edit the previous filter to include only definitions that contain the word set. The modified filter is shown here:

```
GCI | Where-Object {$_.definition -like "set*"}
```

8. The results of this command are shown here:

```
CommandType       Name                    Definition
-----------       ----                    ----------
Alias             sal                     Set-Alias
Alias             sc                      Set-Content
Alias             si                      Set-Item
Alias             sl                      Set-Location
Alias             sp                      Set-ItemProperty
Alias             sv                      Set-Variable
Alias             cd                      Set-Location
Alias             chdir                   Set-Location
Alias             set                     Set-Variable
```

9. Press the up arrow three times, and edit the previous filter to include only names of aliases that are like the letter w. This revised command is seen here:

```
GCI | Where-Object {$_.name -like "*w*"}
```

10. The results from this command are similar to those shown here:

```
CommandType       Name                    Definition
-----------       ----                    ----------
Alias             fw                      Format-Wide
Alias             gwmi                    Get-WmiObject
Alias             where                   Where-Object
Alias             write                   Write-Output
Alias             pwd                     Get-Location
```

11. From the list above, note that *where* is an alias for the *Where-Object* cmdlet. Press the up arrow one time to retrieve the previous command. Edit it to use the *where* alias instead of spelling out the entire *Where-Object* cmdlet name. This revised command is seen here:

```
GCI | where {$_.name -like "*w*"}
```

Caution   When using the *Set-Location* cmdlet to switch to a newly created PSDrive, you must follow the name of the PSDrive with a colon. A trailing forward slash or backward slash is optional. An error will be generated if the colon is left out, as shown in Figure 3-1. I prefer to use the backward slash (\) because it is consistent with normal Windows file system operations.

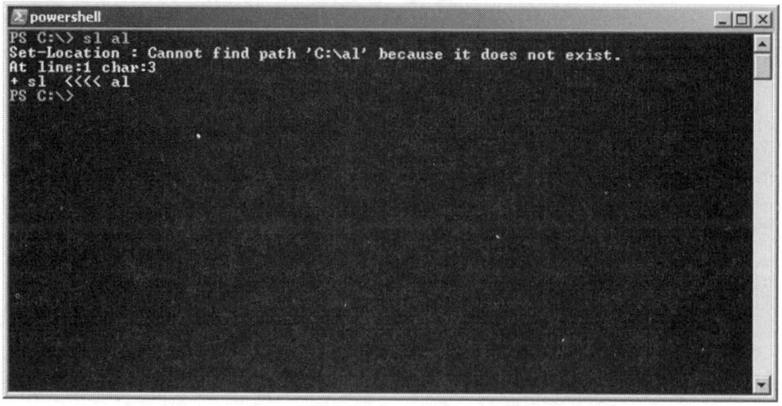

Figure 3-1   Using Set-Location without : results in an error

Understanding the Certificate Provider

In the preceding section, we explored working with the alias provider. Because the file system model applies to the certificate provider in much the same way as it did the alias provider, many of the same cmdlets can be used. To find information about the certificate provider, use the *Get-Help* cmdlet. If you are unsure what articles in *Help* may be related to certificates, you can use the wild card asterisk (*) parameter. This command is shown here:

```
get-help *cer*
```

The certificate provider gives you the ability to sign scripts and allows Windows PowerShell to work with signed and unsigned scripts as well. It also gives you the ability search for, copy, move, and delete certificates. Using the certificate provider, you can even open the Certificates Microsoft Management Console (MMC). The commands used in the procedure are in the ObtainingAListingOfCertificates.txt file.

Obtaining a listing of certificates

1. Open Windows PowerShell.

2. Set your location to the cert PSDrive. To do this, use the *Set-Location* cmdlet, as shown here:

    ```
    Set-Location cert:\
    ```

3. Use the *Get-ChildItem* cmdlet to produce a list of the certificates, as shown here:

    ```
    Get-ChildItem
    ```

4. The list produced is shown here:

    ```
    Location   : CurrentUser
    StoreNames : {?, UserDS, AuthRoot, CA...}

    Location   : LocalMachine
    StoreNames : {?, AuthRoot, CA, AddressBook...}
    ```

5. Use the -recurse argument to cause the *Get-ChildItem* cmdlet to produce a list of all the certificate stores. To do this, press the up arrow key one time, and add the -recurse argument to the previous command. This is shown here:

```
Get-ChildItem -recurse
```

6. Use the -path argument for *Get-ChildItem* to produce a listing of certificates in another store, without having to use the *Set-Location* cmdlet to change your current location. Using the *gci* alias, the command is shown here:

```
GCI -path currentUser
```

7. Your listing of certificate stores will look similar to the one shown here:

```
Name : ?

Name : UserDS

Name : AuthRoot

Name : CA

Name : AddressBook

Name : ?

Name : Trust

Name : Disallowed

Name : _NMSTR

Name : ?????k

Name : My

Name : Root

Name : TrustedPeople

Name : ACRS

Name : TrustedPublisher

Name : REQUEST
```

8. Change your working location to the currentuser\authroot certificate store. To do this, use the *sl* alias followed by the path to the certificate store. This command is shown here:

```
sl currentuser\authroot
```

9. Use the *Get-ChildItem* cmdlet to produce a listing of certificates in the currentuser\authroot certificate store that contain the name C&W in the subject field. Use the *gci* alias to reduce the amount of typing. Pipeline the resulting object to a *Where-Object* cmdlet, but use the *where* alias instead of typing *Where-Object*. The code to do this is shown here:

```
GCI | where {$_.subject -like "*c&w*"}
```

10. On my machine, there are four certificates listed. These are shown here:

```
Thumbprint                                Subject
---------                                 -------
F88015D3F98479E1DA553D24FD42BA3F43886AEF  O=C&W HKT SecureNet CA SGC Root, C=hk
9BACF3B664EAC5A17BED08437C72E4ACDA12F7E7  O=C&W HKT SecureNet CA Class A, C=hk
4BA7B9DDD68788E12FF852E1A024204BF286A8F6  O=C&W HKT SecureNet CA Root, C=hk
47AFB915CDA26D82467B97FA42914468726138DD  O=C&W HKT SecureNet CA Class B, C=hk
```

11. Use the up arrow, and edit the previous command so that it will return only certificates that contain the phrase *SGC Root* in the subject property. The revised command is shown here:

```
GCI | where {$_.subject -like "*SGC Root*"}
```

12. The resulting output on my machine contains an additional certificate. This is shown here:

```
Thumbprint                                Subject
---------                                 -------
F88015D3F98479E1DA553D24FD42BA3F43886AEF  O=C&W HKT SecureNet CA SGC Root, C=hk
687EC17E0602E3CD3F7DFBD7E28D57A0199A3F44  O=SecureNet CA SGC Root, C=au
```

13. Use the up arrow, and edit the previous command. This time, change the *Where-Object* cmdlet so that it filters on the thumbprint attribute that is equal to F88015D3F98479E1DA553D24FD42BA3F43886AEF. You do not have to type that, however; to copy the thumbprint, you can highlight it and press Enter in Windows PowerShell, as shown in Figure 3-2. The revised command is shown here:

```
GCI | where {$_.thumbprint -eq "F88015D3F98479E1DA553D24FD42BA3F43886AEF"}
```

Figure 3-2 Highlight items to copy using the mouse

> **Troubleshooting**   If copying from inside a Windows PowerShell window does not work, then you probably need to enable Quick Edit Mode. To do this, right-click the PowerShell icon in the upper left-hand corner of the Windows PowerShell window. Choose Properties, and select Quick Edit Mode. This is shown in Figure 3-3.

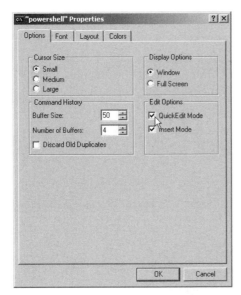

Figure 3-3   Enable Quick Edit Mode to enable Clipboard Support

14. To see all the properties of the certificate, pipeline the certificate object to a *Format-List* cmdlet and choose all the properties. The revised command is shown here:

```
GCI | where {$_.thumbprint -eq "F88015D3F98479E1DA553D24FD42BA3F43886AEF"} |
Format-List *
```

15. The output contains all the properties of the certificate object and is shown here:

```
PSPath            : Microsoft.PowerShell.Security\Certificate::currentuser\aut
                    hroot\F88015D3F98479E1DA553D24FD42BA3F43886AEF
PSParentPath      : Microsoft.PowerShell.Security\Certificate::currentuser\aut
                    hroot
PSChildName       : F88015D3F98479E1DA553D24FD42BA3F43886AEF
PSDrive           : cert
PSProvider        : Microsoft.PowerShell.Security\Certificate
PSIsContainer     : False
Archived          : False
Extensions        : {}
FriendlyName      : CW HKT SecureNet CA SGC Root
IssuerName        : System.Security.Cryptography.X509Certificates.X500Distingu
                    ishedName
NotAfter          : 10/16/2009 5:59:00 AM
NotBefore         : 6/30/1999 6:00:00 AM
HasPrivateKey     : False
PrivateKey        :
```

```
PublicKey         : System.Security.Cryptography.X509Certificates.PublicKey
RawData           : {48, 130, 2, 235...}
SerialNumber      : 00
SubjectName       : System.Security.Cryptography.X509Certificates.X500Distingu
                    ishedName
SignatureAlgorithm : System.Security.Cryptography.Oid
Thumbprint        : F88015D3F98479E1DA553D24FD42BA3F43886AEF
Version           : 1
Handle            : 75655840
Issuer            : O=C&W HKT SecureNet CA SGC Root, C=hk
Subject           : O=C&W HKT SecureNet CA SGC Root, C=hk
```

16. Open the Certificates MMC. This MMC is called Certmgr.msc and can be launched by simply typing the name inside Windows PowerShell, as shown here:

```
Certmgr.msc
```

17. But it is more fun to use the *Invoke-Item* cmdlet to launch the Certificates MMC. To do this, supply the PSDrive name of cert:\ to the *Invoke-Item* cmdlet. This is shown here:

```
Invoke-Item cert:\
```

18. Compare the information obtained from Windows PowerShell with the information displayed in the Certificates MMC. They are the same. The certificate is shown in Figure 3-4.

Figure 3-4 Certmgr.msc can be used to examine certificate properties

19. This concludes this procedure.

Understanding the Environment Provider

The environment provider in Windows PowerShell is used to provide access to the system environment variables. If you open a CMD (command) shell and type **set**, you will obtain a listing of all the environment variables defined on the system. If you use the echo command in the CMD shell to print out the value of %windir%, you will obtain the results seen in Figure 3-5.

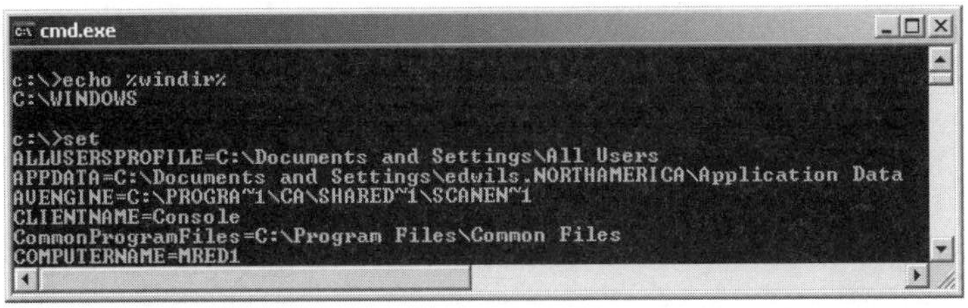

Figure 3-5   Use *set* in a CMD prompt to see environment variables

Environment variables are used by various applications and other utilities as a shortcut to provide easy access to specific files, folders, and configuration data. By using the environment provider in Windows PowerShell, you can obtain a listing of the environment variables. You can also add, change, clear, and delete these variables.

Obtaining a listing of environment variables

1. Open Windows PowerShell.

2. Obtain a listing of the PSDrives by using the *Get-PSDrive* cmdlet. This is shown here:

    ```
    Get-PSDrive
    ```

3. Note that the Environment PSDrive is called *env*. Use the *env* name with the *Set-Location* cmdlet and change to the environment PSDrive. This is shown here:

    ```
    Set-Location env:\
    ```

4. Use the *Get-Item* cmdlet to obtain a listing of all the environment variables on the system. This is shown here:

    ```
    Get-Item *
    ```

5. Use the *Sort-Object* cmdlet to produce an alphabetical listing of all the environment variables by name. Use the up arrow to retrieve the previous command, and pipeline the returned object into the *Sort-Object* cmdlet. Use the property argument, and supply name as the value. This command is shown here:

    ```
    get-item * | Sort-Object  -property name
    ```

6. Use the *Get-Item* cmdlet to retrieve the value associated with the environment variable *windir*. This is shown here:

```
get-item windir
```

7. Use the up arrow and retrieve the previous command. Pipeline the object returned to the *Format-List* cmdlet and use the wild card character to print out all the properties of the object. The modified command is shown here:

```
get-item windir | Format-List *
```

8. The properties and their associated values are shown here:

```
PSPath        : Microsoft.PowerShell.Core\Environment::windir
PSDrive       : Env
PSProvider    : Microsoft.PowerShell.Core\Environment
PSIsContainer : False
Name          : windir
Key           : windir
Value         : C:\WINDOWS
```

9. This concludes this procedure. Do not close Windows PowerShell. Leave it open for the next procedure.

Creating a new environment variable

1. You should still be in the Environment PSDrive from the previous procedure. If not, use the *Set-Location env:* command).

2. Use the *Get-Item* cmdlet to produce a listing of all the environment variables. Pipeline the returned object to the *Sort-Object* cmdlet using the property of name. To reduce typing, use the *gi* alias and the *sort* alias. This is shown here:

```
GI * | Sort -Property Name
```

3. Use the *New-Item* cmdlet to create a new environment variable. The path argument will be dot (.) because you are already on the env:\ PSDrive. The -name argument will be admin, and the value argument will be your given name. The completed command is shown here:

```
New-Item -Path . -Name admin -Value mred
```

4. Use the *Get-Item* cmdlet to ensure the *admin* environment variable was properly created. This command is shown here:

```
Get-Item admin
```

5. The results of the previous command are shown here:

```
Name                    Value
----                    -----
admin                   mred
```

6. Use the up arrow to retrieve the previous command. Pipeline the results to the *Format-List* cmdlet, and choose All Properties. This command is shown here:

```
Get-Item admin | Format-List *
```

7. The results of the previous command include the PSPath, PSDrive, and additional information about the newly created environment variable. These results are shown here:

```
PSPath        : Microsoft.PowerShell.Core\Environment::admin
PSDrive       : Env
PSProvider    : Microsoft.PowerShell.Core\Environment
PSIsContainer : False
Name          : admin
Key           : admin
Value         : mred
```

8. This concludes this procedure. Leave PowerShell open for the next procedure.

Renaming an environment variable

1. Use the *Get-ChildItem* cmdlet to obtain a listing of all the environment variables. Pipeline the returned object to the *Sort-Object* cmdlet and sort the list on the name property. Use the *gci* and *sort* aliases to reduce typing. The code to do this is shown here:

```
GCI | Sort -Property name
```

2. The *admin* environment variable should be near the top of the list of system variables. If it is not, then create it by using the *New-Item* cmdlet. The path argument has a value of dot (.); the name argument has the value of admin; and the value argument should be the user's given name. If this environment variable was created in the previous exercise, then PowerShell will report that it already exists. This is shown here:

```
New-Item -Path . -Name admin -Value mred
```

3. Use the *Rename-Item* cmdlet to rename the *admin* environment variable to *super*. The path argument combines both the PSDrive name and the environment variable name. The NewName argument is the desired new name without the PSDrive specification. This command is shown here:

```
Rename-Item -Path env:admin -NewName super
```

4. To verify that the old environment variable *admin* has been renamed *super*, press the up arrow two or three times to retrieve the *gci | sort -property name* command. This is command is shown here:

```
GCI | Sort -Property name
```

5. This concludes this procedure. Do not close the Windows PowerShell. Leave it open for the next procedure.

Removing an environment variable

1. Use the *Get-ChildItem* cmdlet to obtain a listing of all the environment variables. Pipeline the returned object to the *Sort-Object* cmdlet and sort the list on the name property. Use the *gci* and *sort* aliases to reduce typing. The code to do this is shown here:

```
GCI | Sort -Property name
```

2. The *super* environment variable should be in the list of system variables. If it is not, then create it by using the *New-Item* cmdlet. The path argument has a value of dot (.); the name argument has the value of super; and the value argument should be the user's given name. If this environment variable was created in the previous exercise, then PowerShell will report that it already exists. This is shown here:

```
New-Item -Path . -Name super -Value mred
```

3. Use the *Remove-Item* cmdlet to remove the *super* environment variable. The name of the item to be removed is typed following the name of the cmdlet. If you are still in the env:\ PSDrive, you will not need to supply a -path argument. The command is shown here:

```
Remove-Item super
```

4. Use the *Get-ChildItem* cmdlet to verify that the environment variable *super* has been removed. To do this, press the up arrow 2 or 3 times to retrieve the *gci* | *sort -property name* command. This command is shown here:

```
GCI | Sort -Property name
```

5. This concludes this procedure.

Understanding File System Provider

The file system provider is the easiest Windows PowerShell provider to understand—it provides access to the file system. When Windows PowerShell is launched, it automatically opens on the C:\PSDrive. Using the Windows PowerShell filesystem provider, you can create both directories and files. You can retrieve properties of files and directories, and you can delete them as well. In addition, you can open files and append or overwrite data to the files. This can be done with inline code, or by using the pipelining feature of Windows PowerShell. The commands used in the procedure are in the IdentifyingPropertiesOfDirectories.txt, CreatingFoldersAndFiles.txt, and ReadingAndWritingForFiles.txt files.

Working with directory listings

1. Open Windows PowerShell.

2. Use the *Get-ChildItem* cmdlet to obtain a directory listing of the C:\ drive. Use the *gci* alias to reduce typing. This is shown here:

```
GCI C:\
```

3. Use the up arrow to retrieve the *gci C:* command. Pipeline the object created into a *Where-Object* cmdlet, and look for containers. This will reduce the output to only directories. The modified command is shown here:

```
GCI C:\ | where {$_.psiscontainer}
```

4. Use the up arrow to retrieve the *gci C:\ | where {$_.psiscontainer}* command and use the exclamation point (!), meaning *not*, to retrieve only items in the PSDrive that are not directories. The modified command is shown here:

```
GCI C:\ | where {!$_.psiscontainer}
```

5. This concludes this procedure. Do not close Windows PowerShell. Leave it open for the next procedure.

Identifying properties of directories

1. Use the *Get-ChildItem* cmdlet and supply a value of C:\ for the path argument. Pipeline the resulting object into the *Get-Member* cmdlet. Use the *gci* and *gm* aliases to reduce typing. This command is shown here:

```
GCI  -Path C:\ | GM
```

2. The resulting output contains methods, properties, and more. Filter the output by pipelining the output into a *Where-Object* cmdlet and specifying the *membertype* attribute as equal to property. To do this, use the up arrow to retrieve the previous *gci -path C:\ | gm* command. Pipeline the resulting object into the *Where-Object* cmdlet and filter on the *membertype* attribute. The resulting command is shown here:

```
GCI  -Path C:\ | GM | Where {$_.membertype -eq "property"}
```

3. The previous *gci -path C:\ | gm | where {$_.membertype -eq "property"}* command returns information on both the System.IO.DirectoryInfo and the System.IO.FileInfo objects. To reduce the output to only the properties associated with the System.IO.FileInfo object, we need to use a compound *Where-Object* cmdlet. Use the up arrow to retrieve the *gci -path C:\ | gm | where {$_.membertype -eq "property"}* command. Add the And conjunction and retrieve objects that have a typename that is like *file*. The modified command is shown here:

```
GCI  -Path C:\ | GM | where {$_.membertype -eq "property" -AND $_.typename -like
"*file*"}
```

4. The resulting output only contains the properties for a System.IO.FileInfo object. These properties are shown here:

```
    TypeName: System.IO.FileInfo

Name              MemberType Definition
----              ---------- ----------
Attributes        Property   System.IO.FileAttributes Attributes {get;set;}
CreationTime      Property   System.DateTime CreationTime {get;set;}
CreationTimeUtc   Property   System.DateTime CreationTimeUtc {get;set;}
```

```
Directory          Property    System.IO.DirectoryInfo Directory {get;}
DirectoryName      Property    System.String DirectoryName {get;}
Exists             Property    System.Boolean Exists {get;}
Extension          Property    System.String Extension {get;}
FullName           Property    System.String FullName {get;}
IsReadOnly         Property    System.Boolean IsReadOnly {get;set;}
LastAccessTime     Property    System.DateTime LastAccessTime {get;set;}
LastAccessTimeUtc  Property    System.DateTime LastAccessTimeUtc {get;set;}
LastWriteTime      Property    System.DateTime LastWriteTime {get;set;}
LastWriteTimeUtc   Property    System.DateTime LastWriteTimeUtc {get;set;}
Length             Property    System.Int64 Length {get;}
Name               Property    System.String Name {get;}
```

5.   This concludes this procedure. Do not close Windows PowerShell. Leave it open for the next procedure.

Creating folders and files

1.   Use the *Get-Item* cmdlet to obtain a listing of files and folders. Pipeline the resulting object into the *Where-Object* cmdlet and use the PsIsContainer property to look for folders. Use the name property to find names that contain the word *my* in them. Use the *gi* alias and the *where* alias to reduce typing. The command is shown here:

```
GI * | Where {$_.PsisContainer -AND $_.name -Like "*my*"}
```

2.   If you were following along in the previous chapters, you will have a folder called Mytest off the root of the C:\ drive. Use the *Remove-Item* cmdlet to remove the Mytest folder. Specify the recurse argument to also delete files contained in the C:\Mytest folder. If your location is still set to Env, then change it to C or search for C:\Mytest. The command is shown here:

```
RI mytest -recurse
```

3.   Press the up arrow twice and retrieve the *gi * | where {$_.PsisContainer -AND $_.name -Like "*my*"}* command to confirm the folder was actually deleted. This command is shown here:

```
GI * | Where {$_.PsisContainer -AND $_.name -Like "*my*"}
```

4.   Use the *New-Item* cmdlet to create a folder named Mytest. Use the path argument to specify the path of C:\. Use the name argument to specify the name of Mytest, and use the type argument to tell Windows PowerShell the new item will be a directory. This command is shown here:

```
New-Item -Path C:\ -Name mytest -Type directory
```

5.   The resulting output, shown here, confirms the operation:

```
    Directory: Microsoft.PowerShell.Core\FileSystem::C:\


Mode                LastWriteTime     Length Name
----                -------------     ------ ----
d----         1/4/2007    2:43 AM            mytest
```

6. Use the *New-Item* cmdlet to create an empty text file. To do this, use the up arrow and retrieve the previous *new-item -path C:\ -name Mytest -type directory* command. Edit the path argument so that it is pointing to the C:\Mytest directory. Edit the name argument to specify a text file named Myfile, and specify the type argument as file. The resulting command is shown here:

```
New-Item -Path C:\mytest -Name myfile.txt -type file
```

7. The resulting message, shown here, confirms the creation of the file:

```
    Directory: Microsoft.PowerShell.Core\FileSystem::C:\mytest


Mode                LastWriteTime      Length Name
----                -------------      ------ ----
-a---          1/4/2007   3:12 AM           0 myfile.txt
```

8. This concludes this procedure. Do not close Windows PowerShell. Leave it open for the next procedure.

Reading and writing for files

1. Delete Myfile.txt (created in the previous procedure). To do this, use the *Remove-Item* cmdlet and specify the path argument as C:\Mytest\Myfile.txt. This command is shown here:

```
RI -Path C:\mytest\myfile.txt
```

2. Use the up arrow twice to retrieve the *new-item -path C:\Mytest -name Myfile.txt -type* file. Add the -value argument to the end of the command line, and supply a value of *my file*. This command is shown here:

```
New-Item -Path C:\mytest -Name myfile.txt -Type file -Value "My file"
```

3. Use the *Get-Content* cmdlet to read the contents of Myfile.txt. This command is shown here:

```
Get-Content C:\mytest\myfile.txt
```

4. Use the *Add-Content* cmdlet to add additional information to the Myfile.txt file. This command is shown here:

```
Add-Content C:\mytest\myfile.txt -Value "ADDITIONAL INFORMATION"
```

5. Press the up arrow twice and retrieve the *get-content C:\Mytest\Myfile.txt* command, which is shown here:

```
Get-Content C:\mytest\myfile.txt
```

6. The output from the *get-content C:\Mytest\Myfile.txt* command is shown here:

```
My fileADDITIONAL INFORMATION
```

7. Press the up arrow twice, and retrieve the *add-content C:\mytest\Myfile.txt -value* "ADDI-TIONAL INFORMATION" command to add additional information to the file. This command is shown here:

```
Add-Content C:\mytest\myfile.txt -Value "ADDITIONAL INFORMATION"
```

8. Use the up arrow to retrieve the *get-content C:\Mytest\Myfile.txt* command, which is shown here:

```
Get-Content C:\mytest\myfile.txt
```

9. The output produced is shown here. Notice that the second time, the *"ADDITIONAL INFORMATION"* command was added to a new line.

```
My fileADDITIONAL INFORMATION
ADDITIONAL INFORMATION
```

10. Use the *Set-Information* cmdlet to overwrite the contents of the Myfile.txt file. Specify the value argument as *"Setting information"*. This command is shown here:

```
Set-Content C:\mytest\myfile.txt -Value "Setting information"
```

11. Use the up arrow to retrieve the *get-content C:\Mytest\Myfile.txt* command, which is shown here:

```
Get-Content C:\mytest\myfile.txt
```

12. The output from the *Get-Content* command is shown here:

```
Setting information
```

13. This concludes this procedure.

Understanding the Function Provider

The Function provider provides access to the functions defined in Windows PowerShell. By using the function provider you can obtain a listing of all the functions on your system. You can also add, modify, and delete functions. The function provider uses a file system–based model, and the cmdlets learned earlier also apply to working with functions. The commands used in the procedure are in the ListingAllFunctionsOnTheSystem.txt file.

Listing all functions on the system

1. Open Windows PowerShell.

2. Use the *Set-Location* cmdlet to change the working location to the function PSDrive. This command is shown here:

```
Set-Location function:\
```

3. Use the *Get-ChildItem* cmdlet to enumerate all the functions. Do this by using the *gci* alias, as shown here:

```
GCI
```

4. The resulting list contains many functions that use *Set-Location* to the different drive letters. A partial view of this output is shown here:

```
CommandType     Name                          Definition
-----------     ----                          ----------
Function        prompt                        'PS ' + $(Get-Location) + $(...
Function        TabExpansion                  ...
Function        Clear-Host                    $spaceType = [System.Managem...
Function        more                          param([string[]]$paths);  if...
Function        help                          param([string]$Name,[string[...
Function        man                           param([string]$Name,[string[...
Function        mkdir                         param([string[]]$paths); New...
Function        md                            param([string[]]$paths); New...
Function        A:                            Set-Location A:
Function        B:                            Set-Location B:
Function        C:                            Set-Location C:
Function        D:                            Set-Location D:
```

5. To return only the functions that are used for drives, use the *Get-ChildItem* cmdlet and pipe the object returned into a *Where-Object* cmdlet. Use the default $_ variable to filter on the definition attribute. Use the like argument to search for definitions that contain the word *set*. The resulting command is shown here:

```
GCI | Where {$_.definition -like "set*"}
```

6. If you are more interested in functions that are not related to drive mappings, then you can use the notlike argument instead of like. The easiest way to make this change is to use the up arrow and retrieve the *gci | where {$_.definition -like "set*"}* and then change the filter from *like* to *notlike*. The resulting command is shown here:

```
GCI | Where {$_.definition -notlike "set*"}
```

7. The resulting listing of functions is shown here:

```
CommandType     Name                          Definition
-----------     ----                          ----------
Function        prompt                        'PS' + $(Get-Location) + $(...
Function        TabExpansion                  ...
Function        Clear-Host                    $spaceType = [System.Managem...
Function        more                          param([string[]]$paths);  if...
Function        help                          param([string]$Name,[string[...
Function        man                           param([string]$Name,[string[...
Function        mkdir                         param([string[]]$paths); New...
Function        md                            param([string[]]$paths); New...
Function        pro                           notepad $profile
```

8. Use the *Get-Content* cmdlet to retrieve the text of the *md* function. This is shown here:

```
Get-Content md
```

9. The content of the *md* function is shown here:

```
param([string[]]$paths); New-Item -type directory -path $paths
```

10. This concludes this procedure.

Understanding the Registry Provider

The registry provider provides a consistent and easy way to work with the registry from within Windows PowerShell. Using the registry provider, you can search the registry, create new registry keys, delete existing registry keys, and modify values and access control lists (ACLs) from within Windows PowerShell. The commands used in the procedure are in the UnderstandingTheRegistryProvider.txt file. Two PSDrives are created by default. To identify the PSDrives that are supplied by the registry provider, you can use the *Get-PSDrive* cmdlet, pipeline the resulting objects into the *Where-Object* cmdlet, and filter on the provider property while supplying a value that is like the word registry. This command is shown here:

```
get-psDrive | where {$_.Provider -like "*Registry*"}
```

The resulting list of PSDrives is shown here:

```
Name        Provider    Root                                CurrentLocation
----        --------    ----                                ---------------
HKCU        Registry    HKEY_CURRENT_USER
HKLM        Registry    HKEY_LOCAL_MACHINE
```

Obtaining a listing of registry keys

1. Open Windows PowerShell.

2. Use the *Get-ChildItem* cmdlet and supply the HKLM:\ PSDrive as the value for the path argument. Specify the software key to retrieve a listing of software applications on the local machine. The resulting command is shown here:

   ```
   GCI -path HKLM:\software
   ```

3. A partial listing of similar output is shown here. The corresponding keys, as seen in Regedit.exe, are shown in Figure 3-6.

   ```
       Hive: Microsoft.PowerShell.Core\Registry::HKEY_LOCAL_MACHINE\software

   SKC  VC Name                         Property
   ---  -- ----                         --------
     2   0 781                          {}
     1   0 8ec                          {}
     4   0 Adobe                        {}
    12   0 Ahead                        {}
     2   1 Analog Devices               {ProductDir}
     2   0 Andrea Electronics           {}
     1   0 Application Techniques        {}
   ```

4. This concludes this procedure. Do not close Windows PowerShell. Leave it open for the next procedure.

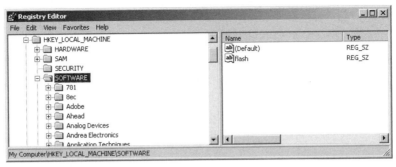

Figure 3-6   A Regedit.exe similar view of HKEY_LOCAL_MACHINE\SOFTWARE

Searching for hotfixes

1. Use the *Get-ChildItem* cmdlet and supply a value for the path argument. Use the HKLM:\ PSDrive and supply a path of Software\Microsoft\Windows NT\CurrentVersion\Hotfix. Because there is a space in Windows NT, you will need to use a single quote (') to encase the command. You can use *Tab completion* to assist with the typing. The completed command is shown here:

```
GCI -Path 'HKLM:\SOFTWARE\Microsoft\Windows NT\CurrentVersion\HotFix'
```

2. The resulting similar list of hotfixes is seen in the output here, in abbreviated fashion:

```
    Hive: Microsoft.PowerShell.Core\Registry::HKEY_LOCAL_MACHINE\SOFTWARE\Micros
oft\Windows NT\CurrentVersion\HotFix


SKC  VC Name                      Property
---  -- ----                      --------
  1   8 KB873333                  {Installed, Comments, Backup Dir, Fix...
  1   8 KB873339                  {Installed, Comments, Backup Dir, Fix...
  1   8 KB883939                  {Installed, Comments, Backup Dir, Fix...
  1   8 KB885250                  {Installed, Comments, Backup Dir, Fix...
```

3. To retrieve information on a single hotfix, you will need to add a *Where-Object* cmdlet. You can do this by using the up arrow to retrieve the previous *gci -path 'HKLM:\SOFTWARE\Microsoft\Windows NT\CurrentVersion\HotFix'* command and pipelining the resulting object into the *Where-Object* cmdlet. Supply a value for the name property, as seen in the code listed here. Alternatively, supply a "KB" number from the previous output.

```
GCI -Path 'HKLM:\SOFTWARE\Microsoft\Windows NT\CurrentVersion\HotFix' | where
{$_.Name -like "*KB928388"}
```

4. This concludes this procedure.

Understanding the Variable Provider

The variable provider provides access to the variables that are defined within Windows PowerShell. These variables include both user-defined variables, such as $mred, and system-defined variables, such as $host. You can obtain a listing of the cmdlets designed to work specifically with variables by using the *Get-Help* cmdlet and specifying the asterisk (*) variable. The commands used in the procedure are in the UnderstandingTheVariableProvider.txt and WorkingWithVariables.txt files. To return only cmdlets, we use the *Where-Object* cmdlet and filter on the category that is equal to cmdlet. This command is shown here:

```
Get-Help *variable | Where-Object {$_.category -eq "cmdlet"}
```

The resulting list contains five cmdlets but is a little jumbled and difficult to read. So let's modify the preceding command and specify the properties to return. To do this, use the up arrow and pipeline the returned object into the *Format-List* cmdlet. Add the three properties we are interested in: name, category, and synopsis. The revised command is shown here:

```
Get-Help *variable | Where-Object {$_.category -eq "cmdlet"} |
Format-List name, category, synopsis
```

The resulting output is much easier to read and understand. It is shown here:

```
Name     : Get-Variable
Category : Cmdlet
Synopsis : Gets the variables in the current console.

Name     : New-Variable
Category : Cmdlet
Synopsis : Creates a new variable.

Name     : Set-Variable
Category : Cmdlet
Synopsis : Sets the value of a variable. Creates the variable if one with the requested
name does not exist.

Name     : Remove-Variable
Category : Cmdlet
Synopsis : Deletes a variable and its value.

Name     : Clear-Variable
Category : Cmdlet
Synopsis : Deletes the value of a variable.
```

Working with variables

1. Open Windows PowerShell.

2. Use the *Set-Location* cmdlet to set the working location to the variable PSDrive. Use the *sl* alias to reduce typing needs. This command is shown here:

   ```
   SL variable:\
   ```

3. Produce a complete listing of all the variables currently defined in Windows PowerShell. To do this, use the *Get-ChildItem* cmdlet. You can use the alias *gci* to produce this list. The command is shown here:

```
Get-ChildItem
```

4. The resulting list is jumbled. Use the up arrow to retrieve the *Get-ChildItem* command, and pipeline the resulting object into the *Sort-Object* cmdlet. Sort on the name property. This command is shown here:

```
Get-ChildItem | Sort {$_.Name}
```

5. The output from the previous command is shown here:

```
Name                          Value
----                          -----
$                             }
?                             True
^                             Get-ChildItem
_
args                          {}
ConfirmPreference             High
ConsoleFileName
DebugPreference               SilentlyContinue
Error                         {System.Management.Automation.ParseException:...
ErrorActionPreference         Continue
ErrorView                     NormalView
ExecutionContext              System.Management.Automation.EngineIntrinsics
false                         False
FormatEnumerationLimit        4
HOME                          C:\Documents and Settings\edwils.NORTHAMERICA
Host                          System.Management.Automation.Internal.Host.In...
input                         System.Array+SZArrayEnumerator
LASTEXITCODE                  0
lastWord                      get-c
line                          get-c
MaximumAliasCount             4096
MaximumDriveCount             4096
MaximumErrorCount             256
MaximumFunctionCount          4096
MaximumHistoryCount           64
MaximumVariableCount          4096
mred                          mred
MyInvocation                  System.Management.Automation.InvocationInfo
NestedPromptLevel             0
null
OutputEncoding                System.Text.ASCIIEncoding
PID                           292
PROFILE                       C:\Documents and Settings\edwils.NORTHAMERICA...
ProgressPreference            Continue
PSHOME                        C:\WINDOWS\system32\WindowsPowerShell\v1.0
PWD                           Variable:\
ReportErrorShowExceptionClass 0
ReportErrorShowInnerException 0
ReportErrorShowSource         1
```

```
ReportErrorShowStackTrace       0
ShellId                         Microsoft.PowerShell
StackTrace                         at System.Number.StringToNumber(String str...
true                            True
VerbosePreference               SilentlyContinue
WarningPreference               Continue
WhatIfPreference                0
```

6. Use the *Get-Variable* cmdlet to retrieve a specific variable. Use the *ShellId* variable. You can use *Tab completion* to speed up typing. The command is shown here:

```
Get-Variable ShellId
```

7. Use the up arrow to retrieve the previous *Get-Variable ShellId* command. Pipeline the object returned into a *Format-List* cmdlet and return all properties. This is shown here:

```
Get-Variable ShellId | Format-List *
```

8. The resulting output includes the description of the variable, value, and other information shown here:

```
Name        : ShellId
Description : The ShellID identifies the current shell.  This is used by #Requires.
Value       : Microsoft.PowerShell
Options     : Constant, AllScope
Attributes  : {}
```

9. Create a new variable called *administrator*. To do this, use the *New-Variable* cmdlet. This command is shown here:

```
New-Variable administrator
```

10. Use the *Get-Variable* cmdlet to retrieve the new administrator variable. This command is shown here:

```
Get-Variable administrator
```

11. The resulting output is shown here. Notice that there is no value for the variable.

```
Name                      Value
----                      -----
administrator
```

12. Assign a value to the new administrator variable. To do this, use the *Set-Variable* cmdlet. Specify the *administrator* variable name, and supply your given name as the value for the variable. This command is shown here:

```
Set-Variable administrator -value mred
```

13. Use the up arrow one time to retrieve the previous *Get-Variable administrator* command. This command is shown here:

```
Get-Variable administrator
```

14. The output displays both the variable name and the value associated with the variable. This is shown here:

```
Name                          Value
----                          -----
administrator                 mred
```

15. Use the *Remove-Variable* cmdlet to remove the administrator variable you previously created. This command is shown here:

```
Remove-Variable administrator
```

16. Use the up arrow one time to retrieve the previous *Get-Variable administrator* command. This command is shown here:

```
Get-Variable administrator
```

17. The variable has been deleted. The resulting output is shown here:

```
Get-Variable : Cannot find a variable with name 'administrator'.
At line:1 char:13
+ Get-Variable <<<< administrator
```

18. This concludes this procedure.

Exploring the Certificate Provider: Step-by-Step Exercises

In this exercise, we explore the use of the Certificate provider in Windows PowerShell.

1. Start Windows PowerShell.

2. Obtain a listing of all the properties available for use with the *Get-ChildItem* cmdlet by piping the results into the *Get-Member* cmdlet. To filter out only the properties, pipeline the results into a *Where-Object* cmdlet and specify the *membertype* to be equal to property. This command is shown here:

```
Get-ChildItem |Get-Member | Where-Object {$_.membertype -eq "property"}
```

3. Set your location to the certificate drive. To identify the certificate drive, use the *Get-PSDrive* cmdlet. Use the *Where-Object* cmdlet and filter on names that begin with the letter c. This is shown here:

```
Get-PSDrive |where {$_.name -like "c*"}
```

4. The results of this command are shown here:

```
Name      Provider      Root                    CurrentLocation
----      --------      ----                    ---------------
C         FileSystem    C:\
cert      Certificate   \
```

5. Use the *Set-Location* cmdlet to change to the certificate drive.

```
Sl cert:\
```

6. Use the *Get-ChildItem* cmdlet to produce a listing of all the certificates on the machine.

```
GCI
```

7. The output from the previous command is shown here:

```
Location   : CurrentUser
StoreNames : {?, UserDS, AuthRoot, CA...}

Location   : LocalMachine
StoreNames : {?, AuthRoot, CA, AddressBook...}
```

8. The listing seems somewhat incomplete. To determine whether there are additional certificates installed on the machine, use the *Get-ChildItem* cmdlet again, but this time specify the recurse argument. Modify the previous command by using the up arrow. The command is shown here:

```
GCI -recurse
```

9. The output from the previous command seems to take a long time to run and produces hundreds of lines of output. To make the listing more readable, pipe the output to a text file, and then open the file in Notepad. The command to do this is shown here:

```
GCI -recurse >C:\a.txt;notepad.exe a.txt
```

10. This concludes this step-by-step exercise.

One Step Further: Examining the Environment Provider

In this exercise, we work with the Windows PowerShell Environment provider.

1. Start Windows PowerShell.

2. Use the *New-PSDrive* cmdlet to create a drive mapping to the alias provider. The name of the new PSDrive will be *al*. The PSProvider is alias, and the root will be dot (.). This command is shown here:

```
new-PSDrive -name al -PSProvider alias -Root .
```

3. Change your working location to the new PSDrive you called *al*. To do this, use the *sl* alias for the *Set-Location* cmdlet. This is shown here:

```
SL al:\
```

4. Use the *gci* alias for the *Get-ChildItem* cmdlet, and pipeline the resulting object into the *Sort-Object* cmdlet by using the *sort* alias. Supply name as the property to sort on. This command is shown here:

```
GCI | Sort -Property name
```

5. Use the up arrow to retrieve the previous *gci | sort -property name* command and modify it to use a *Where-Object* cmdlet to return aliases only when the name is greater than the letter t. Use the *where* alias to avoid typing the entire name of the cmdlet. The resulting command is shown here:

```
GCI | sort -Property name | Where {$_.Name -gt "t"}c
```

6. Change your location back to the C:\ drive. To do this, use the *sl* alias and supply the C:\ argument. This is shown here:

```
SL C:\
```

7. Remove the PSDrive mapping for al. To do this, use the *Remove-PSDrive* cmdlet and supply the name of the PSDrive to remove. Note, this command does not want a trailing colon (:) or colon with backslash (:\). The command is shown here:

```
Remove-PSDrive al
```

8. Use the *Get-PSDrive* cmdlet to ensure the al drive was removed. This is shown here:

```
Get-PSDrive
```

9. Use the *Get-Item* cmdlet to obtain a listing of all the environment variables. Use the path argument and supply env:\ as the value. This is shown here:

```
Get-Item -Path env:\
```

10. Use the up arrow to retrieve the previous command, and pipeline the resulting object into the *Get-Member* cmdlet. This is shown here:

```
Get-Item -Path env:\ | Get-Member
```

11. The results from the previous command are shown here:

```
    TypeName: System.Collections.Generic.Dictionary'2+ValueCollection[[System.St
ring, mscorlib, Version=2.0.0.0, Culture=neutral, PublicKeyToken=b77a5c561934e0
89],[System.Collections.DictionaryEntry, mscorlib, Version=2.0.0.0, Culture=neu
tral, PublicKeyToken=b77a5c561934e089]]

Name            MemberType   Definition
----            ----------   ----------
CopyTo          Method       System.Void CopyTo(DictionaryEntry[] array, Int32...
Equals          Method       System.Boolean Equals(Object obj)
GetEnumerator   Method       System.Collections.Generic.Dictionary`2+ValueColl...
GetHashCode     Method       System.Int32 GetHashCode()
GetType         Method       System.Type GetType()
get_Count       Method       System.Int32 get_Count()
ToString        Method       System.String ToString()
PSDrive         NoteProperty System.Management.Automation.PSDriveInfo PSDrive=Env
PSIsContainer   NoteProperty System.Boolean PSIsContainer=True
PSPath          NoteProperty System.String PSPath=Microsoft.PowerShell.Core\En...
PSProvider      NoteProperty System.Management.Automation.ProviderInfo PSProvi...
Count           Property     System.Int32 Count {get;}
```

12. Press the up arrow twice to return to the *get-item -path env:* command. Use the Home key to move your insertion point to the beginning of the line. Add a variable called *$objEnv* and use it to hold the object returned by the *get-item -path env:* command. The completed command is shown here:

```
$objEnv=Get-Item -Path env:\
```

13. From the listing of members of the environment object, find the count property. Use this property to print out the total number of environment variables. As you type **$o**, try to use *Tab completion* to avoid typing. Also try to use *Tab completion* as you type the *c* in count. The completed command is shown here:

```
$objEnv.Count
```

14. Examine the methods of the object returned by *get-item -path env:*. Notice there is a Get_Count method. Let's use that method. The code is shown here:

```
$objEnv.Get_count
```

15. When this code is executed, however, the results define the method rather than execute the Get_Count method. These results are shown here:

```
MemberType          : Method
OverloadDefinitions : {System.Int32 get_Count()}
TypeNameOfValue     : System.Management.Automation.PSMethod
Value               : System.Int32 get_Count()
Name                : get_Count
IsInstance          : True
```

16. To retrieve the actual number of environment variables, we need to use empty parentheses is at the end of the method. This is shown here:

```
$objEnv.Get_count()
```

17. If you want to know exactly what type of object you have contained in the *$objEnv* variable, you can use the GetType method, as shown here:

```
$objEnv.GetType()
```

18. This command returns the results shown here:

```
IsPublic IsSerial Name                             BaseType
-------- -------- ----                             --------
False    True     ValueCollection                  System.Object
```

19. This concludes this one step further exercise.

Chapter 3 Quick Reference

To	Do This
Produce a listing of all variables defined in a Windows PowerShell session	Use the *Set-Location* cmdlet to change location to the variable PSDrive, then use the *Get-ChildItem* cmdlet
Obtain a listing of all the aliases	Use the *Set-Location* cmdlet to change location to the alias PSDrive, then use the *Get-ChildItem* cmdlet to produce a listing of aliases. Pipeline the resulting object into the *Where-Object* cmdlet and filter on the name property for the appropriate value
Delete a directory that is empty	Use the *Remove-Item* cmdlet and supply the name of the directory
Delete a directory that contains other items	Use the *Remove-Item* cmdlet and supply the name of the directory and specify the recurse argument
Create a new text file	Use the *New-Item* cmdlet and specify the -path argument for the directory location. Supply the name argument, and specify the type argument as file. Example: *new-item -path C:\Mytest -name Myfile.txt -type file*
Obtain a listing of registry keys from a registry hive	Use the *Get-ChildItem* cmdlet and specify the appropriate PSDrive name for the -path argument. Complete the path with the appropriate registry path. Example: *gci -path HKLM:\software*
Obtain a listing of all functions on the system	Use the *Get-ChildItem* cmdlet and supply the PSDrive name of *function:* to the path argument. Example: *gci -path function:*

Chapter 4
Using PowerShell Scripts

After completing this chapter, you will be able to:

- Understand the reasons for writing Windows PowerShell scripts
- Make the configuration changes required to run Windows PowerShell scripts
- Understand how to run Windows PowerShell scripts
- Understand how to break lines
- Understand the use of variables and constants
- Create objects in a Windows PowerShell script
- Call methods in a Windows PowerShell script

With the ability to perform so many actions from inside Windows PowerShell in an interactive fashion, you may wonder, "Why do I need to write scripts?" For many network administrators, one-line PowerShell commands will indeed solve many routine problems. This can become extremely powerful when the commands are combined into batch files and perhaps called from a login script. However, there are some very good reasons to write Windows PowerShell scripts. We will examine them as we move into this chapter. All the scripts mentioned in this chapter can be found in the corresponding scripts folder on the CD.

Why Write Windows PowerShell Scripts

Perhaps the number one reason to write a Windows PowerShell script is to address recurring needs. As an example, consider the activity of producing a directory listing. The simple *Get-ChildItem* cmdlet does a good job, but after you decide to sort the listing and filter out only files of a certain size, you end up with the command shown here:

```
Get-ChildItem c:\fso | Where-Object {$_.Length -gt 1000} | Sort-Object -Property name
```

Even using *Tab Completion*, the previous command requires a bit of typing. One way to shorten it would be to create a user-defined function, and we will examine that technique later. For now, the easiest solution is to write a Windows PowerShell script. The DirectoryListWithArguments.ps1 script is shown here:

DirectoryListWithArguments.ps1
```
foreach ($i in $args)
   {Get-ChildItem $i | Where-Object {$_.length -gt 1000} |
    Sort-Object -property name}
```

The DirectoryListWithArguments.ps1 script takes a single, unnamed argument that allows the script to be modified when it is run. This makes the script much easier to work with and adds flexibility.

An additional reason that network administrators write Windows PowerShell scripts is to run the script as a scheduled task. In the Windows world, there are multiple task scheduler engines. Using the WIN32_ScheduledJob Windows Management Instrumentation (WMI) class, you can create, monitor, and delete scheduled jobs. This WMI class has been available since the Windows NT 4 days. On Windows XP and Windows Server 2003, the *schtasks.exe* utility offers more flexibility than the WIN32_ScheduledJob WMI class. On Windows Vista, a Schedule.Service object is available to simplify configuration of scheduled jobs.

The ListProcessesSortResults.ps1 script is a script that a network administrator may want to schedule to run several times a day. It produces a list of currently running processes and writes the results out to a text file as a formatted and sorted table.

ListProcessesSortResults.ps1

```
$args = "localhost","loopback","127.0.0.1"

foreach ($i in $args)
   {$strFile = "c:\mytest\"+ $i +"Processes.txt"
    Write-Host "Testing" $i "please wait ...";
    Get-WmiObject -computername $i -class win32_process |
    Select-Object name, processID, Priority, ThreadCount, PageFaults, PageFileUsage |
    Where-Object {!$_.processID -eq 0} | Sort-Object -property name |
    Format-Table | Out-File $strFile}
```

One other reason for writing Windows PowerShell scripts is that it makes it easy to store and share both the "secret commands" and the ideas behind the scripts. For example, suppose you develop a script that will connect remotely to workstations on your network and search for user accounts that do not require a password. Obviously, an account without a password is a security risk! After some searching around, you discover the WIN32_UserAccount WMI class and develop a script that performs to your expectation. Because this is likely a script you would want to use on a regular basis, and perhaps share with other network administrators in your company, it makes sense to save it as a script. A sample of such a script is AccountsWith-NoRequiredPassword.ps1, which is seen here.

AccountsWithNoRequiredPassword.ps1

```
$args = "localhost"

foreach ($i in $args)
   {Write-Host "Connecting to" $i "please wait ...";
    Get-WmiObject -computername $i -class win32_UserAccount |
    Select-Object Name, Disabled, PasswordRequired, SID, SIDType |
    Where-Object {$_.PasswordRequired -eq 0} |
    Sort-Object -property name | Write-Host}
```

Enabling Script Support

The DirectoryListWithArguments.ps1 script will not run in Windows PowerShell by default. This is because scripting support is disabled by default in Windows PowerShell. If you attempt to run a Windows PowerShell script when the support has not been enabled, an error will occur, and the script will not run. This error message is seen in Figure 4-1.

```
PS C:\> c:\test.ps1
File C:\test.ps1 cannot be loaded because the execution of scripts is disabled on this system. Pleas
ut_signing" for more details.
At line:1 char:11
+ c:\test.ps1 <<<<
PS C:\> _
```

Figure 4-1   Error generated when attempting to run a Windows PowerShell script when execution policy not set

This is referred to as the *restricted execution policy*. There are four levels of execution policy that can be configured in Windows PowerShell by using the *Set-ExecutionPolicy* cmdlet. These four levels are listed in Table 4-1. The restricted execution policy can be configured by group policy using the "Turn on Script Execution" Group Policy setting in Active Directory. To configure the group policy setting in Active Directory, you can download the required ADM file from *http://www.microsoft.com/downloads*. It can be applied to either the computer object or the user object. The computer object setting takes precedence over other settings.

User preferences for the restricted execution policy can be configured by using the *Set-Execution-Policy* cmdlet, but they will not override settings configured by Group Policy. The resultant set of restricted execution policy settings can be obtained by using the *Get-ExecutionPolicy* cmdlet.

Table 4-1   Script Execution Policy Levels

Level	Meaning
Restricted	Will not run scripts or configuration files
AllSigned	All scripts and configuration files must be signed by a trusted publisher
RemoteSigned	All scripts and configuration files downloaded from the Internet must be signed by a trusted publisher
Unrestricted	All scripts and configuration files will run. Scripts downloaded from the Internet will prompt for permission before running

Just the Steps   To retrieve the script execution policy, use the *Get-ExecutionPolicy* cmdlet.

Retrieving script execution policy

1. Open Windows PowerShell.

2. Use the *Get-ExecutionPolicy* cmdlet to retrieve the effective script execution policy. This is shown here:

```
Get-ExecutionPolicy
```

3. This concludes this procedure. Leave Windows PowerShell open for the next procedure.

> ### Quick Check
>
> **Q. Do Windows PowerShell scripts work by default?**
>
> A. No. Windows PowerShell scripts must be explicitly enabled.
>
> **Q. What cmdlet can be used to retrieve the resultant execution policy?**
>
> A. The *Get-ExecutionPolicy* cmdlet can retrieve the resultant execution policy.
>
> **Q. What cmdlet can be used to set the script execution policy?**
>
> A. The *Set-ExecutionPolicy* cmdlet can be used to set the script execution policy.

Setting script execution policy

1. Use the *Set-ExecutionPolicy* cmdlet to change the script execution policy to unrestricted. This command is shown here:

```
Set-ExecutionPolicy unrestricted
```

2. Use the *Get-ExecutionPolicy* cmdlet to retrieve the current effective script execution policy. This command is shown here:

```
Get-ExecutionPolicy
```

3. The result prints out to Windows PowerShell console as shown here:

```
Unrestricted
```

4. This concludes this procedure.

> **Tip**   If the execution policy on Windows PowerShell is set to restricted, how can you use a script to determine the execution policy? One method is to use VBScript to read from the following registry key: \SOFTWARE\Microsoft\PowerShell\1\ShellIds\Microsoft.PowerShell\ executionPolicy from both the HKLM and the HKCU hives. However, keep in mind these keys only appear after the execution policy has been changed. A script that checks the registry for the execution policy is GetPowerShellExecutionPolicy.vbs, found in the scripts folder for this chapter on the CD-ROMg.

Running Windows PowerShell Scripts

You cannot simply double-click on a Windows PowerShell script and have it run. You cannot type the name in the *Start | Run* dialog box either. If you are inside Windows PowerShell, you can run scripts if you have enabled the execution policy, but you need to type the entire path to the script you wish to run and make sure you include the ps1 extension.

Just the Steps   To run a Windows PowerShell script from inside PowerShell, follow these steps:

1. Type the full path to the script.
2. Include the name of the script.
3. Ensure you include the ps1 extension.

If you need to run a script from outside Windows PowerShell, you need to type the full path to the script, but you must feed it as an argument to the PowerShell.exe program. In addition, you probably want to specify the -noexit argument so that you can read the output from the script. This is shown in Figure 4-2.

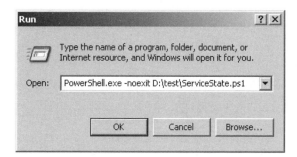

Figure 4-2   Use the -noexit argument for the PowerShell.exe program to keep the console open after a script run

Just the Steps   To run a Windows PowerShell script from outside PowerShell, follow these steps:

1. Type the full path to the script.
2. Include the name of the script.
3. Ensure you include the ps1 extension.
4. Feed this to the PowerShell.exe program.
5. Use the -noexit argument to keep the PowerShell console after script execution.

The RetrieveAndSortServiceState.ps1 script uses the Get-WMIObject cmdlet to make a connection into the WMI service. We will examine WMI as it relates to Windows PowerShell in Chapter 5, Using WMI, and Chapter 6, Querying WMI, but because of the way Windows PowerShell uses cmdlets, you do not need to know everything about a technology to use it in your script. The RetrieveAndSortServiceState.ps1 script will create a list of all the services that are defined on a machine. It then checks to see if they are running, stopped, or disabled and reports the status of the service. The script also collects the service account that the service is running under.

A *Sort-Object* cmdlet is used to perform three sorts on the data: It sorts first by the start mode of the service (that is, automatic, manual, disabled); it sorts next by the state of the service (that is, running, stopped, and so forth); and it then alphabetizes the list by the name of each service in each of the two previous categories. After the sorting process, the script uses a *Format-Table* cmdlet and produces a table output in the console window. The RetrieveAndSortServiceState.ps1 script is shown here, and the Running Scripts Inside Windows PowerShell procedure examines running this script.

The script is designed to run against multiple remote machines, and it holds the names of the destination machines in the system variable $args. As written, it uses two computer names that always refer to the local machine: *localhost* and *loopback*. By using these two names, we can simulate the behavior of connecting to networked computers.

RetrieveAndSortServiceState.ps1

```
$args = "localhost","loopback"

    foreach ($i in $args)
       {Write-Host "Testing" $i "..."
          Get-WmiObject -computer $args -class win32_service |
          Select-Object -property name, state, startmode, startname |
          Sort-Object -property startmode, state, name |
          Format-Table *}
```

> **Note**   For the Running Scripts Inside Windows PowerShell procedure, I copied the Retrieve-AndSortServiceState.ps1 script to the C:\Mytest directory we created in Chapter 3. This makes it much easier to type the path and has the additional benefit of making the examples clearer. To follow the procedures, you will need to either modify the path to the script or copy the RetrieveAndSortServiceState.ps1 script to the C:\Mytest directory.

Running scripts inside Windows PowerShell

1. Open Windows PowerShell.

2. Type the full path to the script you wish to run. For example C:\Mytest. You can use *Tab completion*. On my system, I only had to type C:\My and then press Tab. Add a backslash (\), and type the script name. You can use *Tab completion* for this as well. If you copied the RetrieveAndSortServiceState.ps1 into the C:\Mytest directory, then simply typing **r** and pressing Tab should retrieve the script name. The completed command is shown here:

    ```
    C:\mytest\RetrieveAndSortServiceState.ps1
    ```

3. A partial output from the script is shown here:

```
Testing loopback ...

name            state          startmode        startname
----            -----          ---------        ---------
Alerter         Running        Auto             NT AUTHORITY\Loc...
Alerter         Running        Auto             NT AUTHORITY\Loc...
AudioSrv        Running        Auto             LocalSystem
AudioSrv        Running        Auto             LocalSystem
```

4. This concludes this procedure. Please close Windows PowerShell.

Running scripts outside Windows PowerShell

1. Open the Run dialog box (*Start | Run*, or the Windows Flag key + R, or Ctrl + Esc then R).

2. Type PowerShell and use the -noexit switch. Type the full path to the script. The command for this is shown here:

```
Powershell  -noexit C:\mytest\RetrieveAndSortServiceState.ps1
```

3. This concludes this procedure.

Tip   Add a shortcut to Windows PowerShell in your SendTo folder. This folder is located in the Documents and Settings*%username%* folder. When you create the shortcut, make sure you specify the -noexit switch for PowerShell.exe, or the output will scroll by so fast you will not be able to read it. You can do this by hand, or modify the CreateShortCutToPower-Shell.vbs script from Chapter 1, "Overview of Windows PowerShell."

Quick Check

Q. Which command can you use to sort a list?

A.   The *Sort-Object* cmdlet can be used to sort a list.

Q. How do you use the *Sort-Object* cmdlet to sort a list?

A.   To use the *Sort-Object* cmdlet to sort a list, specify the property to sort on in the property argument.

Understanding Variables and Constants

Understanding the use of variables and constants in Windows PowerShell is fundamental to much of the flexibility of the PowerShell scripting language. Variables are used to hold information for use later in the script. Variables can hold any type of data, including text, numbers, and even objects.

Use of Variables

By default when working with Windows PowerShell, you do not need to declare variables before use. When you use the variable to hold data, it is declared. All variable names must be preceded with a dollar sign ($). There are a number of special variables in Windows PowerShell. These variables are created automatically and have a special meaning. A listing of the special variables and their associated meaning appears in Table 4-2.

Table 4-2   Use of Special Variables

Name	Use
$^	Contains the first token of the last line input into the shell
$$	Contains the last token of the last line input into the shell
$_	The current pipeline object; used in script blocks, filters, *Where-Object*, *ForEach-Object*, and *Switch*
$?	Contains the success/fail status of the last statement
$Args	Used in creating functions requiring parameters
$Error	If an error occurred, the error object is saved in the *$error* variable.
$ExecutionContext	The execution objects available to cmdlets
$foreach	Refers to the enumerator in a *foreach* loop
$HOME	The user's home directory; set to %HOMEDRIVE%\%HOMEPATH%
$Input	Input is piped to a function or code block.
$Match	A hash table consisting of items found by the -match operator
$MyInvocation	Information about the currently executing script or command-line
$PSHome	The directory where PS is installed
$Host	Information about the currently executing host
$LastExitCode	The exit code of the last native application to run
$true	Boolean TRUE
$false	Boolean FALSE
$null	A null object
$this	In the Types.ps1xml file and some script block instances, this represents the current object
$OFS	Output Field Separator used when converting an array to a string
$ShellID	The identifier for the shell. This value is used by the shell to determine the ExecutionPolicy and what profiles are run at Startup
$StackTrace	Contains detailed stack trace information about the last error

In the ReadUserInfoFromReg.ps1 script, there are five variables used. These are listed in Table 4-3.

Table 4-3   ReadUserInfoFromReg.ps1 Variables

Name	Use
$strUserPath	Path to registry subkey "Software\Microsoft\Windows\CurrentVersion\Explorer"
$strUserName	Registry value "Logon User Name"
$strPath	Path to registry subkey "\Volatile Environment"
$strName	An array of Registry values: "LOGONSERVER", "HOMEPATH", "APPDATA", "HOMEDRIVE"
$i	Holds a single registry value name from the *$strName* array of registry values; *$i* gets assigned the value by using the *ForEach* alias.

The ReadUserInfoFromReg.ps1 script uses the *Set-Location* cmdlet to change to the HKCU PSDrive. This makes it easier to work with the registry. After the location has been set to the HKCU drive, the script uses the *Get-ItemProperty* cmdlet to retrieve the data stored in the specified registry key. The *Get-ItemProperty* cmdlet needs two arguments to be supplied: path and name. The path argument receives the registry path that is stored in the *$strUserPath* variable, whereas the name argument receives the string stored in the *$strUserName* variable.

Tip   Because the $strUserPath registry subkey was rather long, I used the grave accent (`) to continue the subkey onto the next line. In addition, because I had to close out the string with quotation marks, I used the plus symbol (+) to concatenate (glue) the two pieces of the string back together.

After the value is retrieved from the registry, the object is pipelined to the *Format-List* cmdlet, which once again uses the string contained in the *$strUserName* variable as the property to display.

Note   The *Format-List* cmdlet is required in the ReadUserInfoFromReg.ps1 script because of the way the *Get-ItemProperty* cmdlet displays the results of its operation—it returns information about the object as well as the value contained in the registry key. The use of *Format-List* mitigates this behavior.

The really powerful aspect of the ReadUserInfoFromReg.ps1 script is that it uses the array of strings contained in the *$strName* variable. To read the values out of the registry, we need to "singularize" the strings contained within the *$strName* variable. To do this, we use the *ForEach-Object* cmdlet (however, we reference it by the alias *foreach*). After we have an individual value from the *$strName* array, we store the string in a variable called *$i*. The *Get-ItemProperty* cmdlet is used in exactly the same manner as it was used earlier. However, this time, we use the string contained in the *$strPath* variable, and the name of the registry key to read is contained in the *$i* variable, whose value will change four times with the execution of each pass through the array.

When the ReadUserInfoFromReg.ps1 script is run, it reads five pieces of information from the registry: the logon user name, the logon server name, the user's home path location, the user's application data store, and the user's home drive mapping. The ReadUserInfoFromReg.ps1 script is shown here:

ReadUserInfoFromReg.ps1

```
$strUserPath = "\Software\Microsoft\Windows\CurrentVersion\" `
               + "Explorer"
$strUserName = "Logon User Name"
$strPath = "\Volatile Environment"
$strName = "LOGONSERVER","HOMEPATH", "APPDATA","HOMEDRIVE"

Set-Location HKCU:\
   Get-ItemProperty -path $strUserPath -name $strUserName |
      Format-List $strUserName
foreach ($i in $strName)
   {Get-ItemProperty -path $strPath -name $i |
      Format-List $i}
```

> **Quick Check**
>
> **Q.   To read a value from the registry, which provider is used?**
>
> A.   The registry provider is used to read from the registry.
>
> **Q.   Which cmdlet is used to retrieve a registry key value from the registry?**
>
> A.   The *Get-ItemProperty* cmdlet is used to retrieve a registry key value from the registry.
>
> **Q.   How do you concatenate two string values?**
>
> A.   You can use the plus symbol (+) to concatenate two string values together.

Exploring strings

1.   Open Windows PowerShell.

2.   Create a variable called *$a* and assign the value "this is the beginning" to it. The code for this is shown here:

```
$a = "this is the beginning"
```

3. Create a variable called *$b* and assign the number 22 to it. The code for this is shown here:

    ```
    $b = 22
    ```

4. Create a variable called *$c* and make it equal to $a + $b. The code for this is shown here:

    ```
    $c = $a + $b
    ```

5. Print out the value of *$c*. The code for this is shown here:

    ```
    $c
    ```

6. The results of printing out *c$* are shown here:

    ```
    this is the beginning22
    ```

7. Modify the value of *$a*. Assign the string "this is a string" to the variable *$a*. This is shown here:

    ```
    $a = "this is a string"
    ```

8. Use the up arrow and retrieve the *$c = $a + $b*. This command is shown here:

    ```
    $c = $a + $b
    ```

9. Now print out the value of *$c*. The command to do this is shown here:

    ```
    $c
    ```

10. Assign the string "this is a number" to the variable *$b*. The code to do this is shown here:

    ```
    $b = "this is a number"
    ```

11. Use the up arrow to retrieve the *$c = $a + $b* command. This will cause Windows PowerShell to re-evaluate the value of $c. This command is shown here:

    ```
    $c = $a + $b
    ```

12. Print out the value of *$c*. This command is shown here:

    ```
    $c
    ```

13. Change the *$b* variable so that it can only contain an integer. (Data type aliases are seen in Table 4-4.) Use the *$b* variable to hold the number 5. This command is shown here:

    ```
    [int]$b = 5
    ```

14. Use the up arrow to retrieve the *$c = $a + $b* command. This command is shown here:

    ```
    $c = $a + $b
    ```

15. Print out the value contained in the *$c* variable, as shown here:

    ```
    $c
    ```

16. Assign the string "this is a string" to the *$b* variable. This command is shown here:

    ```
    $b = "this is a string"
    ```

17. Attempting to assign a string to a variable that has a [int] constraint placed on it results in the error shown here (these results are wrapped for readability):

    ```
    Cannot convert value "this is a number" to type "System.Int32".
    Error: "Input string was not in a correct format."
    At line:1 char:3
    + $b  <<<< = "this is a string"
    ```

18. This concludes this procedure.

These commands are found in the ExploringStrings.txt script in the scripts folder for this chapter.

Table 4-4   Data Type Aliases

Alias	Type
[int]	32-bit signed integer
[long]	64-bit signed integer
[string]	Fixed-length string of Unicode characters
[char]	A Unicode 16-bit character
[bool]	True/false value
[byte]	An 8-bit unsigned integer
[double]	Double-precision 64-bit floating point number
[decimal]	An 128-bit decimal value
[single]	Single-precision 32-bit floating point number
[array]	An array of values
[xml]	Xml objects
[hashtable]	A hashtable object (similar to a dictionary object)

Use of Constants

Constants in Windows PowerShell are like variables—with two important exceptions: their value never changes, and they cannot be deleted. Constants are created by using the *Set-Variable* cmdlet and specifying the option argument to be equal to constant.

Note   When referring to a constant in the body of the script, we must prefix it with the dollar sign ($), just like any other variable. However, when creating the constant (or variable for that matter) by using the *Set-Variable* cmdlet, when we specify the name argument, we do not use the dollar sign.

In the GetHardDiskDetails.ps1 script, we create a constant called *$intDriveType* and assign the value of 3 to it because the WIN32_LogicalDisk WMI class uses a value of 3 in the disktype property to describe a local fixed disk. Because we are not interested in network drives, removable drives, or ram drives, we use the *Where-Object* to return only items that have a drivetype of 3.

> ### Quick Check
>
> **Q. How do you create a constant in a script?**
>
> A. You create a constant in a script by using the *Set-Variable* and specifying the value of constant to the option argument.
>
> **Q. How do you indicate that a variable will only hold integers?**
>
> A. To indicate that a variable will only contain integers, use the [int] in front of the variable name when assigning a value to the variable.

In looking at the GetHardDiskDetails.ps1 script, the value of *$intDriveType* is never changed. It is assigned the value of 3 on the *Set-Variable* line. The *$intDriveType* constant is only used with the *Where* filter line. The value of *$strComputer*, however, will change once for each computer name that is specified in the array *$aryComputers*. In this script, it will change twice. The first time through the loop, it will be equal to *loopback*, and the second time through the loop, it will be equal to *localhost*. However, if you added 250 different computer names, the effect would be the same—the value of *$strComputer* would change each time through the loop.

GetHardDiskDetails.ps1

```
$aryComputers = "loopback", "localhost"
Set-Variable -name intDriveType -value 3 -option constant

foreach ($strComputer in $aryComputers)

   {"Hard drives on: " + $strComputer
   Get-WmiObject -class win32_logicaldisk -computername $strComputer|
      Where {$_.drivetype -eq $intDriveType}}
```

Looping Through Code

A fundamental concept in any programming language is the use of looping techniques. Because everything in Windows PowerShell is an object, looping techniques not only become much more important but also are inherent in the way you use the scripts. Most of the time, you will not have to stop and think, "Do I need to use a looping technique here?" Rather, it will be intuitive, and you will probably find yourself performing the looping without thinking.

Using the *ForEach-Object* Cmdlet

If you were tempted to call this the *for ... each ... next statement* (as it was called in VBScript), then I have good news for you. In Windows PowerShell, there is no "next" required for the *ForEach-Object* cmdlet. Therefore, you will never forget to close out a *for ... each ... next* statement by leaving out the last *next* statement again. This is because Windows PowerShell automatically closes the statement, and the trailing *next* is no longer required. Of course, because everything in Windows PowerShell is an object, *foreach* is actually an alias for the *ForEach-Object* cmdlet.

In the ColorCodeProcessOutput.ps1 script, we use a *ForEach-Object* to produce a color-coded listing of processes running on a local machine that are using more CPU clock cycles than other processes. We use an *if* statement to decide on the color of the text to display. If the amount of CPU time is less than 100, then the color of text is blue. If it is more than 100, then we change the color of the text to red.

The *Write-Host* cmdlet is used to write the output from the script to the Windows PowerShell console. There are several properties available from the *Get-Process* cmdlet. If you wanted to add properties to display, you would simply list them in the first position separated by commas, as we did with *$_.name* and *$_.cpu*. To see all the properties available from *Get-Process*, pipeline *Get-Process* into the *Get-Member* cmdlet, as shown here:

```
Get-Process | Get-Member
```

After you have identified the properties you wish to retrieve, the next argument to supply to the *Write-Host* cmdlet is the foregroundcolor argument.

The color constants listed in Table 4-5 can be used for both the foregroundcolor argument and the backgroundcolor argument of *Write-Host*.

Table 4-5   *Write-Host* **Color Constants**

Black	DarkBlue	DarkGreen	DarkCyan
DarkRed	DarkMagenta	DarkYellow	Gray
DarkGray	Blue	Green	Cyan
Red	Magenta	Yellow	White

Note   Before you run ColorCodeProcessOutput.ps1 script on your machine, you may want to use *Get-Process* with no arguments to see what processes are using the most CPU time, and then adjust the -gt and the -lt arguments in the script accordingly.

ColorCodeProcessOutput.ps1

```
Get-Process |
  ForEach-Object `
    {if ($_.cpu -lt 100)
```

```
     {Write-Host $_.name, $_.cpu -foregroundcolor blue}
elseif ($_.cpu -gt 100)
     {Write-Host $_.name, $_.cpu -foregroundcolor red}}
```

> **Troubleshooting**   If you are unable to run Windows PowerShell scripts, one thing to check is the script execution policy. To do this, use the *Get-ExecutionPolicy* cmdlet.
>
> If the script execution policy is set to Restricted, you will need to change the policy to either Remote Signed or Unrestricted. To do this, you can use the *Set-ExecutionPolicy* cmdlet.

Exploring the *ForEach-Object* cmdlet

1. Open Windows PowerShell.

2. Use the *Get-Service* cmdlet to produce a listing of the name and status of each service defined on your machine. The code to do this is shown here:

   ```
   Get-Service
   ```

3. Pipeline the results from the *Get-Service* cmdlet to a *ForEach-Object*. This code is shown here:

   ```
   ForEach-Object
   ```

4. Use the line continuation special escape sequence to continue the *ForEach-Object* command to the next line. The line continuation character is the grave accent (`` ` ``) and on English language keyboards is found on the same key as the tilde (~). This line is shown here (you will not need to repeat *ForEach-Object* because this is the same line).

   ```
   ForEach-Object `
   ```

5. Open an *if* statement. The condition to be evaluated is "if the status of the service is equal to stopped." The status property will be associated with the current pipeline object and is referenced by the special variable $_. The code to do this is shown here:

   ```
   if ($_.Status -eq "stopped")
   ```

6. Open a script block by using the left curly bracket ({). Use the *Write-Host* cmdlet to write data to the Windows PowerShell console. Write the name and the status of each service. If the service is stopped, we want to specify the foregroundcolor to be red. Use the separator argument and use the comma, a new line, and a Tab. To specify the new line, use the special escape sequence `` `n ``. To specify a Tab, use the special escape sequence `` `t ``. The code to do this is shown here:

   ```
   {Write-Host $_.name, $_.Status -foregroundcolor red -separator ",`n`t"}
   ```

7. For the elseif clause, evaluate whether the status of the service in the current pipeline object is equal to running. This is shown here:

   ```
   elseif ($_.Status -eq "running")
   ```

8. If the service is running, we want to write the name and the status of the service in green by using the foregroundcolor argument of the *Write-Host* cmdlet. Use the separator argument and use the comma, a new line, and a Tab. To specify the new line, use the special escape sequence `n. To specify a Tab, use the special escape sequence`t. The code to do this is shown here:

```
{Write-Host $_.name, $_.Status -foregroundcolor green -separator ",`n`t"}}
```

9. Save your script as *yourname*ColorCodedServiceStatus.ps1. If your script does not work as expected, compare your script with the ColorCodedServiceStatus.ps1 script in the scripts folder for this chapter.

Using the *For* Statement

Similar to the *ForEach-Object* cmdlet, the *for* statement is used to control execution of a script block as long as a condition is true. Most of the time, you will use the *for* statement to perform an action a certain number of times. The line of code shown here is the basic for construction. The parentheses are used to separate the expression being evaluated from the code block contained in curly brackets. The evaluated expression is composed of three sections. In the first part, we create a variable $a and assign the value of 1 to it. In the second section, we have the condition to be evaluated. In the code shown here, as long as the variable $a is less than or equal to 3, the command in the code block section will continue to run. The last portion of the evaluation expression adds 1 to the variable $a. The code block is a simple printout of the word *hello*.

```
for ($a = 1; $a -le 3 ; $a++) {"hello"}
```

The PingArang.ps1 script shown here is very useful because it can be used to ping a range of IP addresses and will tell you whether the computer is responding to Internet control messaging packets (ICMPs). This is helpful for network discovery, or for ensuring that a computer is talking to the network. The $intPing variable is set to 10 and defined as an integer. Next, the $intNetwork variable is assigned the string "127.0.0." and is defined as a string.

The *for* statement is used to execute the remaining code the number of times specified in the $intPing variable. The counter-variable is created on the *for* statement line. This counter-variable, called $i, is assigned the value of 1. As long as $i is less than or equal to the value set in the $intPing variable, the script will continue to execute. The last thing that is done inside the evaluator section of the *for* statement is to add one to the value of $i.

The code block begins with the curly bracket. The first thing that is done inside the code block is to create a variable called $strQuery. The $strQuery is the string that holds the WMI query. The reason for putting this in a separate variable is that it makes it easier to use the $intNetwork variable and the $i counter-variable to create a valid IP address for use in the WMI query that results in a ping.

The *$wmi* variable is used to hold the collection of objects that is returned by the *Get-WmiObject* cmdlet. By using the optional query argument of the *Get-WmiObject* cmdlet, we are able to supply a WMI query. The statuscode property contains the result of the ping operation. A zero (0) indicates success; any other number means the ping failed. To present this information in a clear fashion, we use an *if ... else* statement to evaluate the statuscode property.

PingArange.ps1

```
[int]$intPing = 10
[string]$intNetwork = "127.0.0."

for ($i=1;$i -le $intPing; $i++)
{
$strQuery = "select * from win32_pingstatus where address = '" + $intNetwork + $i + "'"
    $wmi = get-wmiobject -query $strQuery
    "Pinging $intNetwork$i ... "
    if ($wmi.statuscode -eq 0)
       {"success"}
       else
          {"error: " + $wmi.statuscode + " occurred"}
}
```

Using *Do ... While*

The *do ... while* statement is one method for looping through code. The *do ... while* statement evaluates the test condition before running the script block. If the condition is false, then it will not run. If however, it is true, the script will run the loop, evaluate the condition to see whether it is still true, and then run again.

In the CountDownTimer.ps1 script, a *do ... while* loop is used to alternatively pause the script and display the current time as the script counts down to a specified time just like an alarm clock. The script begins by using the variable *$dtmTime* to hold the object that is returned by the *Get-Date* cmdlet. When you supply the values for hour, minute, and second, the *Get-Date* cmdlet will return a dateTime object representing the specified time. The *do ... while* loop evaluates the current time (retrieved by the *Get-Date* cmdlet and stored in the *$dtmCurrent* variable) with the time specified in the *$dtmTime* variable.

If the *$dtmCurrent* time value is less than the time specified in *$dtmTime*, then the script will print out the current time value that is contained in the *$dtmCurrent* variable. To do this, we use the -lt comparison operator. Other comparison operators are seen in Table 4-6. The *Start-Sleep* cmdlet is used to pause script execution for 2 seconds (as indicated by the -s 2 argument). After the while condition has been satisfied, the script will print out the message "time reached", and it uses the ` a special escape sequence to play the alert beep. The CountDownTimer.ps1 script is shown here:

CountDownTimer.ps1

```
$dtmTime = get-date -h 04 -mi 23 -s 00

do {$dtmCurrent = Get-Date -DisplayHint time
"The current time is " + $dtmCurrent
"counting to " + $dtmtime
start-sleep -s 2
} while ($dtmCurrent -lt $dtmTime)
"time reached `a"
```

Table 4-6   Comparison Operators

Operator	Description
-eq	equals
-ne	not equal
-gt	greater than
-ge	greater than or equal to
-lt	less than
-le	less than or equal to
-like	wild card comparison
-notlike	wild card comparison
-match	regular expression comparison
-notmatch	regular expression comparison

Quick Check

Q. **If you want to perform an operation as long as a value is equal to a certain number, what operator do you use?**

A. If you want to perform an operation as long as a value is equal to a certain number, use the -eq operator.

Q. **If you want to sound a beep in a script, what special escape character can you use?**

A. If you want to sound a beep in a script, use the `a special escape character.

Using *Do ... Until*

The *do ... until* statement provides a means of looping through your code until a condition becomes true. The difference between *do ... while* and *do ... until* is that the *do ... until* statement evaluates at the end of the loop. This means the code will always run at least once. A basic *do ... until* command is shown here. The value of *$i* is set to 10. The semicolon is then used to separate the value assignment from *do ... loop*. The curly brackets separate the script block from the rest of the code. Inside the script block, 1 is subtracted from the value of *$i* each time we loop through the code. The double hyphen (–) operator is used to do the subtraction. A string is used to print out a status message that lets us know the current value of *$i*. The *until* block tells the command to continue to run until the value of *$i* is equal to 0.

```
$i = 10; do {$i --; "i is $i"} until ($i -eq 0)
```

In the ReadTxtFile.ps1 script, the variable $i is given a value of 0. The value of $i is then incremented after the script displays one line of text from the text file. The *until* clause evaluates whether the value of $i is equal to the length of the text file. When the length of the text file is the same as the value of $i, then we have reached the end of the file.

ReadTxtFile.Ps1

```
$strTxtFile = "c:\mytest\loopbackprocesses.txt"
$i = 0
$mytext = Get-Content $strTxtFile
do {
   $mytext[$i]
   $i ++
} until ($i -eq $mytext.length)
```

The exploring the *do ... until* procedure will highlight this behavior.

Exploring the *do ... until* statement

1. Open Windows PowerShell.

2. Type the variable $i and assign the value of 0 to it. Use a semicolon to separate this variable assignment from the following command. This code is shown here:

    ```
    $i=0;
    ```

3. Open a *do* loop and add one to the $i variable. Use the special double plus symbol (++) operator. Include the semicolon command separator. This code is shown here:

    ```
    do {$i++;
    ```

4. Print out the string "I is equal to" and include the value of $i. Close out the script block. This code is shown here:

    ```
    "i is equal to $i"}
    ```

5. Add the *until* clause and evaluate the value of $i when it is equal to 0. This code is shown here:

    ```
    until ($i -eq 0)
    ```

6. Before you run this command, realize it will go into a continuous loop. This is because *do ... until* evaluates at the end of the script. The value of $i will have already been incremented to 1 before the evaluation being performed. You can use ^c to break into the loop.

7. Run the command. After a few lines have scrolled past, use ^c to break into the loop.

8. Press the up arrow to retrieve the previous command. This line of code is shown here:

    ```
    $i=0;do {$i++; "i is equal to $i"} until ($i -eq 0)
    ```

9. Convert the *do ... until* loop into a *do ... while* loop. To do this, simply replace the word *until* with *while*. The altered code is shown here:

    ```
    $i=0;do {$i++; "i is equal to $i"} while ($i -eq 0)
    ```

10.   This code runs one time and produces the output shown here:

```
i is equal to 1
```

11.   This concludes this procedure. Commands used are stored in the ExploringDoLoop.txt file.

Making Decisions

Now that we have mastered the process of looping through code, it is time to add some intelligence to our code. There are two statements we can use in our code to add intelligence. The first of the statements is the easiest to use and is the one that makes sense to most people: *if ... elseif ... else*. The reason it is so easy to use is that it is intuitive. We are used to saying things like: "If it is sunny this afternoon, then I will go surfing. In Windows PowerShell, the *then* clause is understood and not specifically used, but the syntax is still very intuitive.

The second decision-making statement is one that at first glance does not make sense: the *switch* statement. The *switch* statement is the Windows PowerShell equivalent to the *select... case* statement from Visual Basic days. When read as an *if ... elseif* statement, *switch* makes sense. The advantage of the syntax is that it is much cleaner, involves less typing, and is easier to troubleshoot.

Using *If ... Elseif ... Else*

The *if ... elseif ... else* statement is used to add decision-making capabilities to the script. This can result in a great deal of flexibility in your script. By using the *if* statement you can evaluate a condition, and if the condition is true, you can take an action. When you add the *else* clause, you are able to evaluate a condition, but can now take two actions depending on how the condition evaluates. When you add *elseif*, you can evaluate a condition, but you now have a plethora of potential outcomes.

The GetCPUinfo.ps1 script illustrates using *if ... elseif ... else*. The script will retrieve information about the CPU on a computer by using the *Get-WmiObject* cmdlet. The *$wmi* variable is used to hold the processor object that is returned. The architecture property of the processor management object only reports a coded value, as seen in Table 4-7. To make the script more readable, an *if ... elseif ... else* statement is used to translate each value with the specific type of processor.

Table 4-7   WIN32_Processor Processor Values

Value	Meaning
0	x86
1	MIPS
2	Alpha
3	PowerPC
6	Intel Itanium
9	x64

GetCPUinfo.ps1

```
$wmi = get-wmiObject win32_processor
if ($wmi.Architecture -eq 0)
   {"This is an x86 computer"}
   elseif($wmi.architecture -eq 1)
      {"This is an MIPS computer"}
   elseif($wmi.architecture -eq 2)
      {"This is an Alapha computer"}
   elseif($wmi.architecture -eq 3)
      {"This is an PowerPC computer"}
   elseif($wmi.architecture -eq 6)
      {"This is an IPF computer"}
   elseif($wmi.architecture -eq 9)
      {"This is an x64 computer"}
else
      {$wmi.architecture + " is not a cpu type I am familiar with"}
   "Current clockspeed is : " + $wmi.CurrentClockSpeed + " MHZ"
   "Max clockspeed is : " + $wmi.MaxClockSpeed  + " MHZ"
   "Current load percentage is: " + $wmi.LoadPercentage + " Percent"
   "The L2 cache size is: " + $wmi.L2CacheSize + " KB"
```

Using *Switch*

In other programming languages, *switch* would be called the *select case* statement. The *switch* statement is used to evaluate a condition against a series of potential matches. In this regard, it is essentially a streamlined *if ... elseif ... else* statement. When using the *switch* statement, the condition to be evaluated is contained inside parentheses. Each condition to be evaluated is then placed inside a curly bracket in the code block. This command is shown here:

```
$a=5;switch ($a) { 4{"four detected"} 5{"five detected"} }
```

In the DisplayComputerRoles.ps1 script shown here, the script begins by using the *$wmi* variable to hold the object that is returned by using the *Get-WmiObject* cmdlet. The domainrole property of the WIN32_ComputerSystem class is returned as a coded value. To produce an output that is more readable, the *switch* statement is used to match the value of the domainrole property to the appropriate text value.

DisplayComputerRoles.ps1

```
$wmi = get-wmiobject win32_computersystem
"computer " + $wmi.name + " is: "
switch ($wmi.domainrole)
   {
   0 {"`t Stand alone workstation"}
   1 {"`t Member workstation"}
   2 {"`t Stand alone server"}
   3 {"`t Member server"}
   4 {"`t Back up domain controller"}
   5 {"`t Primary domain controller"}
   default {"`t The role can not be determined"}
   }
```

Creating Multiple Folders: Step-by-Step Exercises

In this exercise, we explore the use of constants, variables, concatenation, decision making, and looping as we create 10 folders in the C:\Mytest directory. This directory was created earlier. If you do not have this folder on your machine, you can either create it manually or modify both the step-by-step exercise and the one step further exercise to use a folder that exists on your machine.

1. Open Notepad or your favorite Windows PowerShell script editor.

2. Create a variable called *$intFolders* and have it hold the value of 10. The code to do this is shown here:

   ```
   $intFolders = 10
   ```

3. Create a variable called *$intPad*. Do not put anything in the variable yet. This code is shown here:

   ```
   $intPad
   ```

4. Create a variable called *$i* and put the number 1 in it. The code to do this is shown here:

   ```
   $i = 1
   ```

5. Use the *New-Variable* cmdlet to create a variable named *strPrefix*. Use the value argument of the cmdlet to assign the value of "testFolder" to the variable. Use the option argument to make *$strPrefix* into a constant. The code to do this is shown here:

   ```
   New-Variable -Name strPrefix -Value "testFolder" -Option constant
   ```

6. Open a *do ... until* statement. Include the opening curly bracket for the script block. This code is shown here:

   ```
   do {
   ```

7. Begin an *if ... else* statement. The condition to be evaluated is if the variable *$i* is less than 10. The code that does this is shown here:

   ```
   if ($i -lt 10)
   ```

8. Open the script block for the *if* statement. Assign the value of 0 to the variable *$intPad*. This is shown here:

   ```
   {$intPad=0
   ```

9. Use the *New-Item* cmdlet to create a new folder. The new folder will be created in the C:\Mytest directory. The name of the new folder will comprise the *$strPrefix* constant "testFolder", the number 0 from the *$intPad* variable, and the number contained in the *$i* variable. The code that does this is shown here:

   ```
   new-item -path c:\mytest -name $strPrefix$intPad$i -type directory}
   ```

10. Add the *else* clause. This code is shown here:

    ```
    else
    ```

11. The *else* script block is the same as the *if* script block, except it does not include the 0 in the name that comes from the *$intPad* variable. Copy the *New-Item* line of code from the *if* statement and delete the *$intPad* variable from the name argument. The revised line of code is shown here:

```
{new-item -path c:\mytest -name $strPrefix$i -type directory}
```

12. Increment the value of the *$i* variable by 1. To do this, use the double plus symbol (++) operator. The code that does this is shown here:

```
$i++
```

13. Close the script block for the *else* clause and add the *until* statement. The condition that *until* will evaluate is if the *$i* variable is equal to the value contained in the *$intFolders* variable + 1. The reason for adding 1 to *$intFolders* is so the script will actually create the same number of folders as are contained in the *$intFolders* variable. Because this script uses a *do ...until* loop and the value of *$i* is incremented before entering the *until* evaluation, the value of *$i* is always 1 more than the number of folders created. This code is shown here:

```
}until ($i -eq $intFolders+1)
```

14. Save your script as *yourname*CreateMultipleFolders.ps1. Run your script. You should see 10 folders created in the C:\Mytest directory. If you do not, compare your results with the CreateMultipleFolders.ps1 script in the scripts folder for this chapter. This concludes this step-by-step exercise.

One Step Further: Deleting Multiple Folders

In this exercise, we will do the following:

1. Open the *yourname*CreateMultipleFolders.ps1 in Notepad or your favorite script editor. This script was created in the step-by-step exercise.

2. In the *if ... else* statement, the *New-Item* cmdlet is used twice to create folders in the C:\Mytest directory. We want to delete these folders. To do this, we need to change the *New-Item* cmdlet to the *Remove-Item* cmdlet. The two edited script blocks are shown here:

```
{$intPad=0
      remove-item -path c:\mytest -name $strPrefix$intPad$i -type directory}
   else
      {remove-item -path c:\mytest -name $strPrefix$i -type directory}
```

3. The *Remove-Item* cmdlet does not have a name argument. Therefore, we need to remove this argument but keep the code that creates the folder name. We can basically replace -name with a backslash, as shown here:

```
{$intPad=0
      remove-item -path c:\mytest\$strPrefix$intPad$i -type directory}
   else
      {remove-item -path c:\mytest\$strPrefix$i -type directory}
```

4. The *Remove-Item* cmdlet does not take a -type argument. Because this argument is not needed, it can also be removed from both *Remove-Item* statements. The revised script block is shown here:

```
{$intPad=0
    Remove-item -path c:\mytest\$strPrefix$intPad$i}
  else
    {Remove-item -path c:\mytest\$strPrefix$i}
```

5. This concludes this one step further exercise. Save your script as *yourname*DeleteMulti-pleFolders.ps1. Run your script. You should see the 10 previously created folders deleted. If you do not, compare your results with the DeleteMultipleFolders.ps1 script in the scripts folder for this chapter.

Chapter 4 Quick Reference

To	Do This
Retrieve the script execution policy	Use the *Get-ExecutionPolicy* cmdlet
Set the script execution policy	Use the *Set-ExecutionPolicy* cmdlet
Create a variable	Type the variable name in the script
Create a constant	Use the *New-Variable* cmdlet and specify constant for the option argument
Loop through a collection when you do not know how many items are in the collection	Use the *ForEach-Object* cmdlet
Pause execution of a script for a certain amount of time	Use the *Start-Sleep* cmdlet and supply the amount of time to sleep in either seconds or milliseconds
Print out text in color	Use the *Write-Host* cmdlet and supply the appropriate color to the foregroundcolor argument
Read the contents of a text file	Use the *Get-Content* cmdlet and supply the path to the file as the value for the path argument
To produce a beep in a script	Use the `a special escape character sequence inside a string
Delete a folder	Use the *Remove-Item* cmdlet and supply the path to the folder as the value for the path argument

Chapter 5
Using WMI

After completing this chapter, you will be able to:

- Understand the concept of WMI namespaces
- Use the WMI namespaces
- Navigate the WMI namespaces
- Understand the use of WMI providers
- Discover classes supplied by WMI providers
- Use the *Get-WmiObject* cmdlet to perform simple WMI queries
- Produce a listing of all WMI classes
- Perform searches to find WMI classes

The inclusion of Windows Management Instrumentation (WMI) in virtually every operating system released by Microsoft since Windows NT 4.0 should give you an idea of the importance of this underlying technology. From a network management perspective, many useful tasks can be accomplished using just Windows PowerShell, but to truly begin to unleash the power of scripting, you need to bring in additional tools. This is where WMI comes into play. WMI was designed to provide access to many powerful ways of managing Microsoft Windows systems. In this section, we dive into the pieces that make up WMI. We look at several concepts—namespaces, providers, and classes—and show how these concepts can aid us in leveraging WMI in our Windows PowerShell scripts. All the scripts mentioned in this chapter can be found in the corresponding scripts folder on the CD.

In Windows Vista, more than 100 new WMI classes were introduced. In products such as Microsoft Exchange Server, Microsoft SQL Server, and Microsoft Internet Information Server (to mention a few), support for WMI continues to grow and expand. Some of the tasks you can perform with WMI follow:

- Report on drive configuration
- Report on available memory, both physical and virtual
- Back up the event log
- Modify the registry

- Schedule tasks
- Share folders
- Switch from a static to a dynamic IP address

Understanding the WMI Model

WMI is sometimes referred to as a *hierarchical namespace*, in which the layers build on one another like a Lightweight Directory Access Protocol (LDAP) directory used in Active Directory, or the filesystem structure on your hard disk drive. Although it is true that WMI is a hierarchical namespace, the term doesn't really convey the richness of WMI. The WMI model has three sections—resources, infrastructure, and consumers—with the following uses:

- **WMI resources**   Resources include anything that can be accessed by using WMI—the filesystem, networked components, event logs, files, folders, disks, Active Directory, and so on.

- **WMI infrastructure**   The infrastructure comprises three parts: the WMI service, the WMI repository, and the WMI providers. Of these parts, WMI providers are the most important because they provide the means for WMI to gather needed information.

- **WMI consumers**   A consumer "consumes" the data from WMI. A consumer can be a PowerShell or VBScript, an enterprise management software package, or some other tool or utility that executes WMI queries.

Working with Objects and Namespaces

Let's go back to the idea of a namespace introduced earlier in this chapter. You can think of a *namespace* as a way to organize or collect data related to similar items. Visualize an old-fashioned filing cabinet. Each drawer can represent a particular namespace. Inside this drawer are hanging folders that collect information related to a subset of what the drawer actually holds. For example, at home in my filing cabinet, I have a drawer reserved for information related to my woodworking tools. Inside this particular drawer are hanging folders for my table saw, my planer, my joiner, my dust collector, and so on. In the folder for the table saw is information about the motor, the blades, and the various accessories I purchased for the saw (such as an over-arm blade guard).

The WMI namespace is organized in a similar fashion. The NameSpaces are the file cabinets. The Providers are drawers in the file cabinet. The Folders in the drawers of the file cabinet are the WMI classes. These namespaces are shown in Figure 5-1.

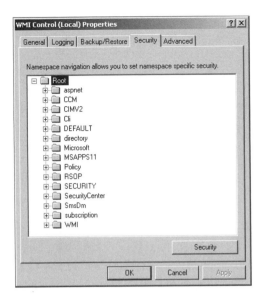

Figure 5-1   WMI namespaces on Windows XP

Namespaces contain objects, and these objects contain properties you can manipulate. Let's use a WMI script, ListWmiNameSpaces.ps1, to illustrate just how the WMI namespace is organized. In the ListWmiNameSpaces.ps1 script, the object returned from the WMI query is contained in the variable $wmi. The Get-WmiObject cmdlet is used to make the connection into the WMI. The class argument is used to specify the class of __Namespace, and the namespace argument is used to specify the the level in the WMI namespace hierarchy. The Get-WmiObject line of code is shown here:

```
$wmi = Get-WmiObject -class __Namespace -namespace root
```

Tip   When the Get-WmiObject cmdlet is run, it returns an object that is an array. We use this to our advantage on the second line of the ListWmiNameSpaces.ps1 script. To easily get the name of the computer the script is run on, we print out the name of the __server property. But because $wmi contains an array, we cannot print out the value directly. We specify element 0 (the first element in the array) by supplying the [0] parameter to the variable. This section of code is shown here:

```
"Listing namespaces on " + $wmi[0].__server +
  " please wait a second "
```

Because all the namespaces are on the same computer, it really does not matter from which element we retrieve the data. All arrays will always have an element 0 populated if they contain any data at all.

The next section of code in the ListWmiNameSpaces.ps1 script displays the progress indicator, which is a listing of dots, one for each namespace enumerated. If simply printing out the progress indicator dots would work, then this section of code would be rather easy; however, it becomes more complex because, by default, everything seems to print each item on a new line. To print out one dot for each item WMI namespace, we need to know how many WMI namespaces there are. This is where Windows PowerShell really shines. Because the object returned was an array, we need to know only how many items are in the array. We can obtain this information by obtaining the value for the length property of the $wmi variable. The *for* statement uses $i as the counter-variable, and will continue until the value of $i is less than or equal to the length of the $wmi array. The last section of the *for* statement increments the value of $i by 1. This section of the code is shown here:

```
for ($i=0;$i -le $wmi.length;$i++)
```

To keep the Windows PowerShell prompt from tangling up with the output from our ListWmiNameSpaces.ps1 script, we add an *if ... else* clause. If the dot does not represent the last namespace on the machine, we print each dot on the same line. We are able to do this by specifying the noNewLine argument from the *Write-Host* cmdlet. If the dot will represent the last namespace, then we want the newline character to be appended. To make the output a little more dramatic, we use the *Start-Sleep* cmdlet and specify an interval of 75 to the millisecond argument. This section of code is shown here:

```
for ($i=0;$i -le $wmi.length;$i++)
   {if ($i -lt $wmi.length)
      {Write-Host -noNewLine "."
      Start-Sleep -m 75}
   else
      {Write-Host "."}
   }
```

The output section of the script pipelines the contents of the $wmi variable into the *Format-List* cmdlet and chooses only the name property. We then use the *Write-Host* cmdlet and supply the value of green for the foregroundcolor argument. We print out the length of the array holding all the WMI namespaces, using the grave accent character (`` ` ``) to continue our line of code to the next line. At the end of the last line of code, we use the `n escape sequence to force a new line. The output section of code is shown here:

```
$wmi | Format-List name
   Write-Host -foregroundColor green "There are" $wmi.length `
   "namespaces on this machine `n"
```

You will want to use the ListWmiNameSpaces.ps1 script to get an idea of the number and variety of WMI namespaces that exist on the computer. This can be a great way to explore and to learn about WMI. The entire contents of the ListWmiNameSpaces.ps1 script is shown here:

ListWmiNameSpaces.ps1

```
$wmi = Get-WmiObject -class __Namespace -namespace root
   "Listing namespaces on " + $wmi[0].__server +
   " please wait a second "
```

```
for ($i=0;$i -le $wmi.length;$i++)
   {if ($i -lt $wmi.length)
      {Write-Host -noNewLine "."
      Start-Sleep -m 75}
   else
      {Write-Host "."}
   }

$wmi | Format-List name
   Write-Host -foregroundColor green "There are" $wmi.length `
   "namespaces on this machine `n"
```

The output from the ListWmiNameSpaces.ps1 script is shown here:

```
Listing namespaces on MRED1 please wait a second
.................

name : ServiceModel

name : SECURITY

name : MSAPPS12

name : CCM

name : RSOP

name : Cli

name : aspnet

name : SecurityCenter

name : WMI

name : CIMV2

name : Policy

name : SmsDm

name : Microsoft

name : DEFAULT

name : directory

name : subscription

name : MSAPPS11


There are 17 namespaces on this machine
```

So what does all this mean? It means that in Windows XP, there are more than a dozen different namespaces from which you could pull information about our server. Understanding that the different namespaces exist is the first step to being able to navigate WMI to find the information you need. Often, students and others new to PowerShell or VBScript work on a WMI script to make the script perform a certain action, which is a great way to learn scripting. However, what they often do not know is which namespace they need to connect to so that they can accomplish their task. When I tell them which namespace to work with, they sometimes reply, "That's fine for you, but how do I know that the such-and-such namespace even exists?" By using the ListWmiNameSpaces.ps1 script, you can easily generate a list of namespaces installed on a particular machine, and armed with that information, search on MSDN, *http://msdn.microsoft.com/library/default.asp,* to see what information it is able to provide.

Listing WMI Providers

Understanding the namespace assists the network administrator with judiciously applying WMI scripting to his or her network duties. However, as mentioned earlier, to access information through WMI, you must have access to a WMI provider. After the provider is implemented, you can gain access to the information that is made available. Two Excel spreadsheets with all the providers and their associated classes from Windows XP and from Windows Server 2003 are in the Supplemental Material folder on the CD-ROM. If you want to know which classes are supported by the RouteProvider, you can click the Filter button and select RouteProvider. This is shown in Figure 5-2.

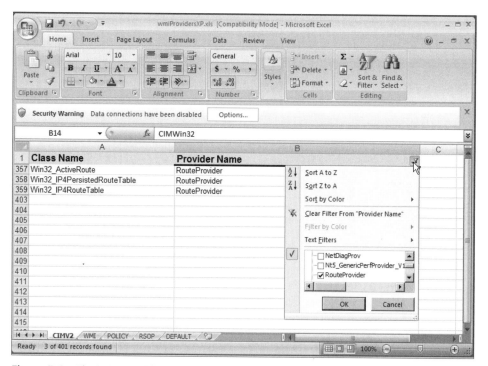

Figure 5-2 The WMIProvidersXP.xls spreadsheet lists classes supported by provider name

Providers in WMI are all based on a template class, or a system class called __provider. Armed with this information, we can look for instances of the __provider class, and we will have a list of all the providers that reside in our WMI namespace. This is exactly what the ListWmiProviders.ps1 script does.

The ListWmiProviders.ps1 script begins by assigning the string Root\cimv2 to the *$wmiNS* variable. This value will be used with the *Get-WmiObject* cmdlet to specify where the WMI query will take place. Note that the WMI namespace Root\cimv2 is the default WMI namespace on Windows 2000, Windows XP, Windows Vista, and Windows Server 2003.

The *Get-WmiObject* cmdlet is used to query WMI. The class provider is used to limit the WMI query to the __provider class. The namespace argument tells the *Get-WmiObject* cmdlet to only look in the Root\cimv2 WMI namespace. The array of objects returned from the *Get-WmiObject* cmdlet is pipelined into the *Sort-Object* cmdlet, where the listing of objects is alphabetized based on the name property. After this process is completed, the reorganized objects are passed to the *Format-List* cmdlet, where the name of each provider is printed out.

ListWmiProviders.ps1

```
$wmiNS = "root\cimV2"
Get-WmiObject -class __Provider -namespace $wmiNS |
    Sort-Object -property Name |
    Format-List name
```

Working with WMI Classes

In addition to working with namespaces, the inquisitive network administrator will want to explore the concept of classes. In WMI parlance, you have core classes, common classes, and dynamic classes. *Core classes* represent managed objects that apply to all areas of management. These classes provide a basic vocabulary for analyzing and describing managed systems. Two examples of core classes are parameters and the *SystemSecurity* class. *Common classes* are extensions to the core classes and represent managed objects that apply to specific management areas. However, common classes are independent from a particular implementation or technology. The *CIM_UnitaryComputerSystem* is an example of a common class. Core and common classes are not used as much by network administrators because they serve as templates from which other classes are derived.

Many of the classes stored in Root\cimv2, therefore, are abstract classes and are used as templates. However, a few classes in Root\cimv2 are dynamic classes used to hold actual information. The important aspect to remember about *dynamic classes* is that instances of a dynamic class are generated by a provider and are therefore more likely to retrieve "live" data from the system.

To produce a simple listing of WMI classes, you can use the *Get-WmiObject* cmdlet and specify the list argument. This code is shown here:

```
Get-WmiObject -list
```

A partial output from the previous command is shown here:

```
Win32_TSGeneralSetting                  Win32_TSPermissionsSetting
Win32_TSClientSetting                   Win32_TSEnvironmentSetting
Win32_TSNetworkAdapterListSetting       Win32_TSLogonSetting
Win32_TSSessionSetting                  Win32_DisplayConfiguration
Win32_COMSetting                        Win32_ClassicCOMClassSetting
Win32_DCOMApplicationSetting            Win32_MSIResource
Win32_ServiceControl                    Win32_Property
```

The following script, ListAllClassesInNameSpace.ps1, returns a list of classes found in the Root\cimv2 namespace. There are more than 900 classes listed in the Root\cimv2 namespace of most computers. The difference between the *Get-WmiObject -list* command and the ListAllClassesInNameSpace.ps1 script, besides length, is flexibility. With the *Get-WmiObject -list* command, you are pretty much limited to retrieving the name of the WMI classes. In the ListAllClassesInNameSpace.ps1 script, you are working directly with the WMI application programming interface (API), and as a result, you have complete flexibility in what information you retrieve and how you present it.

In the ListAllClassesInNameSpace.ps1, the script begins by assigning the shortcut value of dot (.) to the variable *$strComputer*. When used with WMI, the dot in the connection string means to run the command on the local machine. The *$wmiNS* variable holds the value of \Root\cimv2, which is the default WMI namespace in all modern Windows operating systems. The next seven variables are common to all scripts that use the WbemScripting.SWbemLocator method. The variables are listed in Table 5-1.

Table 5-1   Variables Used in ListAllClassesInNameSpace.ps1

Variable Name	Variable Use
$strComputer	Name of computer to run the script on
$wmiNS	WMI namespace containing WMI class used in the script
$strUsr	User name for connection to remote computer
$strPWD	Password of user connecting to remote machine
$strLocl	Language to be used with WMI connection
$strAuth	Credential authority, for example, Kerberos, NTLM
$iFlag	Security flag; used to specify timeout value

After declaring the seven common variables used in all WbemScripting.SWbemLocator scripts, we use the variable *$objLocator* to hold the WbemScripting.SWbemLocator object that is returned by the *New-Object* cmdlet. The *New-Object* command is shown here:

```
$objLocator = New-Object -comobject "WbemScripting.SWbemLocator"
```

The WbemScripting.SWbemLocator object only exposes a single method—the connectServer method. But this method can receive up to seven different arguments.

Because the connectServer method is so heavily parameterized, I decided to define a variable for each parameter. This ensures that parameters that are left out are placed in the correct order—as opposed to just padding a bunch of empty commas. The connectServer method call is shown here:

```
$objWMIService = $objLocator.ConnectServer($strComputer,
    $wmiNS, $strUsr, $strPWD, $strLocl, $strAuth, $iFLag)
```

The connectServer method returns an ISwbemServices object, which is held in the *$objWMIService* variable. The ISwbemServices object exposes a method called subClassesOf. The subClassesOf method returns a collection of WMI classes that is called an ISWbem-ObjectSet. The subClassesOf method call is shown here:

```
$colItems = $objWMIService.subClassesOf()
```

Each WMI class that gets returned is an ISwbemObject, which is adorned with many properties and methods. Each ISwbemObject is contained in the *$objItem* variable. The *$colItems* variable contains a collection. To retrieve the individual properties of the ISwbemObject, we need to have a way to pull a single object from the collection. To do this, we will use the *ForEach-Object* cmdlet. The ForEach-Object statement is seen here. Note that to save a little bit of typing, I decided to use the alias *foreach*.

```
foreach ($objItem In $colItems)
        {
          $objItem.path_.class
        }
```

Each individual object from the collection of objects is called *$objItem*. The ISwbemObject contained in the *$objItem* variable has a property called path_. When we query the path_ property, an ISWbemObjectPath object is returned. The ISWbemObjectPath object has a property called class. To get the name of each class contained in the Root\cimv2 namespace, we simply print out the value of the class property. The line of code that does this is shown here:

```
$objItem.path_.class
```

The completed ListAllClassesInNameSpace.ps1 script is shown here:

ListAllClassesInNameSpace.ps1

```
$strComputer = "."
$wmiNS = "\root\cimv2"
$strUsr ="" #Blank for current security. Domain\Username
$strPWD = "" #Blank for current security.
$strLocl = "MS_409" #US English. Can leave blank for current language
$strAuth = "" #if specify domain in strUsr this must be blank
$iFlag = "0" #only two values allowed: 0 and 128.
```

```
$objLocator = New-Object -comobject "WbemScripting.SWbemLocator"
$objWMIService = $objLocator.ConnectServer($strComputer,
    $wmiNS, $strUsr, $strPWD, $strLocl, $strAuth, $iFLag)


$colItems = $objWMIService.subClassesOf()
   Write-Host "There are: " $colItems.count " classes in $wmiNS"
   foreach ($objItem In $colItems)
          {
             $objItem.path_.class
          }
```

Exploring the WMI object

1. Open the ListAllClassesNameSpaces.ps1 script in Notepad.exe or some other script editor and save it as *yourname*ExploringWmiObjects.ps1. The ExploringWmiObjects.ps1 script can be found in the scripts folder for this chapter.

2. Your script right now should look like the following:

```
$strComputer = "."
$wmiNS = "\root\cimv2"
$strUsr ="" #Blank for current security. Domain\Username
$strPWD = "" #Blank for current security.
$strLocl = "MS_409" #US English. Can leave blank for current language
$strAuth = "" #if specify domain in strUsr this must be blank
$iFlag = "0" #only two values allowed: 0 and 128.

$objLocator = New-Object -comobject "WbemScripting.SWbemLocator"
$objWMIService = $objLocator.ConnectServer($strComputer, `
    $wmiNS, $strUsr, $strPWD, $strLocl, $strAuth, $iFLag)


$colItems = $objWMIService.subClassesOf()
   Write-Host "There are: " $colItems.count " classes in $wmiNS"
   foreach ($objItem In $colItems)
          {
             $objItem.path_.class
          }
```

3. Run the script, but after a second, press Ctrl-c to halt execution of the script. You will see an output similar to the following:

```
There are:  1000  classes in \root\cimv2
__SystemClass
__thisNAMESPACE
__Provider
__Win32Provider
__IndicationRelated
__EventGenerator
__TimerInstruction
__IntervalTimerInstruction
__AbsoluteTimerInstruction
__Event
__NamespaceOperationEvent
__NamespaceDeletionEvent
__NamespaceCreationEvent
```

```
__NamespaceModificationEvent
__InstanceOperationEvent
__MethodInvocationEvent
__InstanceCreationEvent
__InstanceModificationEvent
```

4. Comment out everything below the New-Object line statement in your script. The revised script is shown here:

```
$strComputer = "."
$wmiNS = "\root\cimv2"
$strUsr ="" #Blank for current security. Domain\Username
$strPWD = "" #Blank for current security.
$strLocl = "MS_409" #US English. Can leave blank for current language
$strAuth = "" #if specify domain in strUsr this must be blank
$iFlag = "0" #only two values allowed: 0 and 128.

$objLocator = New-Object -comobject "WbemScripting.SWbemLocator"
# $objWMIService = $objLocator.ConnectServer($strComputer, `
#   $wmiNS, $strUsr, $strPWD, $strLocl, $strAuth, $iFLag)
#
# $colItems = $objWMIService.subClassesOf()
# Write-Host "There are: " $colItems.count " classes in $wmiNS"
#     foreach ($objItem In $colItems)
#             {
#                 $objItem.path_.class
#             }
```

5. Save and run the script. You should not see any output, nor should you see any errors.

6. On the line below the New-Object line in your script (where the first line of commented code resides), add a line that pipelines the object contained in the *$objLocator* variable to the *Get-Member* cmdlet. This code is shown here:

```
$objLocator | Get-Member
```

7. The results from the previous command are shown here:

```
    TypeName: System.__ComObject#{76a6415b-cb41-11d1-8b02-00600806d9b6}

Name           MemberType Definition
----           ---------- ----------
ConnectServer  Method     ISWbemServices ConnectServer (string, string, strin...
Security_      Property   ISWbemSecurity Security_ () {get}
```

8. Remove the comments from the connectServer method call. These two lines of code are shown here:

```
$objWMIService = $objLocator.ConnectServer($strComputer, `
    $wmiNS, $strUsr, $strPWD, $strLocl, $strAuth, $iFLag)
```

9. Save and run the script. You should see exactly the same results you saw the previous time.

10. Pipeline the object contained in the *$objWMIService* variable to the *Get-Member* cmdlet. The code to do this is shown here:

```
$objWMIService | Get-Member
```

11. Save and run the script. The results from this command are shown here:

```
   TypeName: System.__ComObject#{76a6415b-cb41-11d1-8b02-00600806d9b6}

Name          MemberType Definition
----          ---------- ----------
ConnectServer Method     ISWbemServices ConnectServer (string, string, strin...
Security_      Property   ISWbemSecurity Security_ () {get}


   TypeName: System.__ComObject#{d2f68443-85dc-427e-91d8-366554cc754c}

Name                     MemberType Definition
----                     ---------- ----------
AssociatorsOf             Method     ISWbemObjectSet AssociatorsOf (string,...
AssociatorsOfAsync        Method     void AssociatorsOfAsync (IDispatch, st...
Delete                    Method     void Delete (string, int, IDispatch)
DeleteAsync               Method     void DeleteAsync (IDispatch, string, i...
ExecMethod                Method     ISWbemObject ExecMethod (string, strin...
ExecMethodAsync           Method     void ExecMethodAsync (IDispatch, strin...
ExecNotificationQuery     Method     ISWbemEventSource ExecNotificationQuer...
ExecNotificationQueryAsync Method    void ExecNotificationQueryAsync (IDisp...
ExecQuery                 Method     ISWbemObjectSet ExecQuery (string, str...
ExecQueryAsync            Method     void ExecQueryAsync (IDispatch, string...
Get                       Method     ISWbemObject Get (string, int, IDispatch)
GetAsync                  Method     void GetAsync (IDispatch, string, int,...
InstancesOf               Method     ISWbemObjectSet InstancesOf (string, i...
InstancesOfAsync          Method     void InstancesOfAsync (IDispatch, stri...
Put                       Method     ISWbemObjectPath Put (ISWbemObjectEx, ...
PutAsync                  Method     void PutAsync (ISWbemSink, ISWbemObjec...
ReferencesTo              Method     ISWbemObjectSet ReferencesTo (string, ...
ReferencesToAsync         Method     void ReferencesToAsync (IDispatch, str...
SubclassesOf              Method     ISWbemObjectSet SubclassesOf (string, ...
SubclassesOfAsync         Method     void SubclassesOfAsync (IDispatch, str...
Security_                  Property   ISWbemSecurity Security_ () {get}
```

12. Remove the comment character from the line that calls the subClassesOf() method. On the next line following that line of code, pipeline the object contained in the *$colItems* variable to the *Get-Member* cmdlet. These two lines of code are shown here:

```
$colItems = $objWMIService.subClassesOf()
$colItems | Get-Member
```

13. Save and run the script. The resulting output is shown here:

```
   TypeName: System.__ComObject#{76a6415b-cb41-11d1-8b02-00600806d9b6}

Name          MemberType Definition
----          ---------- ----------
ConnectServer Method     ISWbemServices ConnectServer (string, string, strin...
Security_      Property   ISWbemSecurity Security_ () {get}
```

TypeName: System.__ComObject#{d2f68443-85dc-427e-91d8-366554cc754c}

Name	MemberType	Definition
AssociatorsOf	Method	ISWbemObjectSet AssociatorsOf (string,...
AssociatorsOfAsync	Method	void AssociatorsOfAsync (IDispatch, st...
Delete	Method	void Delete (string, int, IDispatch)
DeleteAsync	Method	void DeleteAsync (IDispatch, string, i...
ExecMethod	Method	ISWbemObject ExecMethod (string, strin...
ExecMethodAsync	Method	void ExecMethodAsync (IDispatch, strin...
ExecNotificationQuery	Method	ISWbemEventSource ExecNotificationQuer...
ExecNotificationQueryAsync	Method	void ExecNotificationQueryAsync (IDisp...
ExecQuery	Method	ISWbemObjectSet ExecQuery (string, str...
ExecQueryAsync	Method	void ExecQueryAsync (IDispatch, string...
Get	Method	ISWbemObject Get (string, int, IDispatch)
GetAsync	Method	void GetAsync (IDispatch, string, int,...
InstancesOf	Method	ISWbemObjectSet InstancesOf (string, i...
InstancesOfAsync	Method	void InstancesOfAsync (IDispatch, stri...
Put	Method	ISWbemObjectPath Put (ISWbemObjectEx, ...
PutAsync	Method	void PutAsync (ISWbemSink, ISWbemObjec...
ReferencesTo	Method	ISWbemObjectSet ReferencesTo (string, ...
ReferencesToAsync	Method	void ReferencesToAsync (IDispatch, str...
SubclassesOf	Method	ISWbemObjectSet SubclassesOf (string, ...
SubclassesOfAsync	Method	void SubclassesOfAsync (IDispatch, str...
Security_	Property	ISWbemSecurity Security_ () {get}

TypeName: System.__ComObject#{269ad56a-8a67-4129-bc8c-0506dcfe9880}

Name	MemberType	Definition
AssociatorsAsync_	Method	void AssociatorsAsync_ (IDispatch, string, str...
Associators_	Method	ISWbemObjectSet Associators_ (string, string, ...
Clone_	Method	ISWbemObject Clone_ ()
CompareTo_	Method	bool CompareTo_ (IDispatch, int)
DeleteAsync_	Method	void DeleteAsync_ (IDispatch, int, IDispatch, ...
Delete_	Method	void Delete_ (int, IDispatch)
ExecMethodAsync_	Method	void ExecMethodAsync_ (IDispatch, string, IDis...
ExecMethod_	Method	ISWbemObject ExecMethod_ (string, IDispatch, i...
GetObjectText_	Method	string GetObjectText_ (int)
GetText_	Method	string GetText_ (WbemObjectTextFormatEnum, int...
InstancesAsync_	Method	void InstancesAsync_ (IDispatch, int, IDispatc...
Instances_	Method	ISWbemObjectSet Instances_ (int, IDispatch)
PutAsync_	Method	void PutAsync_ (IDispatch, int, IDispatch, IDi...
Put_	Method	ISWbemObjectPath Put_ (int, IDispatch)
ReferencesAsync_	Method	void ReferencesAsync_ (IDispatch, string, stri...
References_	Method	ISWbemObjectSet References_ (string, string, b...
Refresh_	Method	void Refresh_ (int, IDispatch)
SetFromText_	Method	void SetFromText_ (string, WbemObjectTextForma...
SpawnDerivedClass_	Method	ISWbemObject SpawnDerivedClass_ (int)
SpawnInstance_	Method	ISWbemObject SpawnInstance_ (int)
SubclassesAsync_	Method	void SubclassesAsync_ (IDispatch, int, IDispat...
Subclasses_	Method	ISWbemObjectSet Subclasses_ (int, IDispatch)
Derivation_	Property	Variant Derivation_ () {get}
Methods_	Property	ISWbemMethodSet Methods_ () {get}
Path_	Property	ISWbemObjectPath Path_ () {get}

```
Properties_          Property    ISWbemPropertySet Properties_ () {get}
Qualifiers_          Property    ISWbemQualifierSet Qualifiers_ () {get}
Security_            Property    ISWbemSecurity Security_ () {get}
SystemProperties_    Property    ISWbemPropertySet SystemProperties_ () {get}
```

14. If we were to use the *Get-Member* cmdlet to discover the members of object contained in the *$objItem* variable, we would see the list printed out 1,000 times because the *$colItems* variable contains 1,000 instances of classes on my machine. To avoid this situation, we will use a different method than the subClassesOf() method. Save your script with a new name. Call your new script *yourname*GetWmiObject.ps1.

15. Under the *$wmiNS* variable, create a new variable. Call the variable *$wmiClass* and assign the string WIN32_Service to it. This line of code is shown here:

```
$wmiClass = "WIN32_Service"
```

16. To limit the output of the *Get-Member* cmdlets to only the members of the WIN32_Service class, comment out the two Get-Member lines of code that print out the members of $objLocator and $objWmiService. This section of code is shown here:

```
$objLocator = New-Object -comobject "WbemScripting.SWbemLocator"
#$objLocator | Get-Member
$objWMIService = $objLocator.ConnectServer($strComputer,
    $wmiNS, $strUsr, $strPWD, $strLocl, $strAuth, $iFLag)
#$objWMIService | Get-Member
```

17. Rename the *$colItems* variable to *$objItem* because the variable will be used to hold only a single object. Change the Subclasses() method to the Get method. Have the Get method retrieve the WMI class contained in the *$wmiClass* variable. This revised line of code is shown here:

```
$objItem = $objWMIService.Get($wmiClass)
```

18. Pipeline the $objItem object to the *Get-Member* cmdlet. This line of code is shown here:

```
$objItem | Get-Member
```

19. Save and run your script. The output will look like the following:

```
    TypeName: System.__ComObject#{269ad56a-8a67-4129-bc8c-0506dcfe9880}

Name                MemberType  Definition
----                ----------  ----------
AssociatorsAsync_   Method      void AssociatorsAsync_ (IDispatch, string, str...
Associators_        Method      ISWbemObjectSet Associators_ (string, string, ...
Clone_              Method      ISWbemObject Clone_ ()
CompareTo_          Method      bool CompareTo_ (IDispatch, int)
DeleteAsync_        Method      void DeleteAsync_ (IDispatch, int, IDispatch, ...
Delete_             Method      void Delete_ (int, IDispatch)
ExecMethodAsync_    Method      void ExecMethodAsync_ (IDispatch, string, IDis...
ExecMethod_         Method      ISWbemObject ExecMethod_ (string, IDispatch, i...
GetObjectText_      Method      string GetObjectText_ (int)
GetText_            Method      string GetText_ (WbemObjectTextFormatEnum, int...
InstancesAsync_     Method      void InstancesAsync_ (IDispatch, int, IDispatc...
Instances_          Method      ISWbemObjectSet Instances_ (int, IDispatch)
PutAsync_           Method      void PutAsync_ (IDispatch, int, IDispatch, IDi...
Put_                Method      ISWbemObjectPath Put_ (int, IDispatch)
```

```
ReferencesAsync_      Method      void ReferencesAsync_ (IDispatch, string, stri...
References_           Method      ISWbemObjectSet References_ (string, string, b...
Refresh_              Method      void Refresh_ (int, IDispatch)
SetFromText_          Method      void SetFromText_ (string, WbemObjectTextForma...
SpawnDerivedClass_    Method      ISWbemObject SpawnDerivedClass_ (int)
SpawnInstance_        Method      ISWbemObject SpawnInstance_ (int)
SubclassesAsync_      Method      void SubclassesAsync_ (IDispatch, int, IDispat...
Subclasses_           Method      ISWbemObjectSet Subclasses_ (int, IDispatch)
Derivation_           Property    Variant Derivation_ () {get}
Methods_              Property    ISWbemMethodSet Methods_ () {get}
Path_                 Property    ISWbemObjectPath Path_ () {get}
Properties_           Property    ISWbemPropertySet Properties_ () {get}
Qualifiers_           Property    ISWbemQualifierSet Qualifiers_ () {get}
Security_             Property    ISWbemSecurity Security_ () {get}
SystemProperties_     Property    ISWbemPropertySet SystemProperties_ () {get}
```

20. If your results are not similar to the output shown, compare your script with the GetWmiObject.ps1 script.

Querying WMI

In most situations, when you use WMI, you are performing some sort of query. Even when you're going to set a particular property, you still need to execute a query to return a dataset that enables you to perform the configuration. (A *dataset* includes the data that come back to you as the result of a query, that is, it is a set of data.) In this section, you'll look at the methods used to query WMI.

Just the Steps   To query WMI:

1. Specify the computer name.
2. Define the namespace.
3. Connect to WMI by using *Get-WMIObject*.
4. Specify the query by supplying a value for the filter argument or the query argument.
5. Use *Format-List* or another cmdlet to clean up the output.

In the QueryDesktop.ps1 script, we define three variables that are used to hold the arguments for the *Get-WmiObject* cmdlet. These variables are $wmiQuery, which holds the WMI query; $wmiNS, which holds the WMI namespace that contains the WIN32_Desktop WMI class; and $strComputer, which holds the name of the computer we wish to query. In this case, we are using the shortcut dot (.), which means we are going to query only the local computer. We could have left out both the WMI namespace and the computer name if we wanted to rely on the default computer configuration. The $wmiQuery contains the WMI query, which is written in the WMI query language (WQL). WQL is a subset of Transact SQL (T-SQL), with special modifications to make it more appropriate for working with WMI. The line of code that contains the WMI query is shown here:

```
$wmiQuery = "Select * from Win32_Desktop"
```

The WMI class WIN32_Desktop represents the properties and user-defined configuration settings of the standard Windows desktop. The screensaver timeout value and the secure screensaver properties are particularly important. The *$objWMIService* variable is used to hold the object returned by the *Get-WmiObject* cmdlet. This object is then pipelined to the *Format-List* cmdlet. These two lines of code are shown here:

```
$objWMIService = Get-WmiObject -computer $strComputer -namespace
$wmiNS -query $wmiQuery
$objWMIService | Format-List *
```

The completed QueryDeskTop.ps1 script is shown here:

QueryDesktop.ps1

```
$wmiQuery = "Select * from Win32_Desktop"
$wmiNS = "root\cimv2"
$strComputer = "."
$objWMIService = Get-WmiObject -computer $strComputer -namespace
$wmiNS -query $wmiQuery
$objWMIService | Format-List *
```

Modifying the QueryDesktop.ps1 script

1. Open the QueryDesktop.ps1 script in Notepad.exe or your favorite script editor. Save the script as *yourname*ModifiedDesktop.ps1.

2. Run the *yourname*ModifiedDesktop.ps1 script. It should run without errors and will produce an output that is similar to the one shown here:

```
__GENUS             : 2
__CLASS             : Win32_Desktop
__SUPERCLASS        : CIM_Setting
__DYNASTY           : CIM_Setting
__RELPATH           : Win32_Desktop.Name="NT AUTHORITY\\SYSTEM"
__PROPERTY_COUNT    : 21
__DERIVATION        : {CIM_Setting}
__SERVER            : MRED1
__NAMESPACE         : root\cimv2
__PATH              : \\MRED1\root\cimv2:Win32_Desktop.Name="NT AUTHORITY\\SY
                      STEM"
BorderWidth         : 1
Caption             :
CoolSwitch          : True
```

3. Because we are not interested in all the system properties, add the property argument to the *Format-List* cmdlet and choose the name property. This modified line of code is shown here:

```
$objWMIService | Format-List -property name
```

4. Save and run your script. Your output will only contain the name of each profile stored on your machine. It will be similar to the one shown here:

```
name : NT AUTHORITY\SYSTEM

name : NT AUTHORITY\LOCAL SERVICE
```

```
name : NT AUTHORITY\NETWORK SERVICE

name : NWTRADERS\mred

name : .DEFAULT
```

5. To retrieve the name of the screensaver, add the property screensaverexecutable to the *Format-List* command. This is shown here:

```
$objWMIService | Format-List -property name, screensaverexecutable
```

6. Save and run your script.

7. To identify whether the screensaver is secure, you need to query the screensaversecure property. This modified line of code is shown here:

```
$objWMIService | Format-List -property name, screensaverexecutable,
    screensaverSecure
```

8. If you want to retrieve all the properties related to screensavers, you can use a wild card asterisk (*) screen. Delete the two screensaver properties and replace them with the wild card, as shown here:

```
$objWMIService | Format-List -property name, screen*
```

9. Save and run your script. If it does not run properly, compare it to the ModifiedDesktop.ps1 script.

Obtaining Service Information: Step-by-Step Exercises

In this exercise, we will explore the use of the *Get-WmiObject* cmdlet as we retrieve user information from WMI.

1. Start Windows PowerShell by using *Start | Run | PowerShell*.

2. From the Windows PowerShell prompt, use the *Get-Service* cmdlet to obtain a listing of all the services and their associated status. The command to do this is *Get-Service*. This is shown here:

```
Get-Service
```

3. A partial listing of the output from this command is shown here:

```
Status   Name          DisplayName
------   ----          -----------
Running  Alerter       Alerter
Running  ALG           Application Layer Gateway Service
Stopped  AppMgmt       Application Management
Stopped  aspnet_state  ASP.NET State Service
Running  AudioSrv      Windows Audio
Running  BITS          Background Intelligent Transfer Ser...
```

4. Use the *Sort-Object* cmdlet to sort the listing of services. Specify the status property for the *Sort-Object*. To do this, pipeline the results of the *Get-Service* cmdlet into the *Sort-Object* cmdlet. Use the *sort* alias for the *Sort-Object* cmdlet to reduce the amount of typing. The results are shown here:

```
Get-Service |sort -property status
```

5. A partial output from this command is shown here:

```
Status    Name              DisplayName
------    ----              -----------
Stopped   RasAuto           Remote Access Auto Connection Manager
Stopped   RDSessMgr         Remote Desktop Help Session Manager
Stopped   odserv            Microsoft Office Diagnostics Service
Stopped   ose               Office Source Engine
```

6. Use the *Get-Service* cmdlet to produce a listing of services. Sort the resulting list of services alphabetically by name. To do this, use the *Sort-Object* cmdlet to sort the listing of services by name property. Pipeline the object returned by the *Get-Services* cmdlet into the *Sort-Object* cmdlet. The command to do this, using the *sort* alias for *Sort-Object*, is shown here:

```
Get-Service |sort -property name
```

7. A partial output of this command is shown here:

```
Status    Name              DisplayName
------    ----              -----------
Running   Alerter           Alerter
Running   ALG               Application Layer Gateway Service
Stopped   AppMgmt           Application Management
Stopped   aspnet_state      ASP.NET State Service
Running   AudioSrv          Windows Audio
Running   BITS              Background Intelligent Transfer Ser...
```

8. Use the *Get-Service* cmdlet to produce a listing of services. Sort the object returned by both the name and the status of the service. The command to do this is shown here:

```
Get-Service |sort status, name
```

9. A partial output of this command is shown here:

```
Status    Name              DisplayName
------    ----              -----------
Stopped   AppMgmt           Application Management
Stopped   aspnet_state      ASP.NET State Service
Stopped   Browser           Computer Browser
Stopped   CcmExec           SMS Agent Host
Stopped   CiSvc             Indexing Service
```

10. Use the *Get-Service* cmdlet to return an object containing service information. Pipeline the resulting object in to a *Where-Object* cmdlet. Look for the word *server* in the display name. The resulting command is shown here:

```
Get-Service | where {$_.DisplayName -match "server"}
```

11. The resulting listing is shown here:

```
Status   Name              DisplayName
------   ----              -----------
Running  DcomLaunch        DCOM Server Process Launcher
Running  InoRPC            eTrust Antivirus RPC Server
Running  InoRT             eTrust Antivirus Realtime Server
Running  InoTask           eTrust Antivirus Job Server
Stopped  lanmanserver      Server
Stopped  MSSQL$SQLEXPRESS   SQL Server (SQLEXPRESS)
Stopped  MSSQLServerADHe... SQL Server Active Directory Helper
Stopped  SQLBrowser        SQL Server Browser
Stopped  SQLWriter         SQL Server VSS Writer
```

12. Use the *Get-Service* cmdlet to retrieve a listing of service objects. Pipeline the resulting object to the *Where-Object*. Use the equals argument to return an object that represents the Alerter service. The code that does this is shown here:

```
Get-Service | where {$_.name -eq "alerter"}
```

13. Use the up arrow to retrieve the previous command that retrieves the Alerter service. Store the resulting object in a variable called *$a*. This code is shown here:

```
$a=Get-Service | where {$_.name -eq "alerter"}
```

14. Pipeline the object contained in the *$a* variable into the *Get-Member* cmdlet. You can use the *gm* alias to simplify typing. This code is shown here:

```
$a | gm
```

15. Using the object contained in the *$a* variable, obtain the status of the Alerter service. The code that does this is shown here:

```
$a.status
```

16. If the Alerter service is running, then stop it. To do so, use the *Stop-Service* cmdlet. Instead of pipelining the object in the *$a* variable, we use the -inputobject argument from the *Stop-Service* cmdlet. The code to do this is shown here:

```
Stop-Service -InputObject $a
```

17. If the Alerter service was stopped, then use the *Start-Service* cmdlet instead of the *Stop-Service* cmdlet. Use the -inputobject argument to supply the object contained in the *$a* variable to the cmdlet. This is shown here:

```
Start-Service -InputObject $a
```

18. Query the status property of the object contained in the *$a* variable to confirm that the Alerter services' status changed. This is shown here:

```
$a.status
```

If you are working with a service that has its Startup Type set to Disabled, then Power-Shell will not be able to start it and will return an error.

19. This concludes this step-by-step exercise. If you have any problems with any of the commands in this exercise, refer to the StepByStep.txt file in the scripts folder for this chapter.

One Step Further: Working with Printers

In this exercise, we will explore the use of WMI to obtain information about printers defined on your machine. As we do this, we will examine the use of several Windows PowerShell cmdlets that can dramatically simplify the use of WMI in our scripting.

1. Start Windows PowerShell by using *Start | Run | PowerShell*.

2. Open Notepad.exe or your favorite script editor.

3. Open the WmiTemplate.ps1 file from the scripts folder for this chapter and save it as *your-name*WorkingWithPrinters.ps1. Refer to the WorkingWithPrinters.ps1 script already in this chapter's script folder to see a sample of a completed solution to this exercise.

4. Modify the $wmiQuery line to query the WIN32_Printer class. The revised line is shown here:

```
$wmiQuery = "Select * from win32_Printer"
```

5. Save and run the script. Your output will be similar to the following partial output:

```
Status                  : Unknown
Name                    : Lexmark 4039 Plus PS
__GENUS                 : 2
__CLASS                 : Win32_Printer
__SUPERCLASS            : CIM_Printer
__DYNASTY               : CIM_ManagedSystemElement
__RELPATH               : Win32_Printer.DeviceID="Lexmark 4039 Plus PS"
__PROPERTY_COUNT        : 86
__DERIVATION            : {CIM_Printer, CIM_LogicalDevice, CIM_LogicalEleme
                          nt, CIM_ManagedSystemElement}
__SERVER                : MRED1
__NAMESPACE             : root\cimv2
__PATH                  : \\MRED1\root\cimv2:Win32_Printer.DeviceID="Lexmar
```

6. Change the script so that it only prints out the name of each printer. To do this, add the name property to the *Format-List* cmdlet, as shown here:

```
$objWMIServices | Format-List name
```

7. Save and run your script. You will see an output similar to the following:

```
name : Microsoft XPS Document Writer

name : Lexmark 4039 Plus PS
```

8. To determine where each printer is defined, add the portname property to the *Format-List* cmdlet. This is shown here:

```
$objWMIServices | Format-List name, portname
```

9. Save and run the script. The resulting output will be similar to the one shown here:

```
name     : Microsoft XPS Document Writer
portname : XPSPort:

name     : Lexmark 4039 Plus PS
portname : IP_192.168.1.89
```

10. To identify the capabilities of each printer, add the capabilitydescriptions property to the output. To do this, revise the Format-List line, as shown here:

```
$objWMIServices | Format-List name, portname, capabilitydescriptions
```

11. The resulting output is shown here:

```
name                    : Microsoft XPS Document Writer
portname                : XPSPort:
capabilitydescriptions : {Copies, Color, Duplex, Collate}

name                    : Lexmark 4039 Plus PS
portname                : IP_192.168.1.89
capabilitydescriptions : {Copies, Color, Duplex, Collate}
```

12. To determine whether there are other properties you may be interested in using from the WIN32_Printer WMI class, you can pipeline the object contained in the *$objWmiServices* variable to the *Get-Member* cmdlet. To reduce typing, use the *gm* alias, as shown here:

```
$objWMIServices | GM
```

13. If you find additional interesting properties, add them to the Format-List line as we did with the name, portname, and capabilitydescriptions properties. Some you may wish to investigate include driverName, ServerName, HorizontalResolution, and Vertical-Resolution.

14. This concludes this one step further exercise.

Chapter 5 Quick Reference

To	Do This
Find the default WMI namespace on a computer	Use the advanced tab from the WMI Control Properties dialog box
Browse WMI classes on a computer	Use the *Get-WmiObject* cmdlet with the list argument
Make a connection into WMI	Use the *Get-WmiObject* cmdlet in your script
Use a shortcut name for the local computer	Use a dot (.) and assign it to the variable holding the computer name in the script
Find detailed information about all WMI classes on a computer	Use the Platform SDK: *http://msdn2.microsoft.com/ en-us/library/aa394582.aspx*
Find the default WMI namespace on a computer	Use the advanced Tab from the WMI Control Properties dialog box
List all the namespaces on a computer	Query for a class named __NameSpace
List all providers installed in a particular namespace	Query for a class named __Win32Provider
List all the classes in a particular namespace on a computer	Use the list argument for *the Get-WmiObject* cmdlet
Quickly retrieve similarly named properties from a class	Use the *Format-List* cmdlet and supply a wild card asterisk (*) for the property argument

Chapter 6
Querying WMI

After completing this chapter, you will be able to:

- Understand the different methods for querying WMI
- Use the *Select-Object* cmdlet to create a WMI query
- Configure the filter argument to limit information returned by WMI
- Configure the WMI query to return selected properties
- Use the *Where-Object* cmdlet to improve performance of WMI
- Leverage both hardware classes and system classes to configure machines

After network administrators and consultants get their hands on a couple of Windows Management Instrumentation (WMI) scripts, they begin to arrange all kinds of scenarios for use. This is both a good thing and a bad thing. The good thing is that WMI is powerful technology that can be leveraged in a quick manner to solve a lot of real problems. The bad thing is that a poorly written WMI script can adversely affect the performance of everything it touches— from client machines logging onto the network for the first time to huge infrastructure servers that provide the basis for mission-critical messaging applications. In this chapter, we examine the fundamentals of querying WMI in an effective manner. Along the way, we examine some of the more useful WMI classes and add to our Windows PowerShell skills. All the scripts mentioned in this chapter can be found in the corresponding scripts folder on the CD.

Alternate Ways to Connect to WMI

In Chapter 5, "Using WMI," we learned about using the *Get-WmiObject* cmdlet to produce some basic WMI queries. We also looked briefly at connecting to WMI using the SWbemLocator object. When we make a connection to WMI by either method, it is important to realize there are default values being specified for the WMI connection.

The default values are stored in the following registry location: HKEY_LOCAL_MACHINE\ SOFTWARE\Microsoft\WBEM\Scripting. There are two keys: Default Impersonation Level and Default Damespace. Default Impersonation Level is set to a default of 3, which means that WMI impersonates the logged-on user. The Default Namespace is set to *Root\cimv2*. In reality, these are pretty good defaults. The default computer is the local machine, so you don't need to specify the computer name when you're simply running against the local machine.

> **Tip** Use default WMI values to simplify your WMI scripts. If you only want to return infor-
> mation from the local machine, the WMI class resides in the default namespace, and you
> intend to impersonate the logged-on user, then the defaults are perfect.

SmallBios.ps1

```
Get-WmiObject win32_bios
```

When we use the *Get-WmiObject* cmdlet and only supply the name of the WMI class, then
we are relying on the default values: default computer, default WMI namespace, and default
impersonation level. The SmallBios.ps1 script produces the information shown here, which
is the main information you would want to see about the bios: the version, name, serial
number, and maker.

```
SMBIOSBIOSVersion : Version 1.40
Manufacturer      : TOSHIBA
Name              : v1.40
SerialNumber      : 55061728HU
Version           : TOSHIB - 970814
```

The amazing thing is that you can obtain such useful information by typing about 15
characters on the keyboard (using *Tab completion*). To do this in VBScript would require
much more typing. However, if you want to retrieve different information from the
WIN32_Bios WMI class, or if you would like to see a different kind of output, then you
will need to work with the *Format* cmdlets. This is illustrated next in the retrieving properties procedure.

Retrieving properties

1. Open Windows PowerShell.

2. Use the *Get-WmiObject* cmdlet to retrieve the default properties of the
    WIN32_ComputerSystem WMI class.

    ```
    Get-WmiObject win32_computersystem
    ```

3. The results, with the default properties, are shown here:

    ```
    Domain              : nwtraders.com
    Manufacturer        : TOSHIBA
    Model               : TECRA M3
    Name                : MRED1
    PrimaryOwnerName    : Mred
    TotalPhysicalMemory : 2146680832
    ```

4. If you are only interested in the name and the make and model of the computer, then you
    will need to pipeline the results into a *Format-List* cmdlet and choose only the properties
    you wish. This revised command is shown here:

    ```
    Get-WmiObject win32_computersystem | Format-List name,model, manufacturer
    ```

5. The results are shown here:

```
name        : MRED1
model       : TECRA M3
manufacturer : TOSHIBA
```

6. If you are interested in all the properties from the WIN32_computersystem class, you have several options. The first is to use the up arrow and modify the *Format-List* cmdlet. Instead of choosing three properties, change it to an asterisk (*). This revised command is shown here:

```
Get-WmiObject win32_computersystem | Format-List *
```

7. The results from this command are shown here. Notice, however, that although the results seem impressive at first, they quickly degenerate into seemingly meaningless drivel. Note the number of classes that begin with double underscore, such as __CLASS. These are system properties that get attached to every WMI class when they are created. Although useful to WMI gurus, they are less exciting to normal network administrators.

```
AdminPasswordStatus        : 0
BootupState                : Normal boot
ChassisBootupState         : 3
KeyboardPasswordStatus     : 0
PowerOnPasswordStatus      : 0
PowerSupplyState           : 3
PowerState                 : 0
FrontPanelResetStatus      : 0
ThermalState               : 3
Status                     : OK
Name                       : MRED1
PowerManagementCapabilities :
PowerManagementSupported   :
__GENUS                    : 2
__CLASS                    : Win32_ComputerSystem
__SUPERCLASS               : CIM_UnitaryComputerSystem
__DYNASTY                  : CIM_ManagedSystemElement
__RELPATH                  : Win32_ComputerSystem.Name="MRED1"
__PROPERTY_COUNT           : 54
__DERIVATION               : {CIM_UnitaryComputerSystem, CIM_ComputerSystem, C
                             IM_System, CIM_LogicalElement...}
__SERVER                   : MRED1
__NAMESPACE                : root\cimv2
__PATH                     : \\MRED1\root\cimv2:Win32_ComputerSystem.Name="MRE
                             D1"
AutomaticResetBootOption   : True
AutomaticResetCapability   : True
BootOptionOnLimit          :
BootOptionOnWatchDog       :
BootROMSupported           : True
Caption                    : MRED1
CreationClassName          : Win32_ComputerSystem
CurrentTimeZone            : 60
DaylightInEffect           : False
Description                : AT/AT COMPATIBLE
Domain                     : northamerica.corp.microsoft.com
```

```
DomainRole                 : 1
EnableDaylightSavingsTime  : True
InfraredSupported          : False
InitialLoadInfo            :
InstallDate                :
LastLoadInfo               :
Manufacturer               : TOSHIBA
Model                      : TECRA M3
NameFormat                 :
NetworkServerModeEnabled   :
NumberOfProcessors         : 1
OEMLogoBitmap              :
OEMStringArray             : {PTM30U-0H001V59,SQ003648A83,138}
PartOfDomain               : True
PauseAfterReset            : -1
PrimaryOwnerContact        :
PrimaryOwnerName           : Mred
ResetCapability            : 1
ResetCount                 : -1
ResetLimit                 : -1
Roles                      :
SupportContactDescription  :
SystemStartupDelay         : 15
SystemStartupOptions       : {"Microsoft Windows XP Professional" /noexecute=o
                             ptin /fastdetect}
SystemStartupSetting       : 0
SystemType                 : X86-based PC
TotalPhysicalMemory        : 2146680832
UserName                   : NORTHAMERICA\edwils
WakeUpType                 : 6
Workgroup                  :
```

8. To remove the system properties from the list, use the up arrow to retrieve the *Get-WmiObject win32_computersystem | Format-List ** command. Delete the asterisk in the *Format-List* command and replace it with an expression that limits the results to property names that are returned to only those that begin with the letters a through z. This command is shown here:

    ```
    Get-WmiObject win32_computersystem | Format-List [a-z]*
    ```

9. To see a listing of properties that begin with the letter d, use the up arrow to retrieve the *Get-WmiObject win32_computersystem | Format-List [a-z]** command and change the *Format-List* cmdlet to retrieve only properties that begin with the letter d. To do this, substitute d* for [a-z]*. The revised command is shown here:

    ```
    Get-WmiObject win32_computersystem | Format-List D*
    ```

10. Retrieve a listing of all the properties and their values from the WIN32_computersystem WMI class that begin with either the letter d or the letter t. Use the up arrow to retrieve the previous *Get-WmiObject win32_computersystem | Format-List D** command. Use a comma to separate the t* from the previous command. The revised command is shown here:

    ```
    Get-WmiObject win32_computersystem | Format-List d*,t*
    ```

11. This concludes the retrieving properties procedure.

> **Tip**   After you use the *Get-WmiObject* cmdlet for a while, you may get tired of using *Tab completion* and having to type **Get-W<tab>**. It may be easier to use the default alias of *gwmi*. This alias was discovered by using the following command:
>
> ```
> Get-Alias | where {$_.definition -eq 'Get-WmiObject'}
> ```

Working with disk drives

1. Open Windows PowerShell.

2. Use the *gwmi* alias to retrieve the default properties for each drive defined on your system. To do this, use the WIN32_LogicalDisk WMI class. This command is shown here:

   ```
   gwmi win32_logicaldisk
   ```

3. The result of the *gwmi win32_logicaldisk* command is shown here:

   ```
   DeviceID      : C:
   DriveType     : 3
   ProviderName  :
   FreeSpace     : 6164701184
   Size          : 36701163520
   VolumeName    : c

   DeviceID      : D:
   DriveType     : 3
   ProviderName  :
   FreeSpace     : 11944701952
   Size          : 23302184960
   VolumeName    : d

   DeviceID      : E:
   DriveType     : 5
   ProviderName  :
   FreeSpace     :
   Size          :
   VolumeName    :
   ```

4. To limit the disks returned by the WMI query to only local disk drives, we can supply a value of 3 for the drive type property. Use the up arrow to retrieve the previous command. Add the drivetype property to the filter parameter of the *Get-WMIObject* cmdlet with a value of 3. This revised command is shown here:

   ```
   gwmi win32_logicaldisk -filter drivetype=3
   ```

5. The resulting output from the *gwmi win32_logicaldisk -filter drivetype=3* command is shown here:

   ```
   DeviceID      : C:
   DriveType     : 3
   ProviderName  :
   FreeSpace     : 6163599360
   Size          : 36701163520
   VolumeName    : c
   ```

```
DeviceID      : D:
DriveType     : 3
ProviderName  :
FreeSpace     : 11944701952
Size          : 23302184960
VolumeName    : d
```

6. Open Notepad.exe, or some other script editor, and save the file as yournameLogical Disk.ps1.

7. Use the up arrow in PowerShell to retrieve the *gwmi win32_logicaldisk -filter drivetype=3* command. Highlight it with your mouse, and press Enter.

8. Paste the command into the *yourname*LogicalDisk.ps1 script.

9. Declare a variable called *$objDisk* at the top of your script. This command is shown here:

```
$objDisk
```

10. Use the *$objDisk* variable to hold the object returned by the command you copied from your PowerShell console. As we are planning on saving the script, replace the *gwmi* alias with the actual name of the cmdlet. The resulting command is shown here:

```
$objDisk=Get-WmiObject win32_logicaldisk -filter drivetype=3
```

11. Use the *Measure-Object* cmdlet to retrieve the minimum and the maximum values for the freespace property. To do this, pipeline the previous object into the *Measure-Object* cmdlet. Specify freespace for the property argument, and use the minimum and the maximum switches. Use the pipeline character to break your code into two lines. This command is shown here:

```
$objDisk=Get-WmiObject win32_logicaldisk -filter drivetype=3 |
   Measure-Object -property freespace -Minimum -Maximum
```

12. Print out the resulting object that is contained in the *$objDisk* variable. This command is shown here:

```
$objDisk
```

13. The resulting printout on my computer is shown here:

```
Count    : 2
Average  :
Sum      :
Maximum  : 11944701952
Minimum  : 6163550208
Property : freespace
```

14. To dispose of the empty properties, pipeline the previous command into a *Select-Object* cmdlet. Choose the property and the minimum and maximum properties. Use the pipeline character to break your code into multiple lines The revised command is shown here:

```
$objDisk=Get-WmiObject win32_logicaldisk -filter drivetype=3 |
   Measure-Object -property freespace  -Minimum -Maximum |
   Select-Object -Property property, maximum, minimum
```

15. Save and run the script. Notice how the output is spread over the console. To tighten up
     the display, pipeline the resulting object into the *Format-Table* cmdlet. Use the autosize
     switch. The revised command is shown here:

```
$objDisk=Get-WmiObject win32_logicaldisk -filter drivetype=3 |
    Measure-Object -property freespace  -Minimum -Maximum |
    Select-Object -Property property, maximum, minimum |
    Format-Table -autosize
```

16. Save and run the script. The output on my computer is shown here:

```
Property      Maximum      Minimum
--------      -------      -------
freespace 11944685568 6164058112
```

17. If your results are not similar, compare *yourname*LogicalDisk.ps1 with LogicalDisk.ps1.

> **Note**   The WMI class WIN32_LogicalDisk property DriveType can have a value of 0 to 6
> inclusive. The most useful of these values are as follows: 3 local disk, 4 network drive, 5 com-
> pact disk, and 6 ram disk.

Tell Me Everything About Everything!

When novices first write WMI scripts, they nearly all begin by asking for every property from
every instances of a class. For example, the queries will say "tell me everything about every
process". (This is also referred to as the infamous "select * query".) This approach can often
return an overwhelming amount of data, particularly when you are querying a class such as
installed software or processes and threads. Rarely would one need to have so much data.
Typically, when looking for installed software, you're looking for information about a *particular* software package.

There are, however, several occasions when I want to use the "tell me everything about all
instances of a particular class" query, including the following:

■ During development of a script to see representative data

■ When troubleshooting a more directed query, for example, when I'm possibly trying to
   filter on a field that does not exist

■ When the returned data are so few that being more precise doesn't make sense

> **Just the Steps**   **To return all information from all instances**
> 1. Make a connection to WMI by using the *Get-WmiObject* cmdlet
> 2. Use the query argument to supply the WQL query to the *Get-WmiObject* cmdlet
> 3. In the query, use the *Select* statement to choose everything: *Select **.
> 4. In the query, use the *From* statement to indicate the class from which you wish to retrieve
>   data. For example, *From Win32_Share*.

In the next script, you make a connection to the default namespace in WMI and return all the information about all the shares on a local machine. This is actually good practice because, in the past, numerous worms have propagated through unsecured shares, and you might have unused shares around—a user might create a share for a friend and then forget to delete it. In the script that follows, called ListShares.ps1, all the information about shares present on the machine are reported. The information returned by the ListShares.ps1 will include the properties for the WIN32_Share class which are detailed in Table 6-1.

ListShares.Ps1

```
$strComputer = "."
$wmiNS = "root\cimv2"
$wmiQuery = "Select * from win32_share"

$objWMIServices = Get-WmiObject -computer $strComputer -namespace $wmiNS `
    -query $wmiQuery
 $objWMIServices | Format-List *
```

Table 6-1 Win32_Share Properties

Data Type	Property	Meaning
Boolean	*AllowMaximum*	Allow maximum number of connections? True or false
string	*Caption*	Short, one-line description
string	*Description*	Description
datetime	*InstallDate*	When the share was created (optional)
uint32	*MaximumAllowed*	Number of concurrent connections allowed Only valid when *AllowMaximum* is set to false
string	*Name*	Share name
string	*Path*	Physical path to the share
string	*Status*	Current status of the share: degraded, OK, or failed
uint32	*Type*	Type of resource shared: disk, file, printer, etc.

Quick Check

Q. What is the syntax for a query that returns all properties of a given object?

A. *Select* * returns all properties of a given object.

Q. What is one reason for using *Select* * instead of a more directed query?

A. In troubleshooting, *Select* * is useful because it returns any available data. In addition, *Select* * is useful in trying to characterize the data that might be returned from a query.

Selective Data from All Instances

The next level of sophistication (from using *Select **) is to return only the properties you are interested in. This is a more efficient strategy. For instance, in the previous example, you entered *Select ** and were returned a lot of data you weren't necessarily interested in. Suppose you want to know only what shares are on each machine.

> **Just the Steps**   **To select specific data**
>
> 1. Make a connection to WMI by using the *Get-WmiObject* cmdlet
> 2. Use the query argument to supply the WMI query to the *Get-WmiObject* cmdlet
> 3. In the query, use the *Select* statement to choose the specific property you are interested in, for example, *Select name.*
> 4. In the query, use the *From* statement to indicate the class from which you want to retrieve data, for example, *From Win32_Share.*

Only two small changes in the ListShares.ps1 script are required to enable garnering specific data through the WMI script. In place of the asterisk in the *Select* statement assigned at the beginning of the script, substitute the property you want. In this case, only the name of the shares is required.

The second change is to eliminate all unwanted properties from the Output section. The strange thing here is the way that PowerShell works. In the *Select* statement, we selected only the name property. However, if we were to print out the results without further refinement, we would retrieve unwanted system properties as well. By using the *Format-List* cmdlet and selecting only the property name, we eliminate the unwanted excess. Here is the modified ListNameOnlyShares.ps1 script:

ListNameOnlyShares.Ps1

```
$strComputer = "."
$wmiNS = "root\cimv2"
$wmiQuery = "Select name from win32_Share"

$objWMIServices = Get-WmiObject -computer $strComputer -namespace $wmiNS `
    -query $wmiQuery
$objWMIServices | Sort-Object -property name | Format-List -property name
```

Selecting Multiple Properties

If you're interested in only a certain number of properties, you can use *Select* to specify that. All you have to do is separate the properties by a comma. Suppose you run the preceding script and find a number of undocumented shares on one of the servers—you might want a little bit more information, such as the path to the share and how many people are allowed to connect to it. By default, when a share is created, the "maximum allowed" bit is set, which basically says anyone who has rights to the share can connect. This can be a problem because if too many people connect to a share, they can degrade the performance of the server. To preclude such an eventuality, I always specify a maximum number of connections to the server. The commands to list these properties are in the ListNamePathShare.ps1 script.

> **Note**   I occasionally see people asking whether spaces or namecase in the property list matter. In fact, when I first started writing scripts and they failed, I often modified spacing and capitalization in feeble attempts to make the script work. Spacing and capitalization *do not matter* for WMI properties.

ListNamePathShare.ps1

```
$strComputer = "."
$wmiNS = "root\cimv2"
$wmiQuery = "Select name,path, AllowMaximum from win32_share"

$objWMIServices = Get-WmiObject -computer $strComputer -namespace $wmiNS `
   -query $wmiQuery
$objWMIServices | Sort-Object -property name |
Format-List -property name,path,allowmaximum
```

Working with running processes

1. Open Windows PowerShell.

2. Use the *Get-Process* cmdlet to obtain a listing of processes on your machine. The command is shown here:

   ```
   Get-Process
   ```

3. A portion of the results from the previous command is shown here:

Handles	NPM(K)	PM(K)	WS(K)	VM(M)	CPU(s)	Id	ProcessName
101	5	1132	3436	32	0.03	660	alg
439	7	1764	2856	60	6.05	1000	csrss
121	5	912	3532	37	0.22	1256	ctfmon
629	19	23772	23868	135	134.13	788	explorer
268	7	12072	18344	109	1.66	1420	hh

4. To return information about the explorer process, use the name argument. This command is shown here:

   ```
   Get-Process -name explorer
   ```

5. The results of this command are shown here:

```
Handles  NPM(K)   PM(K)     WS(K) VM(M)   CPU(s)    Id ProcessName
-------  ------   -----     ----- -----   ------    -- -----------
    619      18   21948     22800   115   134.28   788 explorer
```

6. Use the *Get-WmiObject* cmdlet to retrieve information about processes on the machine. Pipe the results into the *more* function, as shown here:

```
Get-WmiObject win32_process |more
```

7. You will notice that the results go on for page after page. The last few lines of one of those pages is shown here:

```
QuotaPagedPoolUsage        : 0
QuotaPeakNonPagedPoolUsage : 0
QuotaPeakPagedPoolUsage    : 0
ReadOperationCount         : 0
<SPACE> next page; <CR> next line; Q quit
```

8. To retrieve information only about the Explorer.exe process, use the filter argument and specify that the name property is equal to Explorer.exe. The revised command is shown here:

```
Get-WmiObject win32_process -Filter "name='explorer.exe'"
```

9. To display a table that is similar to the one produced by *Get-Process*, use the up arrow to retrieve the previous *Get-WmiObject* command. Copy it to the clipboard by selecting it with the mouse and then pasting it into Notepad or some other script editor. Pipeline the results into the *Format-Table* cmdlet and choose the appropriate properties, as shown here. Saving this command into a script makes it easier to work with later. It also makes it easier to write the script by breaking the lines instead of just typing one long command. I called the script ExplorerProcess.ps1, and it is shown here:

```
Get-WmiObject win32_process -Filter "name='explorer.exe'" |
Format-Table handlecount,quotaNonPagedPoolUsage, PeakVirtualSize,
WorkingSetSize, VirtualSize, UserModeTime,KernelModeTime,
ProcessID, Name
```

10. This concludes the working with running processes procedure.

> **Caution**   When using the filter argument of the *Get-WmiObject* cmdlet, pay attention to the use of quotation marks. The filter argument is surrounded by double quotation marks. The value being supplied for the property is surrounded by single quotes. Example: -Filter "name='explorer.exe'". This can cause a lot of frustration if not followed exactly.

Adding logging

1. Open Windows PowerShell.

2. Use the alias for the *Get-WmiObject* cmdlet and supply the WIN32_logicalDisk class as the argument to it. Use the redirection arrow (>) to redirect output to a file called Diskinfo.txt. Place this file in the C:\Mytest folder. This command is shown here:

```
gwmi win32_logicaldisk >c:\mytest\DiskInfo.txt
```

3. Use the up arrow and retrieve the previous command. This time, change the class name to WIN32_OperatingSystem and call the text file OSinfo.txt. This command is shown here:

```
gwmi win32_operatingsystem >c:\mytest\OSinfo.txt
```

4. Use the up arrow and retrieve the previous *gwmi WIN32_operatingsystem* command. Change the WMI class to WIN32_ComputerSystem and use two redirection arrows (>>) to cause the output to append to the file. Use Notepad to open the file, but include this command separated by a semicolon. This is illustrated here. The command is continued to the next line by using the grave accent character (`) for readability.

```
gwmi win32_ComputerSystem >>c:\mytest\OSinfo.txt; `
notepad c:\mytest\OSinfo.txt
```

5. This concludes the adding logging procedure.

> **Quick Check**
>
> **Q. To select specific properties from an object, what do you need to do on the *Select* line?**
>
> A. You need to separate the specific properties of an object with a comma on the *Select* line of the execQuery method.
>
> **Q. To avoid error messages, what must be done when selecting individual properties on the *Select* line?**
>
> A. Errors can be avoided if you make sure each property used is specified in the select line. For example, the WMI query is just like a paper bag that gets filled with items that are picked up using the *Select* statement. If you do not put something in the paper bag, you cannot pull anything out of the bag. In the same manner, if you do not "select" a property, you cannot later print or sort on that property. This is exactly the way that an SQL *Select* statement works.
>
> **Q. What can you check for in your script if it fails with an "object does not support this method or property" error?**
>
> A. If you are getting an "object does not support this method or property" error messages, you might want to ensure you have referenced the property in your *Select* statement before to trying to work with it in an Output section.

Choosing Specific Instances

In many situations, you will want to limit the data you return to a specific instance of that class in the dataset. If you go back to your query and add a *Where* clause to *Select* statement, you'll be able to greatly reduce the amount of information returned by the query. Notice that in the value associated with the *wmiQuery*, you added a dependency that indicated you wanted only information with share name *C$*. This value is not case sensitive, but it must be surrounded with single quotation marks, as you can see in the *wmiQuery* string in the following script. These single quotation marks are important because they tell WMI that the value is a string value and not some other programmatic item. Because the addition of the *Where* statement was the only thing you really added to the ListShares.ps1 script, we do not provide a long discussion of the ListSpecificShares.ps1 script.

ListSpecificShares.ps1

```
$strComputer = "."
$wmiNS = "root\cimv2"
$wmiQuery = "Select * from win32_share where name='c$'"

$objWMIServices = Get-WmiObject -computer $strComputer -namespace $wmiNS
  -query $wmiQuery
$objWMIServices | Format-List *
```

Just the Steps   To limit specific data

1. Make a connection to WMI.

2. Use the *Select* statement in the WMIQuery argument to choose the specific property you are interested in, for example, *Select name*.

3. Use the *From* statement in the WMIQuery argument to indicate the class from which you want to retrieve data, for example, *From Win32_Share*.

4. Add a *Where* clause in the WMIQuery argument to further limit the dataset that is returned. Make sure the properties specified in the *Where* clause are first mentioned in the *Select* statement, for example, *Where name*.

5. Add an evaluation operator. You can use the equals sign (=), or the less than (<) or greater than (>) symbols, for example, *Where name = 'C$'*

Eliminating the WMIQuery argument

1. Open Notepad or some other Windows PowerShell script editor.

2. Declare a variable called *$strComputer* and assign the WMI shortcut dot (.) to it. The shortcut dot means connect to the WMI service on the local computer. This command is shown here:

```
$strComputer = "."
```

3. Declare another variable and call it *$wmiClass*. Assign the string "WIN32_Share" to the variable. This code is shown here:

```
$wmiClass = "win32_Share"
```

4. Declare a variable and call it *$wmiFilter*. This variable will be used to hold the string that will contain the WMI filter to be used with the *Get-WmiObject* command. The variable and the associated string value are shown here:

```
$wmiFilter = "name='c$'"
```

5. Declare a variable called *objWMIServices* and assign the object that is returned from the *Get-WmiObject* cmdlet to the variable. Specify the computer argument and supply the value contained in the *$strComputer* variable to it. At the end of the line, use the grave accent character (`) to indicate line continuation. This line of code is shown here:

```
$objWMIServices = Get-WmiObject -computer $strComputer `
```

6. Use the class argument to supply the class name for the WMI query to the *Get-WmiObject* cmdlet. The class name to query is contained in the *$wmiClass* variable. On the same line, use the filter argument to supply the filter string contained in the *$wmiFilter* variable to the *Get-WmiObject* cmdlet. This line of code is shown here:

```
-class $wmiClass -filter $wmiFilter
```

7. On the next line, use the object contained in the *$objWMIServices* variable and pipeline it to the *Format-List* cmdlet. Use the asterisk to tell the *Format-List* cmdlet you wish to retrieve all properties. This line of code is shown here:

```
$objWMIServices | Format-List *
```

8. The completed script is shown here:

```
$strComputer = "."
$wmiClass = "win32_Share"
$wmiFilter = "name='c$'"
$objWMIServices = Get-WmiObject -computer $strComputer `
   -class $wmiClass -filter $wmiFilter
   $objWMIServices | Format-List *
```

9. A sample output is shown here:

```
Status            : OK
Type              : 2147483648
Name              : C$
__GENUS           : 2
__CLASS           : Win32_Share
__SUPERCLASS      : CIM_LogicalElement
__DYNASTY         : CIM_ManagedSystemElement
```

10. If your results are not similar, compare your script with the ShareNoQuery.ps1 script.

11. This completes the eliminating the WMIQuery argument procedure.

Utilizing an Operator

One of the nice things you can do is use greater than and less than operators in your evalua-tion clause. What is so great about greater than? It makes working with alphabetic characters and numeric characters easy. If you work on a server that hosts home directories for users (which are often named after their user names), you can easily produce a list of all home direc-tories from the letters D through Z by using the > D operation. Keep in mind that D$ is greater than D, and if you really want shares that begin with the letter E, then you could say greater than or equal to E. This command would look like >='E'.

ListGreaterThanShares.ps1

```
$strComputer = "."
$wmiNS = "root\cimv2"
$wmiQuery = "Select name from win32_Share where name > 'd'"

$objWMIServices = Get-WmiObject -computer $strComputer `
   -namespace $wmiNS -query $wmiQuery
   $objWMIServices | Sort-Object -property name |
   Format-List -property name
```

Identifying service accounts

1. Open Notepad, or some other script editor.

2. On the first line, declare a variable called *$strComputer*. Use the dot (.) WMI shortcut to point to the local computer. This line of code is shown here:

    ```
    $strComputer = "."
    ```

3. On the next line, declare a variable called *$wmiNS*. Assign the string "Root\cimv2" to the variable. This will cause the WMI query to use the Root\cimv2 WMI namespace. This line of code is shown here:

    ```
    $wmiNS = "root\cimv2"
    ```

4. On the next line, declare a variable called *$wmiQuery*. You will select only the startname property and the name property from the WIN32_Service WMI class. This line of code is shown here:

    ```
    $wmiQuery = "Select startName, name from win32_service"
    ```

5. On the next line, declare the *$objWMIServices* variable. Use the *$objWMIServices* variable to hold the object that comes back from using the *Get-WmiObject* cmdlet. Use the com-puter argument of the *Get-WmiObject* cmdlet to point the query to the local computer. To do this, use the dot (.) value that is contained in the variable *$strComputer*. Because we will continue the command on the next line, use the grave accent (`) character to tell Windows PowerShell to continue the command on the next line. The code that does this is shown here:

    ```
    $objWMIServices = Get-WmiObject -computer $strComputer `
    ```

6. Use the namespace argument of the *Get-WmiObject* cmdlet to specify the WMI namespace specified in the *$wmiNS* variable. Use the query argument of the *Get-WmiObject* cmdlet to specify the WMI query contained in the variable *$wmiQuery*. This code is shown here:

```
-namespace $wmiNS -query $wmiQuery
```

7. Use the object that comes back from the *Get-WmiObject* cmdlet that is contained in the *$objWMIServices* variable and pipeline it into the *Sort-Object*. Use the *Sort-Object* cmdlet to sort the list first by the startName property and second by the name property. Place the pipeline character at the end of the line because we will pipeline this object into another cmdlet. The code that does this is shown here:

```
$objWMIServices | Sort-Object startName, name |
```

8. Finally, we will receive the pipelined object into the *Format-List* cmdlet. We first format the list by the name property from WIN32_Service and second print out the startName. This code is shown here:

```
Format-List name, startName
```

9. The completed script is shown here:

```
$strComputer = "."
$wmiNS = "root\cimv2"
$wmiQuery = "Select startName, name from win32_service"

$objWMIServices = Get-WmiObject -computer $strComputer `
    -namespace $wmiNS -query $wmiQuery
    $objWMIServices | Sort-Object startName, name |
    Format-List name, startName
```

10. Save the script as *yourname*IdentifyServiceAccounts.ps1. Run the script. You should see an output similar to the one shown here. If not, compare your script to the IdentifyServiceAccounts.ps1 script.

```
name       : BITS
startName : LocalSystem

name       : Browser
startName : LocalSystem

name       : CcmExec
startName : LocalSystem

name       : CiSvc
startName : LocalSystem
```

11. This completes the identifying service accounts procedure.

Logging service accounts

1. Open the IdentifyServiceAccounts.ps1 script in Notepad or your favorite script editor. Save the script as *yourname*IdentifyServiceAccountsLogged.ps1.

2. Declare a new variable called *$strFile*. This variable will be used for the filePath argument of the *Out-File* cmdlet. Assign the string "C:\Mytest\ServiceAccounts.txt" to the *$strFile* variable. This code is shown here:

```
$strFile = "c:\mytest\ServiceAccounts.txt"
```

3. Under the line of code where you declared the *$strFile* variable, use the *New-Variable* cmdlet to create a constant called constASCII. When you assign the constASCII value to the name argument of the *New-Variable* cmdlet, remember you leave off the dollar sign. Use the value argument of the *New-Variable* cmdlet to assign the value of "ASCII" to the constASCII constant. Use the option argument and supply constant as the value for the argument. The completed command is shown here:

```
New-Variable -name constASCII -value "ASCII" `
   -option constant
```

4. At the end of the Format-List line, place the pipeline character (|). This is shown here:

```
Format-List name, startName |
```

5. On the next line, use the *Out-File* cmdlet to produce an output file containing the results of the previous command. Use the filepath argument to specify the path and file name to create. Use the value contained in the *$strFile* variable. To ensure that the output file is easily read, we want to use ASCII encoding. To do this, use the encoding argument of the *Out-File* cmdlet and supply the value contained in the *$constASCII* variable. Use the grave accent character (`) to indicate the command will continue to the next line. The resulting code is shown here:

```
Out-File -filepath $strFile -encoding $constASCII `
```

6. On the next line, use two arguments of the *Out-File* cmdlet. The first argument tells Out-File to append to a file if it exists. The second argument tells Out-File not to overwrite any existing files. This code is shown here:

```
-append -noClobber
```

7. Save and run your script. You should see a file called ServiceAccounts.txt in your Mytest directory on the C:\ drive. The contents of the file will be similar to the output shown here:

```
name      : AppMgmt
startName : LocalSystem

name      : AudioSrv
startName : LocalSystem

name      : BITS
startName : LocalSystem
```

8. If you do not find an output similar to this, compare your script with IdentifyServiceAccountsLogged.ps1.

9. This concludes the logging service accounts procedure.

Where Is the Where?

To more easily modify the *Where* clause in a script, substitute the *Where* clause with a variable. This configuration can be modified to include command-line input as well. This is shown in the ListSpecificWhere.ps1 script.

ListSpecificWhere.ps1

```
$strComputer = "."
$wmiNS = "root\cimv2"
$strWhere = "'ipc$'"
$wmiQuery = "Select * from win32_Share where name="+$strWhere

"Properties of Share named: " + $strWhere

$objWMIServices = Get-WmiObject -computer $strComputer `
    -namespace $wmiNS -query $wmiQuery
    $objWMIServices |
    Format-List -property [a-z]*
```

Quick Check

Q. To limit the specific data returned by a query, what WQL technique can be utilized?

A. The *Where* clause of the WMIquery argument is very powerful in limiting the specific data returned by a query.

Q. What are three possible operators that can be employed in creating powerful *Where* clauses?

A. The equals sign (=) and the greater than (>) and the less than (<) symbols can be used to evaluate the data before returning the dataset.

Working with Software: Step-by-Step Exercises

In this exercise, we explore the use of WIN32_product and classes provided by the Windows installer provider.

1. Open Notepad or your favorite script editor.

2. At the top of your script, declare a variable called *$strComputer*. Assign the WMI shortcut dot character (.) to indicate you want to connect to WMI on your local machine. This line of code is shown here:

    ```
    $strComputer = "."
    ```

3. On the next line, declare the variable *$wmiNS*, which will be used to hold the WMI namespace for your query. Assign the string "Root\cimv2" to the variable. This line of code is shown here:

    ```
    $wmiNS = "root\cimv2"
    ```

4. On the next line, you will use the variable $wmiQuery to hold your WMI query. This query will select everything from the WIN32_Product WMI class. This code is shown here:

```
$wmiQuery = "Select * from win32_product"
```

5. Because this query can take a rather long time to complete (depending on the speed of your machine, CPU load, and number of installed applications), let's use the *Write-Host* cmdlet to inform the user that the script could take a while to run. As long as we are using Write-Host, let's have a little fun and specify the foregroundcolor argument of the *Write-Host* cmdlet, which will change the color of our font. I chose blue, but you can choose any color you wish. The foregroundcolor argument is mentioned in Chapter 4, "Using PowerShell Scripts," and permitted values for this argument are in Table 4-5. Use the `n escape sequence to specify a new line at the end of your command. I used the grave accent character (`) to break the line of code for readability, but this certainly is not necessary for you. The completed code is shown here:

```
Write-Host "Counting Installed Products. This" `
    "may take a little while. " -foregroundColor blue `n
```

6. On the next line, use the variable *$objWMIServices* to hold the object that is returned by the *Get-WmiObject* cmdlet. Supply the computer argument with the value contained in the *$strComputer* variable. Use the grave accent to continue to the next line. This code is shown here:

```
$objWMIServices = Get-WmiObject -computer $strComputer `
```

7. On the next line, use the namespace argument to specify the WMI namespace for the WMI query. Use the value contained in the *$wmiNS* variable. Use the query argument to *supply the WMI query contained in the $wmiQuery variable to the Get-WmiObject cmdlet.* This line of code is shown here:

```
-namespace $wmiNS -query $wmiQuery
```

8. Use the *for* statement to print out a progress indicator. Use the variable *$i* as the counter. Continue counting until the value of *$i* is less than or equal to the value of the count property of the IwbemObjectSet object contained in the *$objWMIServices* variable. (If you need to review the use of the *for* statement, refer to Chapter 4.) The *for* statement code is shown here:

```
for ($i=1; $i -le $objWMIServices.count;$i++)
```

9. The code that will be run as a result of the *for* statement uses the *Write-Host* cmdlet. We will write "/\" to the console. To keep the *Write-Host* cmdlet from writing everything on a new line, use the noNewLine argument. To make the progress bar different from the first prompt, use the foregroundcolor argument and specify an appropriate color. I chose red. This line of code is shown here:

```
{Write-Host "/\" -noNewLine -foregroundColor red}
```

10. Use the *Write-Host* cmdlet to print out the number of installed applications on the machine. To make the value a little easier to read, use two `n escape sequences to produce two blank lines from the progress indicator. This line of code is shown here:

```
Write-Host `n`n "There are " $objWMIServices.count `
   " products installed."
```

11. Save and run your script. Call it *yourname*CountInstalledApplications.ps1. You should see an output similar to the one shown here. If you do not, compare it with CountInstalledApplications.ps1.

```
Counting Installed Products. This may take a little while.
```

```
There are 87 products installed.
```

12. Now we are going to add a timer to our script to see how long it takes to execute. On the fourth line of your script, under the $wmiQuery line, declare a variable called *$dteStart* and assign the date object that is returned by the *Get-Date* cmdlet to it. This line of code is shown here:

```
$dteStart = Get-Date
```

13. At the end of your script, under the last *Write-Host* command, declare a variable called *$dteEnd* and assign the date object that is returned by the *Get-Date* cmdlet to it. This line of code is shown here:

```
$dteEnd = Get-Date
```

14. Declare a variable called *$dteDiff* and assign the date object that is returned by the *New-TimeSpan* cmdlet to it. Use the *New-TimeSpan* cmdlet to subtract the two date objects contained in the *$dteStart* and *$dteEnd* variables. The *$dteStart* variable will go first. This command is shown here:

```
$dteDiff = New-TimeSpan $dteStart $dteEnd
```

15. Use the *Write-Host* cmdlet to print out the total number of seconds it took for the script to run. This value is contained in the totalSeconds property of the date object held in the *$dteDiff* variable. This command is shown here:

```
Write-Host "It took " $dteDiff.totalSeconds " Seconds" `
   " for this script to complete"
```

16. Save your script as *yourname*CountInstalledApplicationsTimed.ps1. Run your script and compare your output with that shown here. If your results are not similar, then compare your script with the CountInstalledApplicationsTimed.ps1 script.

```
Counting Installed Products. This may take a little while.

/\/\/\/\/\/\/\/\/\/\/\/\/\/\/\/\/\/\/\/\/\/\/\/\/\
/\/\/\/\/\/\/\/\/\/\/\/\/\/\/\/\/\/\/\/\/\/\/\/\/\
/\/\/\/\/\/\/\

There are 87 products installed.
It took 120.3125 Seconds for this script to complete
```

17. This concludes this step-by-step exercise.

One Step Further: Windows Environment Settings

In this exercise, we explore Windows environmental settings.

1. Open Windows PowerShell.

2. Use the *Get-WmiObject* cmdlet to view the common properties of the WIN32_Environment WMI class. Use the *gwmi* alias to make it easier to type. This command is shown here:

```
gwmi win32_environment
```

3. The partial output from this command is shown here:

```
VariableValue            Name                  UserName
-------------            ----                  --------
C:\PROGRA~1\CA\SHARED~1... AVENGINE             <SYSTEM>
%SystemRoot%\system32\c... ComSpec              <SYSTEM>
NO                       FP_NO_HOST_CHECK      <SYSTEM>
```

4. To view all the properties of the WIN32_Environment class, pipeline the object returned by the *Get-WmiObject* cmdlet to the *Format-List* cmdlet while specifying the asterisk. Use the up arrow to retrieve the previous *gwmi* command. This command is shown here:

```
gwmi win32_environment | Format-List *
```

5. The output from the previous command will be similar to that shown here:

```
Status          : OK
Name            : TMP
SystemVariable  : False
__GENUS         : 2
__CLASS         : Win32_Environment
__SUPERCLASS    : CIM_SystemResource
```

6.   Scroll through the results returned by the previous command, and examine the properties and their associated values. It appears that the most important information from the
class is Name, UserName, and VariableValue. Use the up arrow to retrieve the previous
gwmi command and change *Format-List* to *Format-Table*. After the *Format-Table* cmdlet,
type the three variables we want to retrieve: *Name, VariableValue*, and *Username*. This
command is shown here:

```
gwmi win32_environment | Format-Table name, variableValue, userName
```

7.   The results from this command will be similar to the partial results shown here:

```
name                    variableValue             userName
----                    -------------             --------
AVENGINE                C:\PROGRA~1\CA\SHARED~1... <SYSTEM>
ComSpec                 %SystemRoot%\system32\c... <SYSTEM>
FP_NO_HOST_CHECK        NO                         <SYSTEM>
INOCULAN                C:\PROGRA~1\CA\ETRUST~1    <SYSTEM>
```

8.   Use the up arrow to retrieve the previous *gwmi* command and delete the variable *user-
Name* and the trailing comma. This command is shown here:

```
gwmi win32_environment | Format-Table name, variableValue
```

9.   The results from this command will be similar to the ones shown here:

```
name                              variableValue
----                              -------------
AVENGINE                          C:\PROGRA~1\CA\SHARED~1\SCANEN~1
ComSpec                           %SystemRoot%\system32\cmd.exe
FP_NO_HOST_CHECK                  NO
INOCULAN                          C:\PROGRA~1\CA\ETRUST~1
```

10.   Notice how the spacing is a little strange. To correct this, use the up arrow to retrieve the
previous command. Add the autosize argument to the *Format-Table* command. You can
use *Tab completion* to finish the command by typing **-a <tab>**. The completed command
is shown here:

```
gwmi win32_environment | Format-Table name, variableValue -AutoSize
```

11.   Now that we have a nicely formatted list, let's compare the results with those produced
by the Environment provider. To do this, we will use the Env PSdrive. Use the *Set-Location* cmdlet to set your location to the Env PSdrive. The command to do this is shown
here. (You can, of course, use the *sl* alias if you prefer.)

```
Set-Location env:
```

12.   Use the *Get-ChildItem* cmdlet to produce a listing of all the environmental variables on
the computer. The command to do this is shown here:

```
Get-ChildItem
```

13. A partial output from the *Get-ChildItem* cmdlet is shown here:

```
Name                        Value
----                        -----
Path                        C:\WINDOWS\system32;C:\WINDOWS;C:\WINDOWS\Sys...
TEMP                        C:\DOCUME~1\EDWILS~1.NOR\LOCALS~1\Temp
```

14. Set your location back to the C:\ drive. The command to do this is shown here:

```
Set-Location c:\
```

15. Retrieve the alias for the *Get-History* cmdlet. To do this, use the *Get-Alias* cmdlet and pipe the resulting object to the *Where-Object*. Use the special variable $_ to indicate the current pipeline object, and look for a match to the definition property that is equal to the *Get-History* cmdlet. The command to do this is shown here:

```
Get-Alias | where {$_.definition -eq "Get-History"}
```

16. The resulting output, shown here, tells us there are three aliases defined for *Get-History*:

```
CommandType     Name                        Definition
-----------     ----                        ----------
Alias           ghy                         Get-History
Alias           h                           Get-History
Alias           history                     Get-History
```

17. Use the up arrow and retrieve the previous *Get-Alias* command. Change the definition from *Get-History* to *Invoke-History*. This command is shown here:

```
Get-Alias | where {$_.definition -eq "Invoke-History"}
```

18. The resulting output, shown here, tells us there are two aliases defined for *Get-History*:

```
CommandType     Name                        Definition
-----------     ----                        ----------
Alias           ihy                         Invoke-History
Alias           r                           Invoke-History
```

19. Use the *Get-History* cmdlet to retrieve a listing of all the commands you have typed into Windows PowerShell. I prefer to use *ghy* for *Get-History* because of similarity with *ihy* (for *Invoke-History*). The *Get-History* command using *ghy* is shown here:

```
ghy
```

20. Examine the output from the *Get-History* cmdlet. You will see a list similar to the one shown here:

```
 1 gwmi win32_environment
 2 gwmi win32_environment | Format-List *
 3 gwmi win32_environment | Format-Table name, variableValue, userName
 4 gwmi win32_environment | Format-Table name, variableValue
 5 gwmi win32_environment | Format-Table name, variableValue -AutoSize
 6 sl env:
 7 gci
 8 sl c:\
 9 Get-Alias | where {$_.definition -eq "Get-History"}
10 Get-Alias | where {$_.definition -eq "Invoke-History"}
```

21. Produce the listing of environmental variables by using the Environment PSdrive. This time, we will do it in a single command. Use *Set-Location* to set the location to the Env: PSdrive. Then continue the command by using a semicolon and then *Get-ChildItem* to produce the list. Use the *sl* alias and the *gci* alias to type this command. The command is shown here:

```
sl env:;gci
```

22. Note that our PSdrive is still set to the Env: PSdrive. Use the *Set-Location* cmdlet to change back to the C:\ PSdrive. This command is shown here:

```
sl c:\
```

23. Use the up arrow to bring up the *sl env:;gci* command, and this time, add another semicolon and another *sl* command to change back to the C:\ PSdrive. The revised command is shown here:

```
sl env:;gci;sl c:\
```

24. You now have an output similar to the one shown here. You are also back at the C:\ PSdrive.

```
Name                         Value
----                         -----
Path                         C:\WINDOWS\system32;C:\WINDOWS;C:\WINDOWS\Sys...
TEMP                         C:\DOCUME~1\EDWILS~1.NOR\LOCALS~1\Temp
SESSIONNAME                  Console
PATHEXT                      .COM;.EXE;.BAT;.CMD;.VBS;.VBE;.JS;.JSE;.WSF;....
```

25. Now use the *ghy* alias to retrieve a history of your commands. Identify the command that contains your previous *gwmi* command that uses *Format-Table* with the autosize argument. This command is shown here:

```
gwmi win32_environment | Format-Table name, variableValue -AutoSize
```

26. Use the *ihy* alias to invoke the history command that corresponds to the command identified in step 25. For me, the command is *ihy 5*, as shown here:

```
Ihy 5
```

27. When the command runs, it prints out the value of the command you are running on the first line. Then you obtain the results normally associated with the command. A partial output is shown here:

```
gwmi win32_environment | Format-Table name, variableValue -AutoSize

name                variableValue
----                -------------
AVENGINE            C:\PROGRA~1\CA\SHARED~1\SCANEN~1
ComSpec             %SystemRoot%\system32\cmd.exe
```

28. Scroll up in Windows PowerShell console, and compare the output from the *gwmi* command you just ran with the output from the *sl env:;gci* command.

29. This concludes this one step further exercise. Commands used in One Step Further: Windows Environment Settings are stored in the OneStepFurtherWindowsEnvironment.txt file.

Chapter 6 Quick Reference

To	Do This
Simplify connecting into WMI while using default security permissions	Use the *Get-WmiObject* cmdlet
To control security when making a remote connection	Specify the impersonation levels in your script
To allow a script to use the credentials of the person launching the script	Use the "impersonate" impersonation level
To allow a script to load a driver	Use the loadDriver privilege
To control security when making a remote connection	Specify the impersonation levels in your script
Get rid of system properties when printing out all properties of a WMI class	Use the *Format-List* cmdlet and specify the property argument must be in range of [a–z]*
Get the current date and time	Use the *Get-Date* cmdlet
Subtract two dates	Use the *New-TimeSpan* cmdlet. Supply two date objects as arguments
Retrieve a listing of all commands typed during a Windows PowerShell session	Use the *Get-History* cmdlet
Run a command from the Windows PowerShell session history	Use the *Invoke-History* cmdlet
Retrieve the minimum and maximum values from an object	Use the *Measure-Object* cmdlet while specifying the property argument as well as the minimum and maximum arguments
Produce paged output from a long scrolling command	Pipeline the resulting object from the command into the *more* function

Chapter 7

Working with Active Directory

After completing this chapter, you will be able to:

- Make a connection into Active Directory
- Understand the use of ADSI providers
- Understand how to work with Active Directory namespaces
- Create organizational units in Active Directory
- Create users in Active Directory
- Create groups in Active Directory
- Modify both users and groups in Active Directory

Network management in the Windows world begins and ends with Active Directory. In this chapter, we cover the user life cycle from a scripting and Active Directory perspective. You will learn how to create organizational units (OUs), users, groups, and computer accounts. We then describe how to modify the users and groups, and finally how to delete the user account. Along the way, you will pick up some more Windows PowerShell techniques. All the scripts mentioned in this chapter can be found in the corresponding scripts folder on the CD.

Creating Objects in Active Directory

The most fundamental object in Active Directory is the OU. One of the most frustrating problems for new network administrators is that by default, when Active Directory is installed, all users are put in the users container, and all computers are put in the computers container—and of course you can not apply Group Policy to a container.

Creating an Organizational Unit

The process of creating an OU in Active Directory will provide the basis for creating other objects in Active Directory because the technique is basically the same. The key to effectively using PowerShell to create objects in Active Directory is using the Active Directory Service Interfaces (ADSI) accelerator.

Just the Steps   **To create an object by using ADSI**

1. Use the [ADSI] accelerator
2. Use the appropriate ADSI provider
3. Specify the path to the appropriate object in Active Directory
4. Use the SetInfo() method to write the changes

The CreateOU.ps1 script shown here illustrates each of the steps required to create an object by using ADSI. The variable *$strClass* is used to hold the class of object to create in Active Directory. For this script, we will be creating an OU. We could just as easily create a user, or a computer—as we will see shortly. We use the variable *$strOUName* to hold the name of the OU we are going to create. For the CreateOU.PS1 script, we are going to create an OU called MyTestOU. Because we will pass this variable directly to the *Create* command, it is important we use the form shown here:

```
$strOUName="ou=MyTestOU"
```

The attribute that is used to create an object in Active Directory is called the *relative distinguished name* (RDN). Standard attribute types are expected by ADSI—such as "ou" for organizational unit. We will look at RDNs in the section on Lightweight Directory Access Protocol (LDAP) names in this chapter. The next line of code in the CreateOU.PS1 script makes the actual connection into Active Directory. To do this, we use the [ADSI] accelerator. The [ADSI] accelerator wants to be given the exact path to your connection point in Active Directory (or some other directory, as we will see shortly) and the name of the ADSI provider. The target of the ADSI operation is called the *ADsPath*.

In the CreateOU.PS1 script, we are connecting to the root of the NwTraders.msft domain, and we are using the LDAP provider. The other providers we can use with ADSI are shown in Table 7-1. After we make our connection into Active Directory, we hold the system. DirectoryServices.DirectoryEntry object in the *$objADSI* variable.

Armed with the connection into Active Directory, we can now use the create method to create our new object. The system.DirectoryServices.DirectoryEntry object that is returned is held in the *$objOU* variable. We use this object on the last line of the script to call the SetInfo() method to write the new object into the Active Directory database. The entire CreateOU.PS1 script is shown here.

CreateOU.PS1

```
$strCLass = "organizationalUnit"
$StrOUName = "ou=MyTestOU"
$objADSI = [ADSI]"LDAP://dc=nwtraders,dc=msft"
$objOU = $objADSI.create($strCLass, $StrOUName)
$objOU.setInfo()
```

ADSI Providers

Table 7-1 lists four providers available to users of ADSI. Connecting to a Microsoft Windows NT 4 system requires using the special *WinNT* provider. During Active Directory migrations, consultants often write a script that copies users from a Windows NT 4 domain to a Microsoft Windows Server 2003 Active Directory OU or domain. In some situations (such as with customized naming schemes), writing a script is easier than using the Active Directory Migration Tool (ADMT).

Table 7-1   ADSI-Supported Providers

Provider	Purpose
WinNT	To communicate with Windows NT 4.0 Primary Domain Controllers (PDCs) and Backup Domain Controllers (BDCs), and with local account databases for Windows 2000 and newer workstations and servers
LDAP	To communicate with LDAP servers, including an Exchange 5.x directory and Windows 2000 Server or Windows Server 2003 Active Directory
NDS	To communicate with Novell Directory Services servers
NWCOMPAT	To communicate with Novell NetWare 3.x servers

The first time I tried using ADSI to connect to a machine running Windows NT, I had a very frustrating experience because of the way the provider was implemented. Type the **WinNT** provider name *exactly* as shown in Table 7-1. It cannot be typed using all lowercase letters or all uppercase letters. All other provider names must be all uppercase letters, but the WinNT name is Pascal-cased, that is, it is partially uppercase and partially lowercase. Remembering this will save a lot of grief later. In addition, you don't get an error message telling you that your provider name is "spelled wrong"–rather, the bind operation simply fails to connect.

 Tip   The ADSI provider names are case sensitive. LDAP is all caps; WinNT is Pascal-cased. Keep this in mind to save a lot of time in troubleshooting.

After the ADSI provider is specified, you need to identify the path to the directory target. This is where a little knowledge of Active Directory comes in handy because of the way the hierarchical naming space is structured. When connecting to an LDAP service provider, you must specify where in the LDAP database hierarchy to make the connection because the hierarchy is a structure of the database itself and not the protocol or the provider. For instance, in the CreateOU.PS1 script, you create an OU that resides off the root of the domain, which is called MyTestOU. This can get confusing, until you realize that the MyTestOU OU is contained in a domain that is called *NWTRADERS.MSFT*. It is vital, therefore, that you understand the hierarchy with which you are working. One tool you can use to make sure you understand the hierarchy of your domain is ADSI Edit.

ADSI Edit is included in the support tools on the Windows Server 2003 disk. It is in the Support\Tools directory, and the tools are installed by clicking Suptools.msi. Installation requires *Help* and other programs to be closed. The installation takes only a couple of minutes and does not require a reboot. After the support tools are installed, you open a blank Micorosoft Management Console (MMC) and add the ADSI Edit snap-in. After you install the snap-in, right-click the ADSI Edit icon, select Connect To, and specify your domain, as illustrated in Figure 7-1.

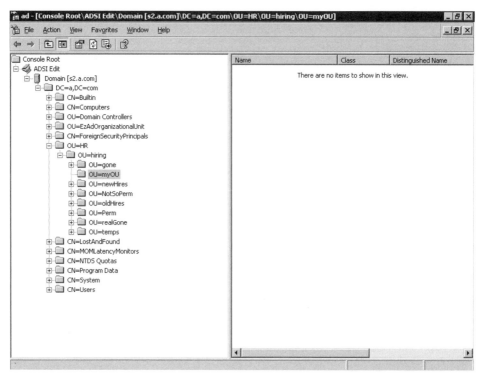

Figure 7-1   Exploring the hierarchy of a forest to ensure the correct path for ADSI

LDAP Names

When specifying the OU and the domain name, you have to use the LDAP naming convention in which the namespace is described as a series of naming parts called *relative distinguished names* (RDNs). The RDN will always be a name part that assigns a value by using the equals sign. When you put together all the RDNs, and the RDNs of each of the ancestors all the way back to the root, you end up with a single globally unique distinguished name.

The RDNs are usually made up of an attribute type, an equal sign, and a string value. Table 7-2 lists some of the attribute types you will see when working with Active Directory. An example of a distinguished name is shown in Figure 7.2.

Table 7-2   Common Relative Distinguished Name Attribute Types

Attribute	Description
DC	Domain Component
CN	Common Name
OU	Organizational Unit
O	Organization Name
Street	Street Address
C	Country Name
UID	User ID

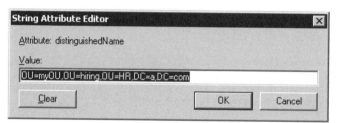

Figure 7-2   Using the string attribute editor in ADSI Edit to quickly verify the distinguished name of a potential target for ADSI scripting

Binding

Whenever you want to do anything with ADSI, you must connect to an object in Active Directory, a process also known as *binding*. Think of binding as being like tying a rope around an object to enable you to work with it. Before you can do any work with an object in Active Directory, you must supply binding information. The *binding string* enables you to use various ADSI elements, including methods and properties. The target of the proposed action is specified as a computer, a domain controller, a user, or another element that resides within the directory structure. A binding string consists of four parts. These parts are illustrated in the following binding string from a sample script:

Accelerator	Variable	Provider	ADsPath
[ADSI]	$objDomain	LDAP://	OU=hr, dc=a, dc=com

> **Note** Avoid a mistake I made early on: make sure that when you finish connecting and creating, you actually commit your changes to Active Directory. Changes to Active Directory are transactional in nature, so your change will roll back if you don't commit it. Committing the change requires you to use the SetInfo() method, as illustrated in the following line from the CreateOU.ps1 script: *$objOU.SetInfo()*. Also keep in mind when calling a method such as SetInfo() that you *must* append empty parentheses () with the method call.

Working with errors

1. Open Notepad or some other Windows PowerShell script editor.

2. On the first line of your script, type a line that will generate an error by trying to create an object called foo. Use the variable *$a* to hold this object. The code to do this is shown here:

   ```
   $a = New-Object foo #creates an error
   ```

3. Print out the value of *$error.count*. The count property should contain a single error when the script is run. This line of code is shown here:

   ```
   $error.count
   ```

4. Save your script as *yourname*WorkWithErrors.ps1. Run your script; you should see it print out the number 1 to let you know there is an error on the Error object.

5. The most recent error will be contained on the variable *error[0]*. Use this to return the CategoryInfo about the error. This code is shown here:

   ```
   $error[0].CategoryInfo
   ```

6. Print out the ErrorDetails of the most recent error. This code is shown here:

   ```
   $error[0].ErrorDetails
   ```

7. Print out the exception information. To do this, print out the value of the Exception property of the *$error* variable. This is shown here:

   ```
   $error[0].Exception
   ```

8. Print out the Fully Qualified Error ID information. This is contained in the FullyQualifiedErrorId property of the *$error* variable. The code to do this is shown here:

   ```
   $error[0].FullyQualifiedErrorId
   ```

9. Print out the invocation information about the error. To do this, use the InvocationInfo property of the *$error* variable. The code to do this is shown here:

   ```
   $error[0].InvocationInfo
   ```

10. The last property to query from *$error* is the TargetObject property. This is shown here:

    ```
    $error[0].TargetObject
    ```

11. Save and run your script. Notice that you will not obtain information from all the properties.

12. The *$error* variable contains information about all errors that occur during the particular Windows PowerShell session, so it is quite likely to contain more than a single error. To introduce an additional error into our script. Try to create a new object called bar. Assign the object that comes back to the variable *$b*. This code is shown here:

```
$b = New-Object bar
```

13. Because we now have more than a single error on the Error object, we need to walk through the collection of errors. To do this, we can use the *for* statement. Use a variable called *$i* as the counter-variable, and proceed until you reach the value of *$error.count*. Make sure you enclose the statement in parentheses and increment the value of *$i* at the end of the statement. The first line of this code is shown here:

```
for ($i = 0 ; $error.count ; $i++)
```

14. Now change each of the *error[0]* statements that print out the various properties of the Error object to use the counter-variable *$i*. Because this will be the code block for the *for* statement, place a curly bracket at the beginning of the first statement and at the end of the last statement. The revised code block is shown here:

```
{$error[$i].CategoryInfo
$error[$i].ErrorDetails
$error[$i].Exception
$error[$i].FullyQualifiedErrorId
$error[$i].InvocationInfo
$error[$i].TargetObject}
```

15. Save and run your script. You will see an output that is similar to the one shown here:

```
New-Object : Cannot find type [foo]: make sure the assembly containing this
 type is loaded.
At D:\BookDocs\WindowsPowerShell\scripts\ch7\WorkWithErrors.ps1:14 char:16
 + $a = New-Object  <<<< foo #creates an error
New-Object : Cannot find type [bar]: make sure the assembly containing this
 type is loaded.
At D:\BookDocs\WindowsPowerShell\scripts\ch7\WorkWithErrors.ps1:15 char:16
 + $b = New-Object  <<<< bar #creates another error

Category   : InvalidType
Activity   : New-Object
Reason     : PSArgumentException
```

16. The first error shown is a result of the Windows PowerShell command interpreter. The last error shown with the category, activity, and reason is a result of our error handling. To remove the first runtime error, use the *$erroractionpreference* variable, and assign the value of "SilentlyContinue" to it. This code is shown here:

```
$erroractionpreference = "SilentlyContinue"
```

17. Save and run your script. You will notice that the runtime error is gone from the top of your screen.

18. To find out how many errors are on the Error object, we can print out the value of *$error.count*. But just having a single number at the top of the screen would be a little

confusing. To take care of that, we must add a descriptive string such as "There are currently " + *$error.count* + " errors. The code to do this is shown here:

```
"There are currently " + $error.count + "errors"
```

19. Save and run your script. You will notice the string prints out at the top of your script, as shown here:

```
There are currently 2 errors
```

20. In your Windows PowerShell Window, use the $error.clear() method to clear the errors from the Error object because it continues to count errors until a new Windows PowerShell Window is opened. This command is shown here:

```
$Error.clear()
```

21. Now comment out the line that creates the bar object. This revised line of code is shown here:

```
#$b = New-Object bar
```

22. Now save and run your script. You will notice the string at the top of your Windows PowerShell window looks a little strange. This is shown here:

```
There are currently 1 errors
```

23. To fix this problem, we need to add some logic to detect if there is one error or more than one error. To do this, we will use an *if ... else* statement. The first line will evaluate if the *$error.count* is equal to 1. If it is, then we will print out there is currently 1 error. This code is shown here:

```
if ($error.count -eq 1)
    {"There is currently 1 error"}
```

24. We can simply use an *else* clause, and add curly brackets around our previous error statement. This revised code is shown here:

```
else
    {"There are currently " + $error.count + "errors"}
```

25. Save and run the script. It should correctly detect there is only one error.

26. Now Remove the comment from the beginning of the line of code that creates the bar object, and run the script. It should detect two errors.

27. This concludes the working with errors procedure. If your script does not produce the desired results, compare it with the WorkWithErrors.ps1 script.

Adding error handling

1. Open the CreateOU.ps1 script, and save it as *yourname*CreateOUwithErrorHandler.ps1.

2. On the first line of the script, use the *$erroractionpreference* variable to assign the SilentlyContinue parameter. This will tell the script to suppress error messages, and continue running the script if possible. This line of code is shown here:

```
$erroractionpreference = "SilentlyContinue"
```

3. To ensure there are no current errors on the Error object, use the clear method. To do this, use the *$error* variable. This line of code is shown here:

```
$error.clear()
```

4. At the end of the script, use an *if* statement to evaluate the error count. If an error has occurred, then the count will not be equal to 0. This line of code is shown here:

```
if ($error.count -ne 0)
```

5. The code block to run, if the condition occurs, should print out a message stating that an error has occurred. It should also print out the CategoryInfo and Invocationinfo properties from the current *$error* variable. The code to do this is shown here:

```
{"An error occurred during the operation. Details follow:"
    $error[0].categoryInfo
    $error[0].invocationinfo
    $error[0].tostring()}
```

6. Save and run your script. You should see an error generated (due to a duplicate attempt to create MyTestOU).

7. Change the OU name to MyTestOU1 and run the script. You should not see an error generated. The revised line of code is shown here:

```
$StrOUName = "ou=MyTestOU1"
```

8. This concludes the adding error handling procedure. If you do not get the results you were expecting, compare your script with the CreateOUWithErrorHandler.ps1 script.

Quick Check

Q.   What is the process of connecting to Active Directory called?

A.   The process of connecting to Active Directory is called binding.

Q.   When specifying the target of an ADSI operation, what is the target called?

A.   The target of the ADSI operation is called the ADsPath.

Q.   An LDAP name is made up of several parts. What do you call each part separated by a comma?

A.   An LDAP name is made up of multiple parts that are called relative distinguished names.

Creating Users

One interesting technique you can use with ADSI is create users. Although using the Graphical User Interface (GUI) to create a single user is easy, using the GUI to create a dozen or more users would certainly not be. In addition, as you'll see, because there is a lot of similarity among ADSI scripts, deleting a dozen or more users is just as simple as creating them. And because you can use the same input text file for all the scripts, ADSI makes creating temporary accounts for use in a lab or school a real snap.

Just the Steps   To create users

1. Use the appropriate provider for your network.
2. Connect to the container for your users.
3. Specify the domain.
4. Specify the User class of the object.
5. Bind to Active Directory.
6. Use the Create method to create the user.
7. Use the Put method to at least specify the sAMAccountName attribute.
8. Use SetInfo() to commit the user to Active Directory.

The CreateUser.ps1 script, which follows, is very similar to the CreateOU.ps1 script. In fact, CreateUser.ps1 was created from CreateOU.ps1, so a detailed analysis of the script is unnecessary. The only difference is that oClass is equal to the "User" class instead of to an "organizationalUnit" class.

Tip   These scripts use a Windows PowerShell trick. When using VBScript to create a user or a group, you must supply a value for the sAMAccountName attribute. When using Windows PowerShell on Windows 2000, this is also the case. With Windows PowerShell on Windows Server 2003, however, the sAMAccountName attribute will be automatically created for you. In the CreateUser.ps1 script, I have included the *$objUser.Put* command, which would be required for Windows 2000, but it is not required in Windows Server 2003.

CreateUser.ps1

```
$strCLass = "User"
$StrName = "CN=MyNewUser"
$objADSI = [ADSI]"LDAP://ou=myTestOU,dc=nwtraders,dc=msft"
$objUser = $objADSI.create($strCLass, $StrName)
$objUser.Put("sAMAccountName", "MyNewUser")
$objUser.setInfo()
```

Quick Check

Q. To create a user, which class must be specified?

A. You need to specify the User class to create a user.

Q. What is the Put method used for?

A. The Put method is used to write additional property data to the object that it is bound to.

Creating groups

1. Open the CreateUser.ps1script in Notepad, and save it as *yourname*CreateGroup.ps1.

2. Declare a variable called *$intGroupType*. This variable will be used to control the type of group to create. Assign the number 2 to the variable. When used as the group type, a type 2 will be a distribution group. This line of code is shown here:

   ```
   $intGroupType = 2
   ```

3. Change the value of *$strClass* from user to group. This variable will be used to control the type of object that gets created in Active Directory. This is shown here:

   ```
   $strGroup = "Group"
   ```

4. Change the name of the *$objUser* variable to *$objGroup* (less confusing that way). This will need to be done in two places, as shown here:

   ```
   $objGroup = $objADSI.create($strCLass, $StrName)
   $objGroup.setInfo()
   ```

5. Above the $objGroup.setInfo() line, use the Put method to create a distribution group. The distribution group is grouptype of 2, and we can use the value held in the *$intGroup-Type* variable. This line of code is shown here:

   ```
   $ObjGroup.put("GroupType",$intGroupType)
   ```

6. Save and run the script. It should create a group called MyNewGroup in the MyTestOU in Active Directory. If the script does not perform as expected, compare you script with the CreateGroup.ps1 script.

7. This concludes the creating groups procedure.

Creating a computer account

1. Open CreateUser.ps1 script in Notepad, and save it as *yourname*CreateComputer.ps1.

2. Change the *$strClass* from "user" to "Computer". The revised command is shown here:

   ```
   $strCLass = "computer"
   ```

3. Change the *$strName* from "CN=MyNewUser" to "CN=MyComputer". This command is shown here:

   ```
   $StrName = "CN=MyComputer"
   ```

4. The [ADSI] accelerator connection string is already connecting to ou=myTestOU and should not need modification.

5. Change the name of the *$objUser* variable used to hold the object that is returned from the Create method to *$objComputer*. This revised line of code is shown here:

   ```
   $objComputer = $objADSI.create($strCLass, $StrName)
   ```

6. Use the Put method from the DirectoryEntry object created in the previous line to put the value "MyComputer" in the sAMAccountName attribute. This line of code is shown here:

```
$objComputer.put("sAMAccountName", "MyComputer")
```

7. Use the SetInfo() method to write the changes to Active Directory. This line of code is shown here:

```
$objComputer.setInfo()
```

8. After the Computer object has been created in Active Directory, you can modify the UserAccountControl attribute. The value 4128 in UserAccountControl means the workstation is a trusted account and does not need to change the password. This line of code is shown here:

```
$objComputer.put("UserAccountControl",4128)
```

9. Use the SetInfo() method to write the change back to Active Directory. This line of code is shown here:

```
$objComputer.setinfo()
```

10. Save and run the script. You should see a computer account appear in Active Directory Users and Computers. If your script does not product the expected results, compare it with CreateComputer.ps1.

11. This concludes the creating a computer account procedure.

What Is User Account Control?

User account control is an attribute stored in Active Directory that is used to enable or disable a User Account, Computer Account, or other object defined in Active Directory. It is not a single string attribute; rather, it is a series of flags that get computed from the values listed in Table 7-3. Because of the way the UserAccountControl attribute is created, simply examining the numeric value is of little help, unless you can decipher the individual numbers that make up the large number. These flags, when added together, control the behavior of the user account on the system. In the script CreateComputer.ps1, we set two user account control flags: the ADS_UF_PASSWD_NOTREQD flag and the ADS_UF_WORKSTATION_TRUST_ACCOUNT flag. The password not required flag has a hex value of 0x20, and the the trusted workstation flag has a hex value of 0x1000. When added together, and turned into decimal value, they equal 4128, which is the value actually shown in ADSI Edit.

Table 7-3   **User Account Control Values**

Ads Constant	Value
ADS_UF_SCRIPT	0X0001
ADS_UF_ACCOUNTDISABLE	0X0002
ADS_UF_HOMEDIR_REQUIRED	0X0008
ADS_UF_LOCKOUT	0X0010
ADS_UF_PASSWD_NOTREQD	0X0020
ADS_UF_PASSWD_CANT_CHANGE	0X0040
ADS_UF_ENCRYPTED_TEXT_PASSWORD_ALLOWED	0X0080
ADS_UF_TEMP_DUPLICATE_ACCOUNT	0X0100
ADS_UF_NORMAL_ACCOUNT	0X0200
ADS_UF_INTERDOMAIN_TRUST_ACCOUNT	0X0800
ADS_UF_WORKSTATION_TRUST_ACCOUNT	0X1000
ADS_UF_SERVER_TRUST_ACCOUNT	0X2000
ADS_UF_DONT_EXPIRE_PASSWD	0X10000
ADS_UF_MNS_LOGON_ACCOUNT	0X20000
ADS_UF_SMARTCARD_REQUIRED	0X40000
ADS_UF_TRUSTED_FOR_DELEGATION	0X80000
ADS_UF_NOT_DELEGATED	0X100000
ADS_UF_USE_DES_KEY_ONLY	0x200000
ADS_UF_DONT_REQUIRE_PREAUTH	0x400000
ADS_UF_PASSWORD_EXPIRED	0x800000
ADS_UF_TRUSTED_TO_AUTHENTICATE_FOR_DELEGATION	0x1000000

Working with Users

In this section, you will use ADSI to modify User properties stored in Active Directory. The following list summarizes a few of the items you can change or configure:

- Office and telephone contact information

- Mailing address information

- Department, title, manager, and direct reports (people who report to the user inside the "chain of command")

User information that is stored in Active Directory can easily replace several pieces of disparate information in a single swoop. For instance, you might have an internal Web site that contains a telephone directory; you can put the phone number into Active Directory as an attribute of the User object. You might also have a Web site containing a social roster that includes employees and their hobbies; you can put hobby information in Active Directory as a custom attribute. You can also add to Active Directory information such as an organizational chart. The problem, of course, is that during a migration, information such as a user's title is the last thing the harried mind of the network administrator thinks about. To leverage the investment in Active Directory, you need to enter this type of information because it quickly becomes instrumental in the daily lives of demure users. This is where ADSI and Windows PowerShell really begin to shine. We can update hundreds or even thousands of records easily and efficiently using scripting. Such a task would be unthinkable using conventional point-and-click methods.

> **Just the Steps   To modify user properties in Active Directory**
> 1. Implement the appropriate protocol provider.
> 2. Perform binding to Active Directory.
> 3. Specify the appropriate ADsPath.
> 4. Use the Put method to write selected properties to users.
> 5. Use the SetInfo() method to commit changes to Active Directory.

General User Information

One of the more confusing issues when you use Windows PowerShell to modify information in Active Directory is that the names displayed on the property page do not correspond with the ADSI nomenclature. This was not done to make your life difficult; rather, the names you see in ADSI are derived from LDAP standard naming convention. Although this naming convention makes traditional LDAP programmers happy, it does nothing for the network administrator who is a casual scripter. This is where the following script, ModifyUserProperties.ps1, comes in handy. The LDAP properties corresponding to each field in Figure 7-3 are used in this script.

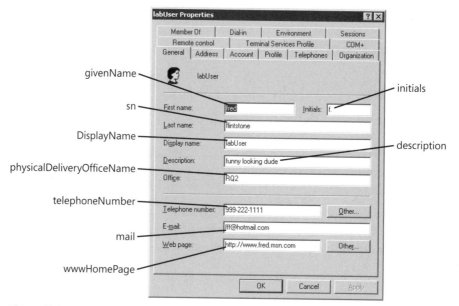

Figure 7-3   ADSI attribute names of the General tab of Active Directory Users and Computers

Some of the names make sense, but others appear to be rather obscure. Notice the series of *objUser.Put* statements. Each lines up with the corresponding fields in Figure 7-3. Use the values to see which display name maps to which LDAP attribute name. The use of all these values is illustrated in ModifyUserProperties.ps1, shown here:

ModifyUserProperties.ps1

```
$objUser = [ADSI]"LDAP://cn=MyNewUser,ou=myTestOU,dc=nwtraders,dc=msft"
$objUser.put("SamaccountName", "myNewUser")
$objUser.put("givenName", "My")
$objUser.Put("initials", "N.")
$objUser.Put("sn", "User")
$objUser.Put("DisplayName", "My New User")
$objUser.Put("description" , "simple new user")
$objUser.Put("physicalDeliveryOfficeName", "RQ2")
$objUser.Put("telephoneNumber", "999-222-1111")
$objUser.Put("mail", "mnu@hotmail.com")
$objUser.Put("wwwHomePage", "http://www.mnu.msn.com")
$objUser.setInfo()
```

> ### Quick Check
>
> **Q.   What is the field name for the user's first name?**
>
> A.   The field for the user's first name is called "*GivenName*". You can find field mapping information in the Platform SDK.
>
> **Q.   Why do you need to do a *SetInfo()* command?**
>
> A.   Without a *SetInfo()* command, all changes introduced during the script are lost because the changes are made to a cached set of attribute values for the object being modified. Nothing is committed to Active Directory until you call *SetInfo()*.

Creating the Address Page

One of the more useful tasks you can perform with Active Directory is exposing address information. This ability is particularly important when a company has more than one location and more than a few hundred employees. I remember one of my first intranet projects was to host a centralized list of employees. Such a project quickly paid for itself because the customer no longer needed an administrative assistant to modify, copy, collate, and distribute hundreds of copies of the up-to-date employee directory—potentially a full-time job for one person. After the intranet site was in place, personnel at each location were given rights to modify the list. This was the beginning of a company-wide directory. With Active Directory, you avoid this duplication of work by keeping all information in a centralized location. The "second page" in Active Directory Users and Computers is the address page, shown in Figure 7-4 with the appropriate Active Directory attribute names filled in.

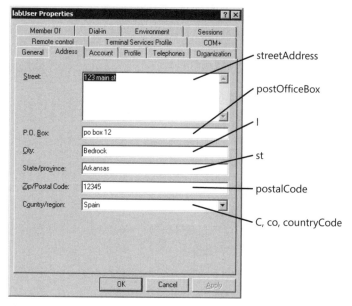

Figure 7-4   Every item on the Address tab in Active Directory Users and Computers can be filled in via ADSI and Windows PowerShell

In the ModifySecondPage.ps1 script, you use ADSI to set the street, post office box, city, state, zip code, c, co, and country values for the User object. Table 7-4 lists the Active Directory attribute names and their mappings to the Active Directory Users and Computers management tool "friendly" display names.

Table 7-4   Address Page Mappings

Active Directory Users and Computers Label	Active Directory Attribute Name
Street	*streetAddress*
P.O. Box	*postOfficeBox*
City	*l* (Note that this is lowercase L.)
State/Province	*st*
Zip/Postal Code	*postalCode*
Country/Region	*c,co,countryCode*

When working with address-type information in Windows PowerShell, the hard thing is keeping track of the country codes. These values must be properly supplied. Table 7-5 illustrates some typical country codes. At times, the country codes seem to make sense; at others times, they do not. Rather than guess, you can simply make the change in Active Directory Users and Computers, and use ADSI Edit to examine the modified value, or you can look them up in ISO 3166-1.

ModifySecondPage.ps1

```
$objUser = [ADSI]"LDAP://cn=MyNewUser,ou=myTestOU,dc=nwtraders,dc=msft"
$objUser.put("streetAddress", "123 main st")
$objUser.put("postOfficeBox", "po box 12")
$objUser.put("l", "Bedrock")
$objUser.put("st", "Arkansas")
$objUser.put("postalCode" , "12345")
$objUser.put("c", "US")
$objUser.put("co", "United States")
$objUser.put("countryCode", "840")
$objUser.setInfo()
```

Table 7-5   ISO 3166-1 Country Codes

Country Code	Country Name
AF	AFGHANISTAN
AU	AUSTRALIA
EG	EGYPT
LV	LATVIA
ES	SPAIN
US	UNITED STATES

Caution   The three country fields are not linked in Active Directory. You could easily have a c code value of US, a co code value of Zimbabwe, and a countryCode value of 470 (Malta). This could occur if someone uses the Active Directory Users and Computers to make a change to the country property. When this occurs, it updates all three fields. If someone later runs a script to only update the country code value, or the co code value, then Active Directory Users and Computers will still reflect the "translated value" of the c code. This could create havoc if your Enterprise Resource Planning (ERP) application uses the co or country code value, and not the c attribute. Best practice is to update all three fields through your script.

Quick Check

Q.   **To set the country name on the address page for Active Directory Users and Computers, what is required?**

A.   To update the country name on the address page for Active Directory Users and Computers, you must specify the c field and feed it a two-letter code that is found in ISO publication 3166.

Q.   **What field name in ADSI is used to specify the city information?**

A.   You set the city information by assigning a value to the l (lowercase) field after making the appropriate connection to Active Directory.

Q.   **If you put an inappropriate letter code in the c field, what error message is displayed?**

A.   None.

Modifying the user profile settings

1. Open the ModifySecondPage.ps1 script, and save it as *yourname*ModifyUserProfile.ps1.

2. The user profile page in Active Directory is composed of four attributes. We can therefore delete all but four of the *$objUser.put* commands. The actual profile attributes are shown in Figure 7-5.

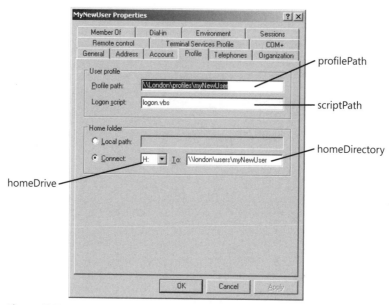

Figure 7-5 ADSI attributes used to fill out the profile page in Active Directory

3. The first attribute we need to supply a value for is the profilePath attribute. This controls where the user's profile will be stored. On my server, the location is \\London\Profiles in a folder named after the user, which in this case is myNewUser. Edit the first of the *$objUser.put* commands you left in your script to match your environment. The modified *$objUser.put* command is shown here:

```
$objUser.put("profilePath", "\\London\profiles\myNewUser")
```

4. The next attribute we need to supply a value for is the scriptpath attribute. This controls which logon script will be run when the user logs on. Even though this attribute is called *scriptpath*, it does not expect an actual path statement (it assumes the script is in sysvol); rather, it simply needs the name of the logon script. On my server, I use a logon script called logon.vbs. Modify the second *$objUser.put* statement in your script to point to a logon script. The modified command is shown here:

```
$objUser.put("scriptPath", "logon.vbs")
```

5. The third attribute that needs to be set for the user profile is called homeDirectory, and it is used to control where the user's home directory will be stored. This attribute needs a Universal Naming Convention (UNC) formatted path to a shared directory. On my

server, each user has a home directory named after their logon user name. These folders are stored under a shared directory called *Users*. Modify the third *$objUser.put* statement in your script to point to the appropriate home directory location for your environment. The completed command is shown here:

```
$objUser.put("homeDirectory", "\\london\users\myNewUser")
```

6. The last user profile attribute that needs to be modified is the homeDrive attribute. The homeDrive attribute in Active Directory is used to control the mapping of a drive letter to the user's home directory. On my server, all users' home drives are mapped to the H: drive (for home). Please note that Active Directory does not expect a trailing backslash for the homeDirectory attribute. Modify the last *$objUser.put* command to map the user's home drive to the appropriate drive letter for your environment. The modified command is shown here:

```
$objUser.put("homeDrive", "H:")
```

7. Save and run your script. If it does not modify the user's profile page as expected, compare your script with the ModifyUserProfile.ps1 script.

8. This concludes the modifying the user profile settings procedure.

Modifying the user telephone settings

1. Open ModifySecondPage.ps1 script, and save the file as *yourname*ModifyTelephone Attributes.ps1.

2. The Telephones tab in Active Directory Users and Computers for a user account is composed of six attributes. These attribute names are shown in Figure 7-6, which also illustrates the field names, as shown in Active Directory Users and Computers on the Telephones tab for the User object. Delete all but six of the *$objUser.put* commands from your script.

3. The first attribute you modify is the homePhone attribute for the MyNewUser user account. To do this, change the value of the first *$objUser.put* command so that it is now writing to the *homePhone* attribute in Active Directory. The phone number for the MyNewUser account is (215) 788-4312. For this example, we are leaving off the country code, and enclosing the area code in parentheses. This is not required, however, for Active Directory. Our modified line of code is shown here:

```
$objUser.Put("homePhone", "(215)788-4312")
```

4. The next telephone attribute in Active Directory is the pager attribute. Our user account has a pager number that is (215) 788-0112. Modify the second *$objUser.put* line of your script to put this value into the *pager* attribute. The revised line of code is shown here:

```
$objUser.Put("pager", "(215)788-0112")
```

5. The third telephone attribute we need to modify on our user account is the mobile telephone attribute. The name of this attribute in Active Directory is *mobile*. The mobile telephone number for our user is (715) 654-2341. Edit the third *$objUser.put* command in your script so that you are writing this value into the mobile attribute. The revised line of code is shown here:

```
$objUser.Put("mobile", "(715)654-2341")
```

6. The fourth telephone attribute that needs to be assigned a value is for the fax machine. The attribute in Active Directory that is used to hold the fax machine telephone number is *facsimileTelephoneNumber*. Our user has a fax number that is (215) 788-3456. Edit the fourth *$objUser.put* command in your script to write the appropriate fax number into the fax attribute in Active Directory. The revised code is shown here:

```
$objUser.Put("facsimileTelephoneNumber", "(215)788-3456")
```

7. The fifth telephone attribute that needs to be assigned a value for our user is the IP address of the user's IP telephone. In Active Directory, this attribute is called *ipPhone*. The myNewUser account has an IP telephone with the IP address of "192.168.6.112". Modify the fifth *$objUser.put* command so that it will supply this information to Active Directory when the script is run. The revised command is shown here:

```
$objUser.Put("ipPhone", "192.168.6.112")
```

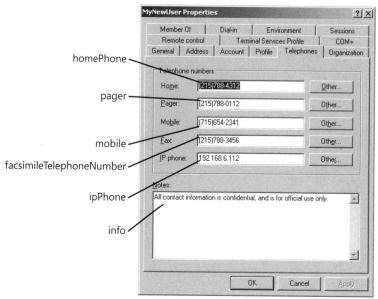

Figure 7-6   Telephone page attributes found in Active Directory

8. Finally, the last telephone attribute is the notes, or the official disclaimer attribute. In Active Directory, this field is called the *info* attribute.

```
$objUser.Put("info", "All contact information is confidential," `
+ "and is for official use only.")
```

9. Save and run your script. You should see the all the properties on the Telephones tab filled in for the MyNewUser account. If this is not the case, you may want to compare your script with the ModifyTelephoneAttributes.ps1 script.

10. This concludes the modifying the user telephone settings procedure.

Creating multiple users

1. Open the CreateUser.ps1 script, and save it as *yourname*CreateMultipleUsers.ps1.

2. On the second line of your script, change the name of the variable *$strName* to *$aryNames* because the variable will be used to hold an array of user names. On the same line, change the CN=MyNewUser username to CN=MyBoss. Leave the quotation marks in place. At the end of the line, place a comma and type in the next user name: **CN=MyDIrect1**, ensuring you encase the name in quotation marks. The third user name is going to be CN=MyDirect2. The completed line of code is shown here:

```
$aryNames = "CN=MyBoss","CN=MyDirect1","CN=MyDirect2"
```

3. Under the $objADSI line that uses the [ADSI] accelerator to connect into Active Directory, and above the $objUser line that creates the user account, place a *foreach* statement. Inside the parentheses, use the variable *$strName* as the single object and *$aryNames* as the name of the array. This line of code is shown here:

```
foreach($StrName in $aryNames)
```

4. Below the *foreach* line, place an opening curly bracket to mark the beginning of the code block. On the line after *$objUser.setinfo()*, close the code block with a closing curly bracket. The entire code block is shown here:

```
{
   $objUser = $objADSI.create($strCLass, $StrName)

   $objUser.setInfo()
}
```

5. Save and run your script. You should see three user accounts—MyBoss, MyDirect1, and MyDirect2—magically appear in the MyTestOU OU. If this does not happen, compare your script with the CreateMultipleUsers.ps1 script.

6. This concludes the creating multiple users procedure.

> **Note**   The interesting thing about Windows PowerShell is that it can read inside a string, find a variable, and substitute the value of the variable, instead of just interpreting the variable as a string literal. Example:
>
> ```
> $objUser = [ADSI]"LDAP://$strUser,$strOU,$strDomain"
> ```

Modifying the organizational settings

1. Open the ModifySecondPage.ps1 script, and save it as *yourname*ModifyOrganizationalPage.ps1.

2. In this script, we are going to modify four attributes in Active Directory, so you can delete all but four of the *$objUser.put* commands from your script. The Organization tab from Active Directory Users and Computers is shown in Figure 7-7, along with the appropriate attribute names.

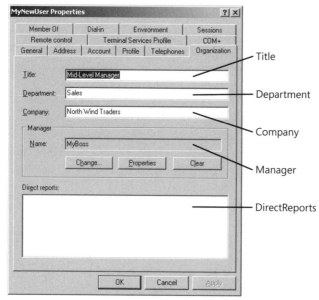

Figure 7-7   Organization attributes in Active Directory

3. To make our script more flexible, we are going to abstract much of the connection string information into variables. The first variable we will use is one to hold the domain name. Call this variable *$strDomain* and assign the value of dc=nwtraders,dc=msft (assuming this is the name of your domain). This code is shown here:

    ```
    $strDomain = "dc=nwtraders,dc=msft"
    ```

4. The second variable you wish to declare is the one that will hold the name of the OU. In this procedure, our users reside in an OU called ou=myTestOU, so you should assign this value to the variable *$strOU*. This line of code is shown here:

    ```
    $strOU = "ou=myTestOU"
    ```

5. The user name we are going to be working with is called MyNewUser. Users are not domain components (dc), nor are they organizational units (ou); rather, they are containers (cn). Assign the string cn=MyNewUser to the variable *$strUser*. This line of code is shown here:

```
$strUser = "cn=MyNewUser"
```

6. The last variable we need to declare and assign a value to is the one that will hold the MyNewUser's manager. His name is myBoss. The line of code that holds this information in the *$strManager* variable is shown here:

```
$strManager = "cn=myBoss"
```

7. So far, we have hardly used even one piece of information from the ModifySecondPage.ps1 script. Edit the *$objUser* line that holds the connection into Active Directory by using the [ADSI] accelerator so that it uses the variables we created for the user, OU, and domain. Windows PowerShell will read the value of the variables instead of interpreting them as strings. This makes it really easy to modify the connection string. The revised line of code is shown here:

```
$objUser = [ADSI]"LDAP://$strUser,$strOU,$strDomain"
```

8. Modify the first *$objUser.put* command so that it assigns the value Mid-Level Manager to the title attribute in Active Directory. This command is shown here:

```
$objUser.put("title", "Mid-Level Manager")
```

9. Modify the second *$objUser.put* command so that it assigns the value of Sales to the department attribute in Active Directory. This command is shown here:

```
$objUser.put("department", "sales")
```

10. Modify the third *$objUser.put* command and assign the string North Wind Traders to the company attribute. This revised line of code is shown here:

```
$objUser.put("company", "North Wind Traders")
```

11. The last attribute we need to modify is the manager attribute. To do this, we will use the last *$objUser.put* command. The manager attribute needs the complete path to the object, so we will use the name stored in *$strManager*, the OU stored in *$strOU*, and the domain stored in *$strDomain*. This revised line of code is illustrated here:

```
$objUser.put("manager", "$strManager,$strou,$strDomain")
```

12. Save and run your script. You should see the Organization tab filled out in Active Directory Users and Computers. The only attribute that has not been filled out is the direct reports attribute on the MyNewUser user. However, if you open the MyBoss user, you will see MyNewUser listed as a direct report for the MyBoss user. If your script does not perform as expected, then compare your script with the ModifyOrganizationalPage.ps1 script.

13. This concludes the modifying the organizational settings procedure.

Deleting Users

There are times when you need to delete user accounts, and with ADSI, you can very easily delete large numbers of users with the single click of a mouse. Some reasons for deleting user accounts follow:

- To clean up a computer lab environment, that is, to return machines to a known state

- To clean up accounts at the end of a school year. Many schools delete all student-related accounts and files at the end of each year. Scripting makes it easy to both create and delete the accounts.

- To clean up temporary accounts created for special projects. If the creation of accounts is scripted, their deletion can also be scripted, ensuring no temporary accounts are left lingering in the directory.

Just the Steps   To delete users

1. Perform the binding to the appropriate OU.
2. Use [ADSI] to make a connection.
3. Specify the appropriate provider and *ADsPath*.
4. Call the Delete method.
5. Specify object class as User.
6. Specify the user to delete by CN.

To delete a user, call the Delete method after binding to the appropriate level in the Active Directory namespace. Then specify both the object class, which in this case is User, and the CN of the user to be deleted. This can actually be accomplished in only two lines of code:

```
$objDomain = [ADSI]($provider + $ou + $domain)
$objDomain.Delete $oClass, $oCn + $oUname
```

If you modify the CreateUser.ps1 script, you can easily transform it into a DeleteUser.ps1 script, which follows. The main change is in the Worker section of the script. The binding string is the same as shown earlier, and is shown here:

```
$objADSI = [ADSI]"LDAP://ou=myTestOU,dc=nwtraders,dc=msft"
```

However, you use the connection that was made in the binding string, and call the Delete method. You specify the class of the object in the *$strClass* variable in the Reference section of the script. You also list the *$strName*. The syntax is Delete(Class, target). The deletion takes effect immediately. No *SetInfo()* command is required. This command is shown here:

```
$objUser = $objADSI.delete($strCLass, $StrName)
```

The DeleteUser.ps1 script entailed only two real changes from the CreateUser.ps1 script. This makes user management very easy. If you need to create a large number of temporary users, you can save the script and then use it to get rid of them when they have completed their project. The complete DeleteUser.ps1 script is shown here.

DeleteUser.PS1

```
strCLass = "User"
$StrName = "CN=MyNewUser"
$objADSI = [ADSI]"LDAP://ou=myTestOU,dc=nwtraders,dc=msft"
$objUser = $objADSI.delete($strCLass, $StrName)
```

Creating Multiple Organizational Units: Step-by-Step Exercises

In this exercise, we will explore the use of a text file to hold the name of multiple OUs we wish to create in Active Directory.

1. Open Notepad or some other script editor.

2. Locate the StepByStep.txt file (this contains the list of OUs your script will create) in the Chapter 7 folder. Make sure you have the exact path to this file. On the first line of your script, create a variable called *$aryText*. Use this variable to hold the object that is returned by the *Get-Content* cmdlet. Specify the path to the StepByStep.txt file as the value of the path argument. The line of code that does this is shown here:

   ```
   $aryText = Get-Content -Path "c:\labs\ch7\stepbystep.txt"
   ```

3. When the *Get-Content* cmdlet is used, it creates an array from a text file. To walk through each element of the array, we will use the *ForEach* cmdlet. Use a variable called *$aryElement* to hold the line from the *$aryText* array. This line of code is shown here:

   ```
   forEach ($aryElement in $aryText)
   ```

4. Begin your code block section by opening a curly bracket. This is shown here:

   ```
   {
   ```

5. Use the variable *$strClass* to hold the string "organizationalUnit" because this is the kind of object we will be creating in Active Directory. The line of code to do this is shown here:

   ```
   $strCLass = "organizationalUnit"
   ```

6. The name of each OU we are going to create comes from each line of the StepByStep.txt file. In our text file, to simplify the coding task, we included ou= as part of each OU name. The *$strOUName* that will be used in the *Create* command is a straight value assignment of one variable to another variable. This line of code is shown here:

   ```
   $StrOUName = $aryElement
   ```

7. The next line of code in our code block is the one that connects into Active Directory by using the [ADSI] accelerator. We are going to use the LDAP provider and connect to the NwTraders.msft domain. We assign the object that is created to the $*objADSI* variable. This line of code is shown here:

```
$objADSI = [ADSI]"LDAP://dc=nwtraders,dc=msft"
```

8. Now we are ready to actually create the OUs in Active Directory. To do this, we will use the Create method. We specify two properties to the Create method: the name of class to create and the name of the object to create. Here, the name of the class is stored in the variable $*strClass*. The name of the object to create is stored in the $*strOUName* variable. The object that is returned is stored in the $*objOU* variable. This line of code is shown here:

```
$objOU = $objADSI.create($strCLass, $StrOUName)
```

9. To write changes back to Active Directory, we use the SetInfo() method. This is shown here:

```
$objOU.setInfo()
```

10. Now we must close the code block. To do this, close it with a curly bracket, as shown here:

```
}
```

11. Save your script as *yourname*StepByStep.ps1. Run your script. You should see five OUs created off the root of your domain. If this is not the case, compare your script with the StepByStep.ps1 script in the Chapter 7 folder.

12. This concludes the creating multiple organizations units step-by-step exercise.

One Step Further: Creating Multivalued Users

In this exercise, we create nine temporary user accounts using concatenation. We specify values for the users from a text file and populate attributes on both the Address tab and the Telephone tab.

1. Open Notepad or your favorite Windows PowerShell script editor.

2. Use the *Get-Content* cmdlet to open the OneStepFurther.txt file. Use the path argument to point to the exact path to the file. Hold the array that is created in a variable called $*aryText*. This line of code is shown here:

```
$aryText = Get-Content -Path "c:\labs\ch7\OneStepFurther.txt"
```

3. Create a variable called $*strUser*. This will be used to determine the class of object to create in Active Directory. Assign the string "user" to this variable. This line of code is shown here:

```
$strCLass = "User"
```

4. Create a variable called $*intUsers*. This variable will be used to determine how many users to create. For this exercise, we will create nine users, so assign the integer 9 to the value of the variable. This code is shown here:

```
$intUsers = 9
```

5. Create a variable called *$strName*. This variable will be used to create the prefix for each user that is created. Because these will be temporary users, called the prefix cn=tempuser. This code is shown here:

```
$strName = "cn=tempUser"
```

6. Create a variable called *$objADSI*. This variable will be used to hold the object that is returned by using the [ADSI] accelerator that is used to make the connection into Active Directory. Specify the LDAP provider, and connect to the MyTestOU that resides in the NwTraders.msft domain. This line of code is shown here:

```
$objADSI = [ADSI]"LDAP://ou=myTestOU,dc=nwtraders,dc=msft"
```

7. Use a *for* loop to count from 1 to 9. Use the $i variable as the counter-variable. When the value of $i is less than or equal to the integer stored in the *$intUsers* variable, exit the loop. Use the $i++ operator to increment the value of $i. This code is shown here:

```
for ($i=1; $i -le $intUsers; $i++)
```

8. Open and close your code block by using curly brackets. This is shown here:

```
{

}
```

9. Between the curly brackets, use the object contained in the *$objADSI* variable to create the class of object stored in the variable *$strClass*. The name of each object will be created by concatenating the *$strName* prefix with the number current in *$i*. Store the object returned by the Create method in the variable *$objUser*. This line of code is shown here:

```
$objUser = $objADSI.create($strCLass, $StrName+$i)
```

10. On the next line in the code block, write the New User object to Active Directory using the SetInfo() method. This line of code is shown here:

```
$objUser.setInfo()
```

11. Open the OneStepFurther.txt file, and examine the contents. Note that each line corresponds to a property in Active Directory. The trick is to ensure that each line in the text file matches each position in the array. Beginning at element, use the array contained in the variable *$aryText* to write the streetaddress, postofficebox, l, st, postalcode, c, co, countrycode, facsimiletelephonenumber, and info attributes for each User object that is created. This section of code, shown here, is placed after the User object is created, and SetInfo() writes it to Active Directory.

```
$objUser.put("streetAddress", $aryText[0])
$objUser.put("postOfficeBox", $aryText[1])
$objUser.put("l", $aryText[2])
$objUser.put("st", $aryText[3])
$objUser.put("postalCode" , $aryText[4])
$objUser.put("c", $aryText[5])
$objUser.put("co", $aryText[6])
```

```
$objUser.put("countryCode", $aryText[7])
$objUser.Put("facsimileTelephoneNumber", $aryText[8])
$objUser.Put("info", $aryText[9])
```

12. Commit the changes to Active Directory by calling the SetInfo() method. This line of code is shown here:

```
$objUser.setInfo()
```

13. Save your script as *yourname*OneStepFurtherPt1.ps1. Run your script, and examine Active Directory Users and Computers. You should find the nine users with attributes on both the Address tab and the Telephones tab. If this is not the case, then compare your script with the OneStepFurtherPt1.ps1 script. After the users are created, proceed to part 2.

14. Save OneStepFurtherPt1.ps1 as *yourname*OneStepFurtherPt2.ps1.

15. Delete the *$aryText* = Get-Content -Path "c:\labs\ch7\OneStepFurther.txt" from the script.

16. Delete everything from inside the code block except for the line of code that creates the User object. This line of code is: $objUser = $objADSI.create($strCLass, $StrName+$i). The code to delete is shown here:

```
$objUser.setInfo()
$objUser.put("streetAddress", $aryText[0])
$objUser.put("postOfficeBox", $aryText[1])
$objUser.put("l", $aryText[2])
$objUser.put("st", $aryText[3])
$objUser.put("postalCode" , $aryText[4])
$objUser.put("c", $aryText[5])
$objUser.put("co", $aryText[6])
$objUser.put("countryCode", $aryText[7])
$objUser.Put("facsimileTelephoneNumber", $aryText[8])
$objUser.Put("info", $aryText[9])
$objUser.setInfo()
```

17. Inside the code block, change the create method in the *$objADSI Create* command to delete, as shown here:

```
$objUser = $objADSI.Delete($strCLass, $StrName+$i)
```

18. Save and run your script. You should see the nine users, created earlier, disappear. If this does not happen, compare your script with the OneStepFurtherPt2.ps1 script.

19. This concludes this one step further exercise.

Chapter 7 Quick Reference

To	Do This
Delete users in an easy fashion	Modify the script you used to create the user, and change the Create method to Delete.
Commit changes to Active Directory when deleting a user	Nothing special is required. Changes take place when deleted.
Find country codes used in Active Directory and Computers	Use ISO 3166
Modify a users first name via ADSI	Add a value to the GivenName attribute. Use the SetInfo() method to write the change to Active Directory. Use the Put method to at least specify the sAMAccountName attribute if using Windows 2000 AD.
Overwrite a field that is already populated in Active Directory	Use the Put method.
Assign a value to a terminal server profile attribute after making a connection into Active Directory	Assign the value to the property. There is no need to use the Put method.
Read a text file and turn it into an array	Use the *Get-Content* cmdlet and specify the path to the file by using the path argument.

Chapter 8
Leveraging the Power of ADO

After completing this chapter, you will be able to:

- Understand the use of ADO in Windows PowerShell scripts
- Connect to Active Directory to perform a search
- Control the way data are returned
- Use compound query filters

Connecting to Active Directory with ADO

In this section, you will learn a special query technique to search Active Directory using ActiveX Data Objects (ADO). The technique is exactly the same technique you will use to search other databases. You will be able to use the results returned by that custom query to perform additional tasks. For example, you could search Active Directory for all users who don't have telephone numbers assigned to them. You could then send that list to the person in charge of maintaining the telephone numbers. Even better, you could modify the search so that it returns the user names and their managers' names. You could then take the list of users with no phone numbers that is returned and send e-mail to the managers to update the phone list in Active Directory. The functionality incorporated in your scripts is primarily limited by your imagination. The following list summarizes uses of the search technology:

- Query Active Directory for a list of computers that meet a given search criterion
- Query Active Directory for a list of users who meet a given search criterion
- Query Active Directory for a list of printers that meet a given search criterion
- Use the data returned from the preceding three queries to perform additional operations

All the scripts mentioned in this chapter can be found in the corresponding scripts folder on the CD.

Just the Steps   **To search Active Directory**

1. Create a connection to Active Directory by using ADO.

2. Use the Open() method of the object to access Active Directory.

3. Create an ADO Command object and assign the ActiveConnection property to the Connection object.

4. Assign the query string to the CommandText property of the Command object.

5. Use the Execute() method to run the query and store the results in a RecordSet object.

6. Read information in the result set using properties of the RecordSet object.

7. Close the connection by using the Close() method of the Connection object.

The script BasicQuery.ps1 (shown later) illustrates how to search Active Directory by using ADO. Keep in mind that BasicQuery.ps1 can be used as a template script to make it easy to perform Active Directory queries using ADO.

The BasicQuery.ps1 script begins with defining the query that will be used. The string is stored in the *$strQuery* variable. When querying Active Directory using ADO, there are two ways the query can be specified. The one used here is called the *Lightweight Directory Access Protocol (LDAP) dialect*. The other means of specifying the query is called the *SQL dialect* and will be explored later in this chapter.

The LDAP dialect string is made up of four parts. Each of the parts is separated by a semicolon. If one part is left out, then the semicolon must still be present. This is actually seen in the BasicQuery.ps1 script because we do not supply a value for the filter portion. This line of code is shown here:

```
$strQuery = "<LDAP://dc=nwtraders,dc=msft>;;name;subtree"
```

Table 8-1 illustrates the LDAP dialect parts. In the BasicQuery.ps1 script, the filter is left out of the query. The base portion is used to specify the exact point of the connection into Active Directory. Here we are connecting to the root of the NwTraders.msft domain. We could connect to an organizational unit (OU) called MyTestOU by using the distinguished name, as shown here:

```
ou=myTestOU,dc=nwtraders,dc=msft
```

Table 8-1   LDAP Dialect Query Syntax

Base	Filter	Attributes	Search Scope
<LDAP://dc=nwtraders,dc=msft>	(objectCategory=computer)	name	subtree

When we create the filter portion of the LDAP dialect query, we specify the attribute name on the left and the value for the attribute we are looking for on the right. If I were looking for every object that had a location of Atlanta, then the filter would look like the one shown here:

```
(l=Atlanta)
```

The attribute portion of the LDAP query is a simple list of attributes you are looking for, each separated by a comma. If after you had found objects in Atlanta, you wanted to know the name and category of the objects, your attribute list would look like the following:

```
Name, objectCategory
```

The search scope is the last portion of the LDAP dialect query. There are three possible values for the search scope. The first is base. If we specify the search scope as base, then it will only return the single that was the target of the query, that is, the base portion of the query. Using base is valuable if you want to determine whether an object is present in active directory.

The second allowable value for the search scope is oneLevel. When you use the search scope of oneLevel, it will return the Child objects of the base of your query. It does not, however, perform a recursive query. If your base is an OU, then it will list the items contained in the OU. But it will not go into any child OUs and list their members. This is an effective query technique and should be considered standard practice.

The last allowable value for the search scope is subtree. Subtree begins at the base of your query and then recurses into everything under the base of your query. It is sometimes referred to in the Platform Software Development Kit (SDK) as the deep search option because it will dig deeply into all sublevels of your Active Directory hierarchy. If you target the domain root, then it will go into every OU under the domain root, and then into the child OUs, and so forth. This should be done with great care because it can generate a great deal of network traffic and a great deal of workload on the server. If you do need to perform such a query, then you should perform the query asynchronously, and use paging to break the result set into smaller chunks. This will level out the network utilization. In addition, you should try to include one attribute that is indexed. If the attributes you are interested in are replicated to the Global Catalog (GC), then you should query the GC instead of connecting to rootDSE (DSA-specific entry). These techniques will all be examined in this chapter.

After the query is defined, we need to create two objects. We will use the *New-Object* cmdlet to create these objects. The first object to create is the ADODB.Connection object. The line of code used to create the Connection object is shown here:

```
$objConnection = New-Object -comObject "ADODB.Connection"
```

This object is a com object and is contained in the variable *$objConnection*. The second object that is needed is the ADODB.Command object. The code to create the Command object is shown here:

```
objCommand = New-Object -comObject "ADODB.Command"
```

After the two objects are created, we need to open the connection into Active Directory. To open the connection, we use the Open method from the ADODB.Connection object. When we call the Open method, we need to specify the name of the provider that knows how to read the Active Directory database. For this, we will use the ADsDSOObject provider. This line of code is shown here:

```
$objConnection.Open("Provider=ADsDSOObject;")
```

After the connection into the Active Directory database has been opened, we need to associate the Command object with the Connection object. To do this, we use the ActiveConnection property of the Command object. The line of code that does this is shown here:

```
$objCommand.ActiveConnection = $objConnection
```

Now that we have an active connection into Active Directory, we can go ahead and assign the query to the command text of the Command object. To do this, we use the CommandText property of the Command object. In the BasicQuery.ps1 script, we use the following line of code to do this:

```
$objCommand.CommandText = $strQuery
```

After everything is lined up, we call the Execute method of the Command object. The Execute method will return a RecordSet object, which is stored in the *$objRecordSet* variable. This line of code is shown here:

```
$objRecordSet = $objCommand.Execute()
```

To examine individual records from the RecordSet object, we use the *do ... until* statement to walk through the collection. The script block of the *do ... until* statement is used to retrieve the Name property from the RecordSet object. To retrieve the specific property, we retrieve the Fields.Item property and specify the property we retrieved from the attributes portion of the query. We then pipeline the resulting object into the *Select-Object* cmdlet and choose both the name and the Value property. This line of code is shown here:

```
$objRecordSet.Fields.item("name") |Select-Object Name,Value
```

To move to the next record in the recordset, we need to use the MoveNext method from the RecordSet object. This line of code is shown here:

```
$objRecordSet.MoveNext()
```

The complete BasicQuery.ps1 script is shown here:

BasicQuery.ps1

```
$strQuery = "<LDAP://dc=nwtraders,dc=msft>;;name;subtree"

$objConnection = New-Object -comObject "ADODB.Connection"
$objCommand = New-Object -comObject "ADODB.Command"
$objConnection.Open("Provider=ADsDSOObject;")
$objCommand.ActiveConnection = $objConnection
$objCommand.CommandText = $strQuery
```

```
$objRecordSet = $objCommand.Execute()

Do
{
    $objRecordSet.Fields.item("name") |Select-Object Name,Value
    $objRecordSet.MoveNext()
}
Until ($objRecordSet.eof)

$objConnection.Close()
```

> ### Quick Check
>
> **Q. What technology is utilized to search Active Directory?**
>
> A. DO is the technology that is used to search Active Directory.
>
> **Q. Which part of the script is used to perform the query?**
>
> A. The command portion of the script is used to perform the query.
>
> **Q. How are results returned from an ADO search of Active Directory?**
>
> A. The results are returned in a recordset.

Creating More Effective Queries

The BasicQuery.ps1 script is a fairly wasteful script in that all it does is produce a list of user names and print them out. Although the script illustrates the basics of making a connection into Active Directory by using ADO, it is not exactly a paradigm of efficiency. ADO, however, is a very powerful technology, and there are many pieces of the puzzle we can use to make the script more efficient and more effective. The first thing we need to do is to understand the objects we have that we can use with ADO. These objects are listed in Table 8-2.

Table 8-2   Objects Used to Search Active Directory

Object	Description
Connection	An open connection to an OLE DB data source such as ADSI
Command	Defines a specific command to execute against the data source
Parameter	An optional collection for any parameters to provide to the Command object
RecordSet	A set of records from a table, a Command object, or SQL syntax A RecordSet object can be created without any underlying Connection object
Field	A single column of data in a recordset
Property	A collection of values supplied by the provider for ADO
Error	Contains details about data access errors. Refreshed when an error occurs in a single operation

When we use ADO to talk to Active Directory, we often are working with three different objects: the Connection object, the Command object, and the RecordSet object. The Command object is used to maintain the connection, pass along the query parameters, and perform such tasks as specifying the page size and search scope and executing the query. The Connection object is used to load the provider and to validate the user's credentials. By default, it utilizes the credentials of the currently logged-on user. If you need to specify alternative credentials, you can use the properties listed in Table 8-3. To do this, we need to use the Properties property of the Connection object. After we have the Connection object, and we use Properties to get to the properties, we then need to use Item to supply value for the specific property item we want to work with.

Table 8-3   Authentication Properties for the Connection Object

Property	Description
User ID	A string that identifies the user whose security context is used when performing the search. (For more information about the format of the user name string, see IADsOpenDSObject::OpenDSObject in the Platform SDK.) If the value is not specified, the default is the logged-on user or the user impersonated by the calling process.
Password	A string that specifies the password of the user identified by "User ID"
Encrypt Password	A Boolean value that specifies whether the password is encrypted. The default is False.
ADSI Flag	A set of flags from the ADS_AUTHENTICATION_ENUM enumeration. The flag specifies the binding authentication options. The default is zero.

Using Alternative Credentials

As network administration becomes more granular, with multiple domains, work groups, OUs, and similar grouping techniques, it becomes less common for everyone on the IT team to be a member of the Domain Admins group. If the script does not impersonate a user who is a member of the Domain Admins group, then it is quite likely it will need to derive permissions from some other source. One method to do this is to supply alternative credentials in the script. To do this, we need to specify certain properties of the Connection object.

Just the Steps   **To create a connection in Active Directory using alternative credentials**

1. Create the ADODB.Connection object
2. Use the Provider property to specify the ADsDSOObject provider
3. Use Item to supply a value for the properties "User ID" and "Password"
4. Open the connection while supplying a value for the name of the connection

The technique outlined in the using alternative credentials step-by-step exercise is shown here. This code is from the QueryComputersUseCredentials.ps1 script, which is developed in the querying active directory using alternative credentials procedure.

```
$objConnection = New-Object -comObject "ADODB.Connection"
$objConnection.provider = "ADsDSOObject"
$objConnection.properties.item("user ID") = $strUser
$objConnection.properties.item("Password") = $strPwd
$objConnection.open("modifiedConnection")
```

Querying Active Directory using alternative credentials

1. Open the QueryComputers.ps1 script in Notepad or in your favorite Windows Power-Shell script editor and save it as *yourname*QueryComputersUseCredentials.ps1.

2. On the first noncommented line, define a new variable called *$strBase*, and use it to assign the LDAP connection string. This variable is used to define the base of the query into Active Directory. For this example, we will connect to the root of the NwTraders.msft domain. To do this, the string is enclosed in angle brackets and begins with the moniker LDAP. The base string is shown here:

   ```
   "<LDAP://dc=nwtraders,dc=msft>"
   ```

   The new line of code is shown here:

   ```
   $strBase = "<LDAP://dc=nwtraders,dc=msft>"
   ```

3. Create a new variable called *$strFilter*. This will be used to hold the filter portion of our LDAP syntax query. Assign a string that specifies the objectCategory attribute when it is equal to the value of computer. This is shown here:

   ```
   $strFilter = "(objectCategory=computer)"
   ```

4. Create a new variable called *$strAttributes* and assign the string of name to it. This variable will be used to hold the attributes to search on in Active Directory. This line of code is shown here:

   ```
   $strAttributes = "name"
   ```

5. Create a variable called *$strScope*. This variable will be used to hold the search scope parameter of our LDAP syntax query. Assign the value of subtree to it. This line of code is shown here:

   ```
   $strScope = "subtree"
   ```

6. Modify the *$strQuery* line of code so that it uses the four variables we created:

   ```
   $strQuery = "<LDAP://dc=nwtraders,dc=msft>;;name;subtree"
   ```

   The advantage of this is that each of the four parameters that are specified for the LDAP syntax query can easily be modified by simply changing the value of the variable. This preserves the integrity of the worker section of the script. The order of the four parameters is base, filter, attributes, and scope. Thus, the revised value to assign to the *$strQuery* variable is shown here:

```
$strQuery = "$strBase;$strFilter;$strAttributes;$strScope"
```

7. Create a new variable called *$strUser* and assign the string "LondonAdmin" to it. This is the name of the useraccount to use to make the connection to Active Directory. This line of code is shown here:

```
$strUser = "LondonAdmin"
```

8. Create a new variable called *$strPassword* and assign the string Password1 to it. This is the password that will be used when connecting into the NwTraders.msft domain by using the LondonAdmin account. This is shown here:

```
$strPwd = "Password1"
```

9. Between *the $objConnection = New-Object -comObject "ADODB.Connection"* command and the *$objCommand = New-Object -comObject "ADODB.Command"* command, insert four blank lines. This space will be used for rearranging the code and for inserting new properties on the Connection object. The revised code is shown here:

```
$objConnection = New-Object -comObject "ADODB.Connection"




$objCommand = New-Object -comObject "ADODB.Command"
```

10. Move the $objConnection.provider = "ADsDSOObject;" line of code from its position below the $objCommand = New-Object −comObject "ADODB.Command" line of code to below the line of code that creates the Connection object. After you have the code moved, remove the trailing semicolon because it is not needed. This revised code is shown here:

```
$objConnection = New-Object -comObject "ADODB.Connection"
$objConnection.provider = "ADsDSOObject"
```

11. Use the Item method of the properties collection of the Connection object to assign the value contained in the *$strUser* variable to the "User ID" property. This line of code is shown here:

```
$objConnection.properties.item("user ID") = $strUser
```

12. Use the Item method of the properties collection of the Connection object to assign the value contained in the *$strPassword* variable to the "Password" property. This line of code is shown here:

```
$objConnection.properties.item("Password") = $strPwd
```

13. The last line of code we need to modify from the old script is the $objConnection.Open("Provider=ADsDSOObject;") line. Because we needed to move the provider string up earlier in the code to enable us to modify the properties, we have already

specified the provider. So, now we only need to open the connection. When we open the connection, we give it a name "modifiedConnection" that we would be able to use later on in the script if we so desired. The revised line of code is shown here:

```
$objConnection.open("modifiedConnection")
```

14. Save and run your script. If it does not perform as expected, compare it with the Query-ComputersUseCredentials.ps1 script.

15. This concludes the querying Active Directory using alternative credentials procedure.

Modifying Search Parameters

A number of search options are available to the network administrator. The use of these search options will have an extremely large impact on the performance of your queries against Active Directory. It is imperative, therefore, that you learn to use the following options. Obviously, not all options need to be specified in each situation. In fact, in many situations, the defaults will perform just fine. However, if a query is taking a long time to complete, or you seem to be flooding the network with unexpected traffic, you might want to take a look at the Search properties in Table 8-4.

Table 8-4   ADO Search Properties for Command Object

Property	Description
Asynchronous	A Boolean value that specifies whether the search is synchronous or asynchronous. The default is False (synchronous). A synchronous search blocks until the server returns the entire result (or for a paged search, the entire page). An asynchronous search blocks until one row of the search results is available, or until the time specified by the Timeout property elapses.
Cache Results	A Boolean value that specifies whether the result should be cached on the client side. The default is True; ADSI caches the resultset. Turning off this option might be desirable for large resultsets.
Chase Referrals	A value from ADS CHASE_REFERRALS_ENUM that specifies how the search chases referrals. The default is ADS_CHASE_REFERRALS EXTERNAL = 0x40. To set ADS_CHASE_REFERRALS_NEVER, set to 0.
Column Names Only	A Boolean value that indicates that the search should retrieve only the name of attributes to which values have been assigned. The default is False.
Deref (dereference) Aliases	A Boolean value that specifies whether aliases of found objects are resolved. The default is False.
PageSize	An integer value that turns on paging and specifies the maximum number of objects to return in a resultset. The default is no page size, which means that after 1000 items have been delivered from Active Directory, that is it. To turn on paging, you must supply a value for page size, and it must be less than the SizeLimit property. (For more information, see PageSize in the Platform SDK, which is available online from *http://msdn2.microsoft.com/*.)

Table 8-4 ADO Search Properties for Command Object

Property	Description
SearchScope	A value from the ADS_SCOPEENUM enumeration that specifies the search scope. The default is ADS_SCOPE_SUBTREE.
SizeLimit	An integer value that specifies the size limit for the search. For Active Directory, the size limit specifies the maximum number of returned objects. The server stops searching once the size limit is reached and returns the results accumulated up to that point. The default is No Limit.
Sort on	A string that specifies a comma-separated list of attributes to use as sort keys. This property works only for directory servers that support the LDAP control for server-side sorting. Active Directory supports the sort control, but this control can affect server performance, particularly when the resultset is large. Be aware that Active Directory supports only a single sort key. The default is No Sorting.
TimeLimit	An integer value that specifies the time limit, in seconds, for the search. When the time limit is reached, the server stops searching and returns the results accumulated to that point. The default is No Time Limit.
Timeout	An integer value that specifies the client-side timeout value, in seconds. This value indicates the time the client waits for results from the server before quitting the search. The default is No Timeout.

In the previous section, when we used alternative credentials in the script, we specified various properties on the Connection object. We will use the same type of procedure to modify search parameters, but this time we will specify values for various properties on the Command object. As an example, suppose we wanted to perform an asynchronous query of Active Directory. We would need to supply a value of true for the asynchronous property. The technique is exactly the same as supplying alternative credentials: create the object, and use the Item method to specify a value for the appropriate property. This piece of code, taken from the AsynchronousQueryComputers.ps1 script, is shown here:

```
$objCommand = New-Object -comObject "ADODB.Command"
$objCommand.ActiveConnection = $objConnection
$objCommand.Properties.item("Asynchronous") = $blnTrue
```

Important When specifying properties for the Command object, ensure you have the active-Connection associated with a valid Connection object before making the assignment. Otherwise, you will get an error stating the property is not valid—which can be very misleading.

Note that you should specify a page size. In Windows Server 2003, Active Directory is limited to returning 1000 objects from the results of a query when no page size is specified. The PageSize property tells Active Directory how many objects to return at a time. When this property is specified, there is no limit on the number of returned objects Active Directory can provide. If you specify a size limit, the page size must be smaller. The exception would be if you want an unlimited size limit of 0, then obviously the PageSize property would be larger than the value of 0. In the SizeLimitQueryUsers.ps1 script, after creating a Command object, associating the connection with the activeConnection property, we use the Item method of the properties collection to specify a size limit of 4. When the script is run, it only returns four users. The applicable portion of the code is shown here:

```
$objCommand = New-Object -comObject "ADODB.Command"
$objCommand.ActiveConnection = $objConnection
$objCommand.Properties.item("Size Limit") = 4
```

Controlling script execution

1. Open the QueryComputersUseCredentials.ps1 script, and save it as *yourname*QueryTimeOut.ps1.

2. Edit the query filter contained in the string that is assigned to the variable *$strFilter* so that the filter will return items when the ObjectCategory is equal to User. The revised line of code is shown here:

    ```
    $strFilter = "(objectCategory=User)"
    ```

3. Delete the line that creates the *$strUser* variable and assigns the LondonAdmin User to it.

4. Delete the line that creates the *$strPwd* variable and assigns the string Password1 to it.

5. Delete the two lines of code that assign the value contained in the *$strUser* variable to the User ID property, and the one that assigns the value contained in the *$strPwd* variable to the Password property of the Connection object. These two lines of code are shown commented-out here:

    ```
    #$objConnection.properties.item("user ID") = $strUser
    #$objConnection.properties.item("Password") = $strPwd
    ```

6. Inside the parentheses of the Open command that opens the Connection object to Active Directory, delete the Reference string that is contained inside it. We are able to delete this string because we did not use it to refer to the connection later in the script. The modified line of code is shown here:

    ```
    $objConnection.open()
    ```

7. Under the line of code that assigns the Connection object that is contained in the *$obj-Connection* variable to the ActiveConnection property of the Command object, we want to add the value of 1 to the TimeLimit property of the Command object. To do this, use the property name TimeLimit, and use the Item method to assign it to the properties collection of the Command object. The line of code that does this is shown here:

    ```
    $objCommand.properties.item("Time Limit")=1
    ```

8. Save and run your script. If it does not produce the desired results, compare it with QueryTimeOut.ps1.

9. This concludes the controlling script execution procedure.

Searching for Specific Types of Objects

One of the best ways to improve the performance of Active Directory searches is to limit the scope of the search operation. Fortunately, searching for a specific type of object is one of the easiest tasks to perform. For example, to perform a task on a group of computers, limit your search to the computer class of objects. To work with only groups, users, computers, or printers, specify the objectClass or the objectCategory attribute in the search filter. The objectCategory attribute is a single value that specifies the class from which the object in Active Directory is derived. In other words, users are derived from an objectCategory called *users*. All the properties you looked at in Chapter 7, "Working with Active Directory," when we were creating objects in Active Directory are contained in a template called an *objectCategory*. When you create a new user, Active Directory does a lookup to find out what properties the user class contains. Then it copies all those properties onto the new user you just created. In this way, all users have the same properties available to them.

> **Just the Steps   To limit the Active Directory search**
>
> 1. Create a connection to Active Directory by using ADO.
> 2. Use the Open method of the object to access Active Directory.
> 3. Create an ADO Command object, and assign the ActiveConnection property to the Connection object.
> 4. Assign the query string to the CommandText property of the Command object.
> 5. In the query string, specify the objectCategory of the target query.
> 6. Choose specific fields of data to return in response to the query.
> 7. Use the Execute method to run the query and store the results in a RecordSet object.
> 8. Read information in the result set using properties of the RecordSet object.
> 9. Close the connection by using the Close method of the Connection object.

In the QueryComputers.ps1 script, you use ADO to query Active Directory with the goal of returning a recordset containing selected properties from all the computers with accounts in the directory.

To make the script easier to edit, we abstracted each of the four parts of the LDAP dialect query into a separate variable. The *$strBase* variable in the QueryComputers.ps1 script is used to hold the base of the ADO query. The base is used to determine where the script will make its connection into Active Directory. The line of code that does this in the QueryComputers.ps1 script is shown here:

```
$strBase = "<LDAP://dc=nwtraders,dc=msft>"
```

The filter is used to remove the type of objects that are returned by the ADO query. In the QueryComputers.ps1 script, we filter on the value of the objectCategory attribute when it has a value of computer. This line of code is shown here:

```
$strFilter = "(objectCategory=computer)"
```

The attributes to be selected from the query are specified in the $strAttributes variable. In the QueryComputers.ps1 script, we choose only the Name attribute. This line of code is shown here:

```
$strAttributes = "name"
```

The search scope determines how deep the query will go. There are three possible values for this: base, oneLevel, and subtree. Base searches only at the level where the script connects. OneLevel tells ADO to go one level below where the $strbase connection is made. Subtree is probably the most commonly used and tells ADO to make a recursive query through Active Directory. This is the kind of query we do in QueryComputers.ps1. This line of code is shown here:

```
$strScope = "subtree"
```

The $strQuery is used to hold the query used to query from Active Directory. When it is abstracted into variables, it becomes easy to modify. The revised code is shown here:

```
$strQuery = "$strBase;$strFilter;$strAttributes;$strScope"
```

The complete QueryComputers.ps1 is shown here:

QueryComputers.ps1

```
$strBase = "<LDAP://dc=nwtraders,dc=msft>"
$strFilter = "(objectCategory=computer)"
$strAttributes = "name"
$strScope = "subtree"
$strQuery = "$strBase;$strFilter;$strAttributes;$strScope"

$objConnection = New-Object -comObject "ADODB.Connection"
$objCommand = New-Object -comObject "ADODB.Command"
$objConnection.Open("Provider=ADsDSOObject;")
$objCommand.ActiveConnection = $objConnection
$objCommand.CommandText = $strQuery
$objRecordSet = $objCommand.Execute()

Do
{
    $objRecordSet.Fields.item("name") |Select-Object Name,Value
    $objRecordSet.MoveNext()
}
Until ($objRecordSet.eof)

$objConnection.Close()
```

Querying multiple attributes

1. Open Notepad or your favorite Windows PowerShell editor.

2. Open QueryComputers.ps1, and save it as *yourname*QueryComputersByName.ps1.

3. Edit the $strFilter line so that it includes the additional attribute name. To do this using the LDAP dialect, we will need to first add an extra set of parentheses around the entire filter expression. This is shown here:

```
$strFilter = "((objectCategory=computer))"
```

4. Between the first set of double parentheses, we will add the ampersand character (&), which will tell the LDAP dialect search filter we want both of the attributes we are getting ready to supply. This is shown here:

```
$strFilter = "(&(objectCategory=computer))"
```

5. At end of the first search filter expression, we want to add a second expression. We want to search by both Computer Type objects and usernames. This modified line of code is shown here:

```
$strFilter = "(&(objectCategory=computer)(name=london))"
```

6. Save and run your script. It should produce a script output that lists all computer accounts named London.

7. This concludes the querying multiple attributes procedure.

What Is Global Catalog?

As you become more proficient in writing your scripts, and as you begin to work your magic on the enterprise on a global scale, you will begin to wonder why some queries seem to take forever and others run rather fast. After configuring some of the parameters you looked at earlier, you might begin to wonder whether you're hitting a Global Catalog (GC) server. A *Global Catalog server* is a server that contains all the objects and their associated attributes from your local domain. If all you have is a single domain, it doesn't matter whether you're connecting to a domain controller or a GC server because the information will be the same. If, however, you are in a multiple domain forest, you might very well be interested in which GC server you are hitting. Depending on your network topology, you could be executing a query that is going across a slow WAN link. You can control replication of attributes by selecting the Global Catalog check box. You can find this option by opening the Active Directory Schema MMC, highlighting the Attributes container. The Active Directory Schema MMC is not available by default in the Administrative Tools program group. For information on how to install it, visit the following URL: *http://technet2.microsoft.com/ WindowsServer/en/library/2218144f-bb92-454e-9334-186ee7c740c61033.mspx?mfr=true.*

In addition to controlling the replication of attributes, the erstwhile administrator might also investigate attribute indexing (Fig. 8-1.) Active Directory already has indexes built on certain objects. However, if an attribute is heavily searched on, you might consider an additional index. You should do this, however, with caution because an improperly placed index is worse than no index at all. The reason for this is the time spent building and maintaining an index. Both of these operations use processor time and disk I/O.

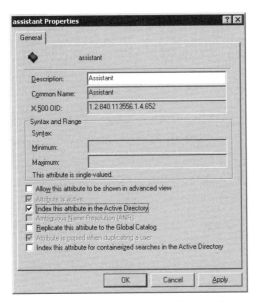

Figure 8-1   Heavily queried attributes often benefit from indexing

Querying a global catalog server

1. Open the BasicQuery.ps1 script in Notepad or another Windows PowerShell editor and save the file as *yourname*QueryGC.ps1

2. On the first noncommented line of your script, declare a variable called *$strBase*. This variable will be used to control the connection into the global catalog server in Active Directory. To do this, instead of using the LDAP moniker, we will use the GC moniker. The rest of the path will be the same because it uses the Distinguished Name of target. For this procedure, let's connect to the OU called MyTestOU in the NwTraders.msft domain. The line of code to do this is shown here:

    ```
    $strBase = <GC://ou=MyTestOU,dc=nwtraders,dc=msft>
    ```

3. On the next line, create a variable called *$strFilter*. This variable will be used to hold the filter portion of the query. The filter will be used to return only objects from Active Directory that have the objectCategory attribute set to User. The line of code that does this is shown here:

    ```
    $strFilter = "(objectCategory=user)"
    ```

4. Create a variable called *$strAttributes* that will be used to hold the attributes to retrieve from Active Directory. For this script, we are only interested in the Name attribute. The line of code that does this is shown here:

```
$strAttributes = "name"
```

5. Create a variable called *$strScope*. This variable will hold the string oneLevel that is used to tell Active Directory that we want the script to obtain a list of the users in the MyTestOU only. We do not need to perform a recursive type of query. This line of code is shown here:

```
$strScope = "oneLevel"
```

6. Modify the *$strQuery* line so that it uses the four variables we defined for each of the four parts of the LDAP dialect query. The four variables are *$strBase, $strFilter, $strAttributes,* and *$strScope* in this order. Make sure you use a semicolon to separate the four parts from one another. Move the completed line of code to the line immediately beneath the $strScope-"oneLevel" line. The completed line of code is shown here:

```
$strQuery = "$strBase;$strFilter;$strAttributes;$strScope"
```

7. Save and run your script. It should run without errors. If it does not produce the expected results, compare your script with the QueryGC.ps1 script.

8. This concludes the querying a global catalog server procedure.

Querying a specific server

1. Open the QueryGC.ps1 script in Notepad or your favorite Windows PowerShell script editor, and save the script as *yourname*QuerySpecificServer.ps1.

2. Edit the string assigned to the *$strBase* variable so that you use the LDAP moniker instead of the GC moniker. After the ://, type the name of the server. Do not use CN=, as would normally be used for the Distinguished Name attribute. Instead, just type the name of the server followed by a forward slash (\). The completed line of code is shown here:

```
$strBase = "<LDAP://London/ou=MyTestOU,dc=nwtraders,dc=msft>"
```

3. Save and run your script. If your script does not work properly, compare it with the QuerySpecificServer.ps1 script.

4. This concludes the querying a specific server procedure.

Querying a specific server by IP address

1. Open the QuerySpecificServer.ps1 script in Notepad or your favorite Windows Power-Shell script editor and save it as *yourname*QuerySpecificServerByIP.ps1.

2. Edit the string that is assigned to the *$strBase* variable so that you are supplying the LDAP moniker with an IP address instead of a Host name. The revised line of code is shown here:

```
$strBase = "<LDAP://192.168.1.1/ou=MyTestOU,dc=nwtraders,dc=msft>"
```

3. Save and run your script. If your script does not run properly, compare it with the QuerySpecificServerByIP.ps1 script.

4. This concludes the querying a specific server by IP address procedure.

Using the base search scope

1. Open the QuerySpecificServer.ps1 script in Notepad, or some other Windows Power-Shell script editor. Save the script as *yourname*SearchBase.ps1.

2. Change the $strScope line so that it will point to base instead of oneLevel. This revised line of code is shown here:

```
$strScope = "base"
```

3. Because a base query connects to a specific object, there is no point in having a filter. Delete the $strFilter line, and remove the *$strFilter* variable from the second position of the *$strQuery* string that is used for the LDAP dialect query. The revised $strQuery line of code is shown here:

```
$strQuery = "$strBase;;$strAttributes;$strScope"
```

4. Because the base query will only return a single object, it does not make sense to perform a *do ... until* loop. Delete the line that has the opening *Do*, and delete the line with the *Until ($objRecordSet.eof)*.

5. Delete the opening and the closing curly brackets. Delete the *$objRecordSet.MoveNext()* command because there are no more records to move to.

6. Go to the *$strAttributes* variable and modify it so that we retrieve both the objectCategory and the Name attributes. The revised line of code is shown here:

```
$strAttributes = "objectCategory,name"
```

7. Copy the $objRecordSet.Fields.item("name") |Select-Object value line of code, and paste it just below the first one. Edit the first $objRecordSet.Fields.item line of code so that it will retrieve the objectCategory attribute from the recordset. The two lines of code are shown here:

```
$objRecordSet.Fields.item("objectCategory") |Select-Object value
$objRecordSet.Fields.item("name") |Select-Object value
```

8. Save and run your script. If it does not perform correctly, compare it with the Search Base.ps1 script.

9. This concludes the using the base search scope procedure.

Using the SQL Dialect to Query Active Directory

For many network professionals, the rather cryptic way of expressing the query into Active Directory is at once confusing and irritating. Because of this confusion, we also have an SQL dialect we can use to query Active Directory. The parts that make up an SQL dialect query are listed in Table 8-5. Of the four parts that can make up an SQL dialect query, only two parts are required: the *Select* statement and the *from* keyword that indicates the base for the search. An example of this use is shown here. A complete script that uses this type of query is the Select-NameSQL.ps1 script.

```
Select name from 'LDAP://ou=MyTestOu,dc=nwtraders,dc=msft'
```

Table 8-5   SQL Dialect

Select	From	Where	Order by
Comma separated list of attributes	AdsPath for the base of the search enclosed in single quotation marks	Optional Used for the filter	Optional. Used for server side sort control. A comma separated list of attributes

The *Where* statement is used to specify the filter for the Active Directory query. This is similar to the filter used in the LDAP dialect queries. The basic syntax of the filter is attributeName = value. But as in any SQL query, we are free to use various operators, as well as *and*, or *or*, and even wild cards. An example of a query using *Where* is shown here (keep in mind this is a single line of code that was wrapped for readability). A complete script that uses this type of query is the QueryComputersSQL.ps1 script.

```
Select name from 'LDAP://ou=MyTestOu,dc=nwtraders,dc=msft'where
objectCategory='computer'
```

The order by clause is the fourth part of the SQL dialect query. Just like the *Where* clause, it is also optional. In addition to selecting the property to order by, you can also specify two keywords: *ASC* for ascending and *DESC* for descending. An example of using the order by clause is shown here. A complete script using this query is the QueryUsersSQL.ps1 script.

```
Select adsPath, cn from 'LDAP://dc=nwtraders,dc=msft' where
objectCategory='user'order by sn DESC
```

The SQLDialectQuery.ps1 script is different from the BasicQuery.ps1 script only in the dialect used for the query language. The script still creates both a Connection object and a Command object, and works with a RecordSet object in the output portion of the script. In the SQLDialectQuery.ps1 script, we hold the SQL dialect query in three different variables. The *$strAttributes* variable holds the select portion of the script. *$strBase* is used to hold the AdsPath attribute, which contains the complete path to the target of operation. The last variable used in holding the query is the *$strFilter* variable, which holds the filter portion of the query. Using these different variables makes the script easier to modify and easier to read. The *$strQuery* variable is used to hold the entire SQL dialect query. If you are curious to see the query put together in its entirety, you can simply print out the value of the variable by adding the $strQuery line under the line where the query is put back together.

SQLDialectQuery.ps1

```
$strAttributes = "Select name from "
$strBase = "'LDAP://ou=MyTestOu,dc=nwtraders,dc=msft'"
$strFilter = " where objectCategory='computer'"
$strQuery = "$strAttributes$strBase$strFilter"

$objConnection = New-Object -comObject "ADODB.Connection"
$objCommand = New-Object -comObject "ADODB.Command"
$objConnection.Open("Provider=ADsDSOObject;")
$objCommand.ActiveConnection = $objConnection
$objCommand.CommandText = $strQuery
$objRecordSet = $objCommand.Execute()

Do
{
    $objRecordSet.Fields.item("name") |Select-Object Name,Value
    $objRecordSet.MoveNext()
}
Until ($objRecordSet.eof)

$objConnection.Close()
```

Creating an ADO Query into Active Directory: Step-by-Step Exercises

In this exercise, we will explore the use of various queries against Active Directory. We will use both simple and compound query filters as we return data, beginning with the generic and moving on to the more specific.

1. Launch the CreateMultipleUsers.ps1 script from the scripts folder for this chapter. This script will create 60 users with city locations from three different cities, and four different departments. We will use the different users and departments and cities in our Active Directory queries. By default, the script will create the users in the MyTestOU in the NwTraders.msft domain. If your Active Directory configuration is different, then edit the Active Directory Service Interfaces (ADSI) connection string shown here. If you are unsure of how to do this, refer back to Chapter 7, "Working with Active Directory."

   ```
   $objADSI = [ADSI]"LDAP://ou=myTestOU,dc=nwtraders,dc=msft"
   ```

2. Open Notepad or another Windows PowerShell script editor.

3. On the first line, declare a variable called *$strBase*. This variable will be used to hold the base for our LDAP syntax query into Active Directory. The string will use angle brackets at the beginning and the end of the string. We will be connecting to the MyTestOU in the NwTraders.msft domain. The line of code that does this is shown here:

   ```
   $strBase = "<LDAP://ou=mytestOU,dc=nwtraders,dc=msft>"
   ```

4. On the next line, declare a variable called *$strFilter*. This variable will hold the string that will be used for the query filter. It will filter out every object that is not a User object. The line of code that does this is shown here:

    ```
    $strFilter = "(objectCategory=User)"
    ```

5. Create a variable called *$strAttributes*. This variable will hold the attribute we wish to retrieve from Active Directory. For this lab, we only want the name of the object. This line of code is shown here:

    ```
    $strAttributes = "name"
    ```

6. On the next line, we need to declare a variable called *$strScope* that will hold the search scope parameter. For this exercise, we will use the subtree parameter. This line of code is shown here:

    ```
    $strScope = "subtree"
    ```

7. On the next line, we put the four variables together to form our query string for the ADO query into Active Directory. Hold the completed string in a variable called *$strQuery*. Inside quotes, separate each of the four variables by a semicolon, which is used by the LDAP dialect to distinguish the four parts of the LDAP dialect query. The line of code to do this is shown here:

    ```
    $strQuery = "$strBase;$strFilter;$strAttributes;$strScope"
    ```

8. Create a variable called *$objConnection*. The *$objConnection* variable will be used to hold an ADODB.Connection COM object. To create the object, use the *New-Object* cmdlet. This line of code is shown here:

    ```
    $objConnection = New-Object -comObject "ADODB.Connection"
    ```

9. Create a variable called *$objCommand* that will be used to hold a new instance of the COM object "ADODB.Command". The code to do this is shown here:

    ```
    $objCommand = New-Object -comObject "ADODB.Command"
    ```

10. Open the Connection object by calling the Open method. Supply the name of the provider to use while opening the connection. For this lab, we will use the AdsDSOObject provider. The line of code that does is shown here:

    ```
    $objConnection.Open("Provider=ADsDSOObject")
    ```

11. Now we need to associate the Connection object we just opened with the ActiveConnection property of the Command object. To do this, simply supply the Connection object contained in the *$objConnection* variable to the ActiveConnection property of the Command object. The code that does this is shown here:

    ```
    $objCommand.ActiveConnection = $objConnection
    ```

12. Now we need to supply the text for the Command object. To do this, we will use the query contained in the variable *$strQuery* and assign it to the CommandText property of the Command object held in the *$objCommand* variable. The code that does this is shown here:

```
$objCommand.CommandText = $strQuery
```

13. It is time to execute the query. To do this, call the Execute method of the Command object. It will return a RecordSet object, so use the variable *$objRecordSet* to hold the RecordSet object that comes back from the query.

```
$objRecordSet = $objCommand.Execute()
```

14. Use a *do ... until* statement to walk through the recordset until you reach the end of file. While you are typing this, go ahead and open and close the curly brackets. This will take four lines of code, which are shown here:

```
Do
{


}
Until ($objRecordSet.eof)
```

15. Inside the curly brackets, retrieve the Name attribute from the recordset by using the Item method from the Fields property. Pipeline the resulting object into a *Select-Object* cmdlet and retrieve only the value property. This line of code is shown here:

```
$objRecordSet.Fields.item("name") |Select-Object Value
```

16. Call the MoveNext method to move to the next record in the RecordSet object contained in the *$objRecordSet* variable. This line of code is shown here:

```
$objRecordSet.MoveNext()
```

17. After the until ($objRecordSet.eof) line of code, call the Close method from the RecordSet object to close the connection into Active Directory. This line of code is shown here:

```
$objConnection.Close()
```

18. Save your script as *yourname*QueryUsersStepByStep.ps1. Run your script. You should see the name of 60 users come scrolling forth from the Windows PowerShell console. If this is not the case, compare your script with the QueryUsersStepByStep.ps1 script. Note, in the QueryUsersStepByStep.ps1 script, there are five $strFilter lines ... only one that is not commented out. This is so you will have documentation on the next steps. When this code is working, it is time to move on to a few more steps.

19. Now we want to modify the filter so that it will only return users who are in the Charlotte location. To do this, copy the $strFilter line and paste it below the current line of code. Now, comment out the original $strFilter. We now want to use a compound query: objects in Active Directory that are of the category user, and a location attribute of Charlotte. From Chapter 7, you may recall the attribute for location is l. To make a compound

query, enter the search parameter inside parentheses, inside the grouping parentheses, after the first search filter. This modified line of code is shown here:

```
$strFilter = "(&(objectCategory=User)(l=charlotte))"
```

20. Save and run your script. Now, we want to add an additional search parameter. Copy your modified $strFilter line, and paste it beneath the line you just finished working on. Comment out the previous $strFilter line. Just after the location filter of Charlotte, add a filter for only users in Charlotte who are in the HR department. This revised line of code is shown here:

```
$strFilter = "(&(objectCategory=User)(l=charlotte)(department=hr))"
```

21. Save and run your script. Now copy your previous $strFilter line of code, and paste it below the line you just modified. This change is easy. You want all users in Charlotte who are not in HR. To make a not query, place the exclamation mark (bang) operator inside the parentheses you wish the operator to affect. This modified line of code is shown here:

```
$strFilter = "(&(objectCategory=User)(l=charlotte)(!department=hr))"
```

22. Save and run your script. Because this is going so well, let's add one more parameter to our search filter. So, once again copy the $strFilter line of code you just modified, and paste it beneath the line you just finished working on. This time, we want users who are in Charlotte or Dallas and who are not in the HR department. To do this, add a l=dallas filter behind the l=charlotte filter. Put parentheses around the two locations, and then add the pipeline character (|) in front of the l=charlotte parameter. This revised line of code is shown here. Keep in mind that it is wrapped for readability, but should be on one logical line in the script.

```
$strFilter = "(&(objectCategory=User)(|(l=charlotte)(l=dallas))(!department=hr))"
```

23. Save and run your script. In case you were getting a little confused by all the copying and pasting, here are all the *$strFilter* commands you have typed in this section of the step-by-step exercise:

```
$strFilter = "(objectCategory=User)"
#$strFilter = "(&(objectCategory=User)(l=charlotte))"
#$strFilter = "(&(objectCategory=User)(l=charlotte)(department=hr))"
#$strFilter = "(&(objectCategory=User)(l=charlotte)(!department=hr))"
#$strFilter = "(&(objectCategory=User)(|(l=charlotte)(l=dallas))(!department=hr))"
```

24. This concludes this step-by-step exercise.

One Step Further: Controlling How a Script Executes Against Active Directory

In this exercise, we will control the way we return data from Active Directory.

1. To make it easier to keep up the number of users returned from our Active Directory queries, run the DeleteMultipleUsers.ps1 script. This will delete the 60 users we created for the previous step-by-step exercise.

2. Run the Create2000Users.ps1 script. This script will create 2000 users for you to use in the MyTestOU OU.

3. Open the QueryUsersStepbyStep.ps1 script and save it as *yourname*OneStepFurther-QueryUsers.ps1.

4. Because we are not interested in running finely crafted queries in this exercise (rather, we are interested in how to handle large amounts of objects that come back), delete all the *$strFilter* commands except for the one that filters out User objects. This line of code is shown here:

```
$strFilter = "(objectCategory=User)"
```

5. Save and run your script. You will see 1000 user names scroll by in your Windows PowerShell console window. After about 30 seconds (on my machine anyway), you will finally see MyLabUser997 show up. The reason it is MyLabUser997 instead of MyLabUser1000 is that this OU already had three users when we started (myBoss, myDirect1, and myDirect2). This is OK; it is easy to see that the query returned the system default of 1000 objects.

6. We know, however, there are more than 2000 users in the MyTestOU, and we have only been able to retrieve 1000 of them. To get past the query limit that is set for Active Directory, we need to turn on paging. This is simple. We assign a value for the PageSize property to be less than the 1000 object limit. To do this, we use the Item method of the properties collection on the Command object and assign the value of 500 to the PageSize property. This line of code is shown here. Place this code just above this line, which creates the RecordSet object: $objRecordSet = $objCommand.Execute().

```
$objCommand.Properties.item("Page Size") = 500
```

7. After you have made the change, save and run your script. You should see all 2000 user objects show up ... however, the results may be a little jumbled. Without using a *Sort-Object* or specifying the Sort property on the server, the values are not guaranteed to be in order. This script takes about a minute or so on my computer.

8. To tell Active Directory we do not want any size limit, specify the SizeLimit property as 0. We can do this by using the Item method of the properties collection on the Command object. This line of code is shown here:

```
$objCommand.Properties.item("Size Limit") = 0
```

9. To make the script a bit more efficient, change the script to perform an asynchronous query (synchronous being the default). This will reduce the network bandwidth consumed and will even out the processor load on your server. To do this, declare a variable called *$blnTrue* and set it equal to the Boolean type. Assign the value –1 to it. Place this code just under the line that creates the *$strQuery* variable. This line of code is shown here:

```
$blnTrue = [bool]-1
```

10. Under the line of code that sets the size limit, use the Item method of the properties collection to assign the value true to the asynchronous property of the Command object.

Use the Boolean value you created and stored in the *$blnTrue* variable. This line of code is shown here:

```
$objCommand.Properties.item("Asynchronous") = $blnTrue
```

11. Save and run your script. You should see the script run perhaps a little faster because it is doing an asynchronous query. If your script does not run properly, compare your script with the OneStepFurtherQueryUsers.ps1 script.

12. To clean up after this lab, run the Delete2000Users.ps1 script. It will delete the 2000 users we created at the beginning of the exercise.

13. This concludes this one step further exercise.

Chapter 8 Quick Reference

To	Do This
Make an ADO connection into Active Directory	Use the ADsDSOObject provider with ADO to talk to Active Directory
Perform an Active Directory query	Use the Field object to hold attribute data
Tell ADO search to cache results on the client side of the connection	Use the "Cache results" property
Directly query a Global Catalog (GC) server	Use GC:// in your connection moniker, instead of using LDAP://, as shown here: `GC://`
Directly query a specific server in Active Directory	Use LDAP:// in your connection moniker, followed by a trailing backslash (/), as shown here: `LDAP://London/`
Query for multiple attributes in Active Directory using the LDAP dialect	Open a set of parentheses. Inside the set of parentheses, type your attribute name and value for each of the attributes you wish to query. Enclose them in parentheses. At the beginning of the expression between the first two sets of parentheses, use the ampersand (&) operator, as shown here: `(&(objectCategory=computer)(name=london))`
Use server side sorting when using the SQL dialect	Use the order by parameter followed by either the ASC or the DESC keyword, as shown here: `'user'order by sn DESC`
Return more than 1000 objects from an Active Directory ADO query	Turn on paging by specifying the PageSize property on the Command object, and supply a value for Size-Limit property
Connect to Active Directory using alternative credentials	Specify the User ID and Password properties on the Connection object

Chapter 9
Managing Exchange 2007

After completing this chapter, you will be able to:

- Understand the Providers included with Exchange 2007
- Use *Get-Command* to obtain a listing of Exchange 2007 cmdlets
- Configure Exchange 2007 recipient settings
- Configure Exchange 2007 storage settings
- Query, configure, and audit policy

The decision by the Microsoft Exchange Server team to base their management tools on Windows PowerShell is a win for customers who desire to apply the flexibility and config-urability of scripting to the management of complex mission-critical networked applications. What this means for Windows PowerShell scripters is that literally everything that can be done using the Graphical User Interface (GUI) can also be done from Windows PowerShell. In some cases, the only way to perform a certain task is through Windows PowerShell. This is the first time that the design of a major application began with the scripting interface in mind, rather than adding the scripting support after the product was completed. All the scripts mentioned in this chapter can be found in the corresponding scripts folder on the CD.

Exploring the Exchange 2007 Cmdlets

When trying to figure out what you can do with a Windows PowerShell enabled application, first examine the cmdlets that are installed with the application. We take several approaches to this task. The easiest way is to use the new alias *Get-ExCommand*. When you use the *Get-ExCommand* cmdlet, you will notice a listing of nearly 385 cmdlets that have been created by the Microsoft Exchange Server 2007 team. These cmdlets have been organized into the Exchange2007Cmdlets.xls spreadsheet (in the Supplemental Material folder), and are grouped around 25 different verbs. These cmdlets allow you to update, uninstall, test, start, stop, suspend, set, add, remove, and perform other kinds of activities on your Exchange server. The only thing you cannot do using the Exchange Server 2007 cmdlets is to create the user or create the group. You can create a new user in Active Directory at the same time you create the mailbox by using the *New-Mailbox* cmdlet, but you cannot create a user account without creating the mailbox. For scripts that can create users and groups, refer to Chapter 7, "Working with Active Directory."

> **Note**   The commands used in this chapter are in a text file named Chapter9Commands.txt. This file includes all commands shown in this chapter. The 'Exchange Management Shell Quick Reference', which lists the common cmdlets, is available at the following URL: *http://www.microsoft.com/downloads.*

The good thing about the *Get-ExCommand* cmdlet is that you can pipeline it to other cmdlets to assist you in searching for exactly the correct cmdlet for a particular job. If, for example, you were looking for cmdlets related to statistics, you could use the following command to retrieve this information:

```
Get-Excommand | Where-Object {$_.name -match "stat"} |
Format-List name,definition
```

When this command runs, you are greeted with a list of seven cmdlets that provide information about statistics. A sample output from the previous command is shown here. You will notice, the good thing about using *Format-List* to format the command output is that the definition of the cmdlet is not truncated, as it is in the default output.

```
Name        : Get-ActiveSyncDeviceStatistics
Definition : Get-ActiveSyncDeviceStatistics [-Identity] <MobileDeviceIdParamete
             r> [-ShowRecoveryPassword] [-Verbose] [-Debug] [-ErrorAction <Acti
             onPreference>] [-ErrorVariable <String>] [-OutVariable <String>] [
             -OutBuffer <Int32>]
             Get-ActiveSyncDeviceStatistics -Mailbox <MailboxIdParameter> [-Sho
             wRecoveryPassword] [-Verbose] [-Debug] [-ErrorAction <ActionPrefer
             ence>] [-ErrorVariable <String>] [-OutVariable <String>] [-OutBuff
             er <Int32>]
```

Configuring Recipient Settings

The most basic aspect of administering any messaging and collaboration is configuring the vast and varied settings that relate to recipients. First, the user account must be "mailbox enabled," which means we need to create a mailbox on the mailbox database for the user account. To do this, we need to use the *Enable-Mailbox* cmdlet. This is illustrated here:

```
Enable-Mailbox -Identity nwtraders\MyNewUser -Database "mailbox database"
```

When this command is run, you will get a prompt back that is shown here. It tells you the name of the user account, the alias assigned, the server name on which the mailbox database resides, and any quota restrictions applied to the account.

```
Name        Alias       ServerName    ProhibitSendQuota
----        -----       ----------    -----------------
MyNewUser   myNewUser   smbex01       unlimited
```

> **Tip**   You cannot mailbox-enable a user account that is disabled. Although this may seem to make sense, keep in mind that often network administrators will create a group of user accounts, and then leave them all disabled for security reasons. Then, when the user calls into the Help desk, the accounts are enabled. In this case, use a single script that logon-enables the user account and at the same time mailbox-enables the user.

Creating the User and the Mailbox

If you want to create the user and the mailbox at the same time, then you can use the *New-Mailbox* cmdlet. This cmdlet, as you might expect, has a large number of parameters owing to the need to supply values for first name, last name, display name, mailbox name, user principal name (UPN) name, and many other optional parameters. An example of using this cmdlet to create a user named MyTestUser2 is shown here:

```
New-Mailbox -Alias myTestUser2 -Database "mailbox database" `
-Name MyTestUser2 -OrganizationalUnit myTestOU -FirstName My `
-LastName TestUser2 -DisplayName "My TestUser2" `
-UserPrincipalName MyTestUser2@nwtraders.com
```

After you run the cmdlet, you will notice that it prompts for the password. It does this because the password parameter is defined as a secureString datatype. If you try to force the password in the command by hard-coding the password as an argument, such as: -password "P@ssword1", you will get an error that says "cannot convert type string to type secureString." This error is shown in Figure 9-1.

Figure 9-1   You cannot convert a string into a secure string

The solution to the above error is to not supply the password argument. In which case, the command will pause, and Windows PowerShell will prompt for the password for the user account. This behavior is shown here in Figure 9-2.

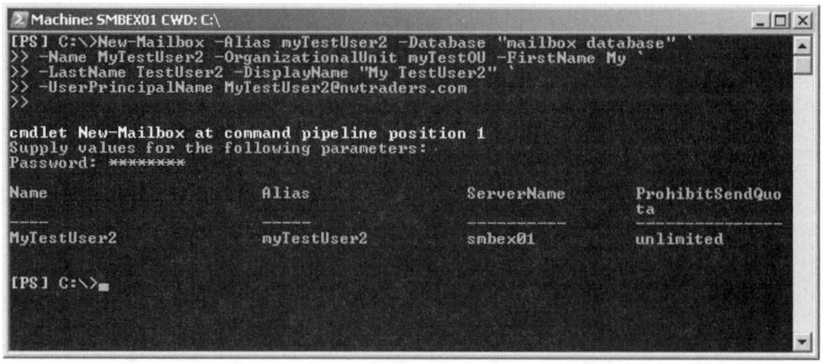

Figure 9-2   The New-Mailbox cmdlet prompts for the password

If we put the command in a script, then it will be easier to create the user, the mailbox, and the password. To do this, we use the *ConvertTo-SecureString* cmdlet to convert a plain text string into an encrypted password that will be acceptable to Exchange 2007. *ConvertTo-SecureString* has two arguments that will enable us to do this; the first argument is the asPlainText argument. This tells the *ConvertTo-SecureString* cmdlet we are supplying a plain text string for it to convert. Because this is not a normal operation, we must also supply the force argument. After we have a secureString for the password, we can supply it to the password argument. This is illustrated in the NewMailboxAndUser.ps1 script.

NewMailboxAndUser.ps1

```
$password = ConvertTo-SecureString "P@ssW0rD!" -asplaintext -force

New-Mailbox -Alias myTestUser2 -Database "mailbox database" `
-Name MyTestUser2 -OrganizationalUnit myTestOU -FirstName My `
-LastName TestUser2 -DisplayName "My TestUser2" `
-UserPrincipalName MyTestUser2@nwtraders.com -password $password
```

Creating multiple new users and mailboxes

1. Open Notepad or your favorite Windows PowerShell script editor.

2. Create a variable called *$password* and use the *ConvertTo-SecureString* cmdlet to create a secure string from the plaintext string "P@ssw0rd1". To ensure this command completes properly, use the force parameter. The code to do this is shown here:

    ```
    $password = ConvertTo-SecureString "P@ssW0rD!" -asplaintext -force
    ```

3. Create a variable called *$strDatabase*. This variable will be used to hold a string that is used to tell the *New-Mailbox cmdlet* on which database to create the new mail-enabled user account. This line of code is shown here:

    ```
    $strDatabase = "Mailbox Database"
    ```

4. On the next line, create a variable called *$strOU*. This variable is used to hold the name of the organizational unit that will hold the new user account. This line of code is shown here:

    ```
    $strOU = "myTestOU"
    ```

5. Create a new variable called *$strDomain*. This variable will hold a string that will be used for the domain portion of the user name to be created. This line of code is shown here:

    ```
    $strDomain = "Nwtraders.msft"
    ```

6. Create a variable called *$strFname,* which will be used to hold the user's first name. This line of code is shown here:

    ```
    $strFname = "My"
    ```

7. Create a variable called *$strLname,* which will be used to hold the user's last name. This line of code is shown here:

    ```
    $strLname = "TestUser"
    ```

8. Use a *for* statement to create a loop that will increment 11 times. Use the variable *$i* as the counter-variable. Start the loop from 0 and continue until it is less than or equal to 10. Use the double plus sign (++) operator to automatically increment the variable *$i.* This code is shown here:

    ```
    for($i=0;$i -le 10;$i++)
    ```

9. Type the opening and closing curly brackets as shown here:

    ```
    {
    }
    ```

10. Between the two curly brackets, use the *New-Mailbox* cmdlet. Use the *$strFname, $strLname,* and *$i* variables to create the user's Alias. Use the *$strDatabase* variable to supply the name for the database argument. Use the *$strFname, $strLname,* and *$i* variables to create name of the account. Use the *$strOU* variable to supply the value for the organizationalunit argument. Use the *$strFname* variable to supply the value for the firstname argument. Use the *$strLname* variable to supply the value for the lastname argument. Use the *$strFname, $strLname,* and *$i* variables to create the value for the displayname argument. To create the userprincipalname argument, use *$strFname, $strLname,* and *$i,* and supply the commercial at sign in parentheses ("@") and the *$strdomain* variable. The last argument that should be supplied is the password contained in the *$password* variable. This line of code is shown here. Note: you can use the grave accent character (`) to break up the line of code for readability purposes, as is done here:

    ```
    New-Mailbox -Alias $strFname$strLname$i  -Database $strDatabase `
    -Name $strFname$strLname$i -OrganizationalUnit $strOU -FirstName `
    $strFname -LastName $strLname -DisplayName $strFname$strLname$i `
    -UserPrincipalName $strFname$strLname$i"@"$strDomain `
    -password $password
    ```

11.   Save your script as *yourname*CreateMultipleUsersAndMailboxes.ps1. Run your script. Go to the Exchange Management Console and click on the Mailbox node. Select Refresh from the Action menu. The new users should appear within a minute or so. If this is not the case, compare your script with the CreateMultipleUsersAndMailboxes.ps1 script.

12.   This concludes the creating multiple new users and mailboxes procedure.

Reporting User Settings

After users are created in Exchange Server 2007, the next step in the user life cycle is to report on their configuration settings. To do this, we can use the *Get-Mailbox* cmdlet. This is shown here:

```
Get-Mailbox
```

When this command is run, it produces a table of output that lists the user name, alias, server name, and other information. A sample of this output is shown here:

```
Name                Alias           ServerName    ProhibitSendQuota
----                -----           ----------    -----------------
Administrator       Administrator   smbex01       unlimited
Claire O'Donnell    claire          smbex01       unlimited
Frank Miller        frank           smbex01       unlimited
Holly Holt          holly           smbex01       unlimited
```

If you are interested in more detailed information, or different information, then you will need to modify the default *Get-Mailbox* command. If you already know the server, and you are only interested in the alias and when the ProhibitSendQuota kicks in, you can use the following command:

```
Get-Mailbox | Format-Table alias, prohibitsendquota –AutoSize
```

This command uses the *Get-Mailbox* cmdlet and pipelines the resulting object into the *Format-Table* cmdlet. It then chooses the alias column and the ProhibitSendQuota column and uses the autosize argument to format the output. A sample of the resulting output is shown here:

```
Alias          ProhibitSendQuota
-----          -----------------
Administrator  unlimited
claire         unlimited
frank          unlimited
holly          unlimited
```

If you use the *Get-Mailbox* cmdlet and supply the alias for a specific user, you will return the same four default columns we obtained earlier. This command is shown here:

```
get-mailbox mytestuser1
```

In reality, you are supplying the string mytestuser1 as the value for the identity argument of the *Get-Mailbox* cmdlet. The command shown here produces the same result:

```
get-mailbox -identity mytestuser1
```

Why is it important to know we are supplying a value for the identity argument of the *Get-Mailbox* cmdlet? There are two reasons: The first is that when you see the identity argument of this cmdlet, you will know what it does; but the second is that there is actually confusion in Exchange Server 2007 about what the identity attribute is and when to use it. For example, technically, the identity of a User object in Exchange Server 2007 would look something like this:

```
nwtraders.com/MyTestOU/MyTestUser1
```

What is interesting is the way I obtained the identity value. Take a look at the syntax of the *Get-Mailbox* cmdlet.

```
get-mailbox -identity mytestuser1 | Format-List identity
```

Remember, this command returned the identity attribute of the User object, so there is confusion between the identity argument of the *Get-Mailbox* cmdlet and the identity attribute used by Exchange Server 2007. But wait, it gets even stranger. When we supply the value for the identity argument and retrieve both the alias and the identity, we have a command that is shown here:

```
get-mailbox -identity mytestuser1 | Format-List alias, identity
```

The data returned from this command are shown here:

```
Alias    : MyTestUser1
Identity : nwtraders.com/MyTestOU/MyTestUser1
```

We could move the commands around a little bit, and create a script that would be very useful from an audit perspective. The FindUnrestrictedMailboxes.ps1 script uses the *Get-Mailbox* cmdlet to retrieve a listing of all user mailboxes. It then uses the *Where-Object* cmdlet to filter out the amount of returned data. It looks for objects that have the ProhibitSendQuota property set to unlimited. It then pipelines the resulting objects to return only the alias of each User object.

FindUnrestrictedMailboxes.ps1

```
"Retrieving users with unrestricted mailbox limits "
"This may take a few minutes ..."
$a = get-mailbox|
   where-object {$_.prohibitSendQuota -eq "unlimited"}

"There are " + $a.length + " users without restrictions."
"They are listed below. `r"

$a | Format-List alias
```

If you were interested in the status of all the quota settings on the Exchange Server, you could revise the script to use the following command:

```
Get-Mailbox | Format-Table alias, *quota
```

Managing Storage Settings

It is a simple fact that the user's need for storage expands to meet the total amount of available storage plus 10%. Without management of storage demands, you will never have enough disk space. Of course, these needs are seldom thought about when the Exchange server is deployed. It is very easy to go from "we have plenty of storage" to "where did all the disk space go?" Everything from attachments to deleted item retention to bulging inboxes demands storage space. Fortunately, we can leverage Windows PowerShell to bring some sanity to the situation.

The first step in working with the storage groups is to find out how many storage groups are defined on the server and their associated names. To do this, use the *Get-StorageGroup* cmdlet, as shown here:

```
Get-StorageGroup
```

When issued with no parameters, the *Get-StorageGroup* cmdlet returns with a listing of all the storage groups defined on the server. This output is shown here:

```
Name                  Server     Replicated      Recovery
----                  ------     ----------      --------
First Storage Group   SMBEX01    None            False
Second Storage Group  SMBEX01    None            False
```

After we have found the storage group we are interested in, we can retrieve all the information from it by using the *Get-StorageGroup* cmdlet to select the first storage group and pipelining the resulting object to the *Format-List* cmdlet. This command is shown here:

```
Get-StorageGroup "first storage group" | Format-List *
```

Examining the Database

Although the storage groups are interesting, what most administrators think about when it comes to Exchange server is the database itself. To retrieve information about the mailbox databases on your server, use the *Get-MailboxDatabase* cmdlet with no arguments. This is shown here:

```
Get-MailboxDatabase
```

The results from this command, shown here, are useful for helping us to identify the name and location of the Exchange Server mailbox database.

```
Name              Server    StorageGroup          Recovery
----              ------    ------------          --------
Mailbox Database  SMBEX01   First Storage Group   False
```

After we have decided which mailbox database to work with, we can pipeline the object returned by the *Get-MailboxDatabase* cmdlet to the *Format-List* cmdlet. This command is shown here:

```
Get-MailboxDatabase | Format-List *
```

This command will return all the properties associated with the mailbox database and the associated values. A sampling of the returned data is shown here:

```
JournalRecipient            :
MailboxRetention            : 30 days
OfflineAddressBook          :
OriginalDatabase            :
```

If, however, we are only interested in storage quota limits, we can modify the command, as shown here:

```
Get-MailboxDatabase | Format-list *quota
```

The results of this command are nice, neat, and succinct, as shown here:

```
ProhibitSendReceiveQuota : 2355MB
ProhibitSendQuota        : 2GB
IssueWarningQuota        : 1945MB
```

Managing Logging

A fundamental aspect of maintenance and troubleshooting involves the configuration and modification of logging settings on Exchange Server 2007. There are 152 different logs that can be configured using Windows PowerShell. In the "old days," merely finding a listing of the Exchange Server log files was a rather specialized and difficult task to accomplish. When a problem arose on the Exchange Server, you had to call a Microsoft Support professional, who would simply walk you through the task of configuring logging, reproducing the problem, and then reading the appropriate log file. After reading the error message in the log file, more often than not, the situation became rather transparent.

In Exchange Server 2007, troubleshooting still consists of configuring the appropriate log file, but now you can easily do that yourself. For instance, to obtain a listing of all the event logs on your server, you use the *Get-EventLogLevel* cmdlet, as shown here:

```
Get-EventLogLevel
```

When this command is run, an output similar to that shown here appears. Notice the format of the Identity property because that is the required parameter to configure the logging level on any particular Exchange log.

```
Identity                             EventLevel
--------                             --------
MSExchange ActiveSync\Requests       Lowest
MSExchange ActiveSync\Configuration  Lowest
MSExchange Antispam\General          Lowest
MSExchange Assistants\Assistants     Lowest
MSExchange Autodiscover\Core         Lowest
```

We can use the name of a specific Exchange log file with *Get-EventLogLevel* to retrieve information about a specific log file. This is shown here, where we obtain the logging level of the routing log:

```
Get-EventLogLevel routing
```

If we try to use the *Set-EventLogLevel* cmdlet to change the logging level to medium as shown here, an error occurs.

```
Set-EventLogLevel routing -Level medium
```

This is rather frustrating because the error that occurs says a specific error log must be supplied. However, we confirmed that the routing log only referred to a single event log.

```
Set-EventLogLevel : Cannot set the EventLog level on more than one category. You must
specify a unique EventSource\Category.
At line:1 char:18 + Set-EventLogLevel  <<<< routing -Level medium
```

To try to identify what Windows PowerShell is expecting for the command, we can look at all the properties of the routing event log. To obtain these properties, we pipe the object returned by the *Get-EventLogLevel* cmdlet to the *Format-List* cmdlet, as shown here:

```
Get-EventLogLevel routing | Format-List *
```

When we examine the properties of the routing event log, we see that is not very complicated. When we use *Get-Help* on the *Set-EventLoglevel,* we see that it wants the Identity property of the log file. As shown here, this would be a lot of typing:

```
Identity    : MSExchangeTransport\routing
IsValid     : True
ObjectState : Unchanged
Name        : Routing
Number      : 4
EventLevel  : Lowest
```

As we discussed earlier, the *Get-EventLogLevel* routing command only returns a single instance of an Exchange event log. We can use this fact to avoid typing. If we store the results of the *Get-EventLogLevel* routing command in a variable, as shown here, we can reuse that variable later:

```
$a = Get-EventLogLevel routing
```

Because the *$a* variable holds only the routing event log, we can now use the Identity property of the Routing Event Log object to refer to that specific log file. As shown here, we can use this reference to the routing event log when we use the *Set-EventLogLevel* cmdlet.

```
Set-EventLogLevel -Identity $a.Identity -Level medium
```

Reporting transport logging levels

1. Open Notepad or your favorite Windows PowerShell script editor.

2. Create a variable called *$aryLog* and use it to hold the object that is returned by using the *Get-EventLogLevel* cmdlet. At the end of the line, use the pipeline character (|) both to pass the object to another object and to break the line for readability. This line of code is shown here:

```
$aryLog = Get-EventLogLevel |
```

3. On the next line, use the *Where-Object* cmdlet to filter the current pipeline object on the Identity property and to do a regular expression match on the word *transport*. The line of code that does this is shown here:

```
where-object {$_.identity -match "transport"}
```

4. On the next line, use the *ForEach* command to walk through the array of Exchange transport logs contained in the *$aryLog* variable. Use the variable *$strLog* as the individual instance of the event log from inside the array. This line of code is shown here:

```
foreach ($strLog in $aryLog)
```

5. On the next line, open the code block with an opening curly bracket. Skip a couple of lines, and close the code block with a closing curly bracket. These two lines of code are shown here:

```
{


}
```

6. Inside the newly created code block, create a variable called *$strLogIdent* and use it to hold the object that is returned by querying the Identity property of the *$strLog* variable. This line of code is shown here:

```
$strLogIdent = $strLog.identity
```

7. On the next line, use the *Get-EventLogLevel* cmdlet. Pass the identity string stored in the *$strLogIdent* variable to the identity argument of the *Get-EventLogLevel* cmdlet. The line of code that does this is shown here:

```
Get-EventLogLevel -identity $strLogIdent
```

8. Save your script as *yourname*ReportTransportLogging.ps1 and run it. You should see a list of 26 transport logs. If this is not the case, compare your script with Report TransportLogging.ps1 script.

9. This concludes the reporting transport logging levels procedure.

Configuring transport logging levels

1. Open Notepad or your favorite Windows PowerShell script editor.

2. On the first line of your script, declare a variable called *$strLevel* and assign the value "medium" to it. This line of code is shown here:

   ```
   $strLevel = "medium"
   ```

3. On the next line in your script, use the *Get-EventLogLevel* cmdlet to get a collection of Event Log objects. At the end of the line, use the pipeline character (|) to pass the object to the next line. At the beginning of the line, use the variable *$aryLog* to hold the resulting object. This line of code is shown here:

   ```
   $aryLog = Get-EventLogLevel |
   ```

4. On the next line, use the *Where-Object* cmdlet to filter the current pipeline object on the Identity property and to do a regular expression match on the word *transport*. The line of code that does this is shown here:

   ```
   where-object {$_.identity -match "transport"}
   ```

5. On the next line, use the *ForEach* command to walk through the array of Exchange transport logs contained in the *$aryLog* variable. Use the variable *$strLog* as the individual instance of the event log from inside the array. This line of code is shown here:

   ```
   foreach ($strLog in $aryLog)
   ```

6. On the next line, open the code block with an opening curly bracket. Skip a couple of lines, and close the code block with a closing curly bracket. These two lines of code are shown here:

   ```
   {


   }
   ```

7. Inside the newly created code block, create a variable called *$strLogIdent* and use it to hold the object that is returned by querying the Identity property of the *$strLog* variable. This line of code is shown here:

   ```
   $strLogIdent = $strLog.identity
   ```

8. On the next line in your script, use the *Set-EventLogLevel* cmdlet to set the logging level of the transport logs. Use the string contained in the *$strLogIdent* variable to supply the specific log identity to the identity argument of the cmdlet. Use the string in the *$strLevel* variable to supply the logging level to the level argument of the *Set-EventLogLevel* cmdlet. This code is shown here:

   ```
   Set-EventLogLevel -identity $strLogIdent -level $strLevel
   ```

9. Save your script as *yourname*ConfigureTransportLogging.ps1. Run your script. After a few seconds, you will see the prompt return, but no output.

10. Run the ReportTransportLogging.ps1 script. You should now see a listing of all the transport logs and see that their logging level has been changed to medium.

11. If you do not see the logging level changed, open the ConfigureTransportLogging.ps1 script and it compare it with yours.

12. This concludes the configuring transport logging levels procedure.

Creating User Accounts: Step-by-Step Exercises

In this exercise, we will explore the use of Windows PowerShell to create several users whose names are contained in a text file.

1. Open Notepad or some other Windows PowerShell script editor.

2. Locate the UserNames.txt file, and ensure you have access to the path to this file. The file contains a listing of users' first and last names. A sample from this file is shown here:

```
Chuck,Adams
Alice,Jones
Bob,Dentworth
```

3. On the first line of your script, create a variable called *$aryUsers* to hold the array of text that is returned by using the *Get-Content* cmdlet to read a text file that contains various user first names and last names. Make sure you edit the string that gets supplied to the path argument of the *Get-Content* cmdlet as required for your computer. This line of code is shown here:

```
$aryUsers = Get-Content -path "c:\ch9\UserNames.txt"
```

4. On the next line of your script, declare a variable called *$password* that will contain the password to use for all your users. For this example, the password is Password01. This line of code is shown here:

```
$password = "Password01"
```

5. On the next line of your script, declare a variable called *$strOU* to hold the organizational unit to place the newly created users. For this example, place the users in the MyTestOU, which was created in Chapter 7, "Working with Active Directory." This line of code is shown here:

```
$strOU = "myTestOU"
```

6. On the next line, declare a variable called *$strDomain*. This variable will be used to hold the domain name of the organization. This will become part of the user's e-mail address. For this example, use NwTraders.msft, as shown here:

```
$strDomain = "nwtraders.msft"
```

7. Now declare a variable called *$strDatabase*. This variable will hold the name of the database where the users' mailboxes will reside. On our system, the database is called Mailbox Database. This line of code is shown here:

```
$strDatabase = "Mailbox Database"
```

8. Use the *ConvertTo-SecureString* cmdlet to convert the string contained in the variable *$password* into a secure string that can be used for the password argument of the *New-Mailbox* cmdlet. To convert a string to a secure string, you need to specify the asplaintext argument for the string contained in the *$password* variable, and use the force argument to force the conversion. Reuse the *$password* variable to hold the newly created secure string. This line of code is shown here:

```
$password = ConvertTo-SecureString $password -asplaintext -force
```

9. Use the *ForEach* statement to walk through the array of text that was created by using the *Get-Content* cmdlet to read the text file. Use the variable *$i* as an individual counter. The variable that holds the array of text from the *Get-Content* cmdlet is *$aryUsers*. This line of code is shown here:

```
foreach ($i in $aryUsers)
```

10. Open and close the code block by using the opening and closing curly brackets, as shown here. You will need space for at least 9 or 10 lines of code, but that can always be added later.

```
{

}
```

11. On the first line inside your code block, use the variable *$newAry* to hold a new array you will create out of one line of text from the *$aryUsers* variable by using the Split method. When you call the Split method, supply a comma to it because the default value of the Split method is a blank *space*. The variable *$i* holds the current line of text from the *$aryUsers* variable. This line of code is shown here:

```
$newAry = $i.split(',')
```

12. The first name is held in the first column in our text file. After this line of text is turned into an array, the first column is addressed as element 0. To retrieve it, we use the name of the new array and enclose the element number in square brackets. Hold the first name in the variable *$strFname*, as shown here:

```
$strFname = $newAry[0]
```

13. The last name is in the second column of the text file and is addressed as element 1 in the new array contained in the *$newAry* variable. Retrieve the value stored in *$newAry[1]* and store it in the variable *$strLname*, as shown here:

```
$strLname = $newAry[1]
```

14. Now we need to use the *New-Mailbox* cmdlet and supply the values for each of the parameters we have hard-coded in the script, and from the first and last name values stored in the text file. The goal is to not have any of the arguments of the *New-Mailbox* cmdlet be hard-coded. This will greatly facilitate changing the script to run in different domains and organization units (OUs), and with additional parameters.

15. On a new line, call the *New-Mailbox* cmdlet. For the alias argument, create the user's alias by concatenating the first name contained in the *$strFname* variable with the last name contained in the *$strLname* variable. The database that will hold the user's mailbox is the one supplied in the *$strDatabase* variable. Because the command will stretch for several lines, use the line continuation command (the grave accent character [`]) at the end of the line. This line of code is shown here:

```
New-Mailbox -Alias $strFname$strLname -Database $strDatabase
```

16. The next line of our *New-Mailbox* command creates the user name attribute. To do this, concatenate the first name and last name. The organizational unit name is stored in the *$strOU* variable. Continue the command to the next line. This line of code is shown here:

```
-Name $strFname$strLname -OrganizationalUnit $strOU
```

17. The next line is easy. The value for the firstname argument is stored in *$strFname*, and the value for the lastname argument is stored in the *$strLname* variable. Use line continuation to continue the command to the next line. This code is shown here:

```
FirstName $strFname -LastName $strLname
```

18. The displayname for these users will be the first name and the last name concatenated. To do this, use the first name stored in *$strFname* and the last name stored in *$strLname*. Continue the command to the next line, as shown here:

```
-DisplayName $strFname$strLname `
```

19. The userprincipalname value is composed of the first name concatenated with the last name separated from the domain name stored in the *$strDomain* variable by the commercial at symbol (@). It looks like an e-mail address but is not the same thing. Our code to create this is shown here:

```
-UserPrincipalName $strFname$strLname"@"$strDomain `
```

20. The value for the password argument is stored in the *$password* variable. This is the last parameter we need to supply for this command.

```
-password $password
```

21. Save your script as *yourname*CreateUsersFromTxt.ps1. Run your script. If it does not produce the desired results, then compare it with CreateUsersFromTxt.ps1 script.

22. This concludes this step-by-step exercise.

One Step Further: Configuring Message Tracking

In this exercise, we will examine the use of Windows PowerShell to configure message tracking on an Exchange 2007 server.

1. Open Notepad or another Windows PowerShell script editor.

2. Declare a variable called *$dteMaxAge* and use the timespan accelerator to convert a string type into a timespan data type. Set the timespan to be equal to 30 days, 0 hours, 0 minutes, and 0 seconds. The line of code that does this is shown here:

```
$dteMaxAge = [timespan]"30.00:00:00"
```

3. On the next line, create a variable called *$intSize* and use it to hold the value 50MB. The *Set-MailboxServer* cmdlet expects a value with both the number and suffix to indicate whether the number is megabytes or kilobytes or some other size of number. To do this, use the following code:

```
$intSize = 50MB
```

4. On the next line, use the variable *$strLogPath* to hold the string representing the path for storing the message tracking logs. This needs to be a path that is local to the actual Exchange server. To do this, we used the following code:

```
$strLogPath = "c:\x2kLogs"
```

5. Use the variable *$aryServer* to hold a collection of Exchange mailbox servers obtained by using the *Get-MailboxServer* cmdlet. This line of code is shown here:

```
$aryServer = Get-MailboxServer
```

6. Use the *ForEach* statement to walk through the collection of Exchange servers held in the *$aryServer* variable. Use the variable *$strServer* as the counter-variable while you go through the array. This line is code is shown here:

```
foreach ($strServer in $aryServer)
```

7. Open and close the code block by typing an opening curly bracket and a closing curly bracket, as shown here:

```
{
}
```

8. Use the variable *$strServer* to hold the Identity property that is returned by querying the Identity property from the object contained in the *$strServer* variable. This line of code is shown here:

```
$strServer = $strServer.identity
```

9.   On the next line, use the *Set-MailboxServer* cmdlet and supply the value for the identity argument with the string contained in the *$strServer* variable. Use the grave accent character (`) to continue the command to the next line. The code that does this is shown here:

```
Set-MailboxServer -identity $strServer
```

10.   On the next line, use the MessageTrackingLogEnabled argument to turn on message tracking. To do this, use the value *$true* as the value for the MessageTrackingLogEnabled argument. The line of code that does this is shown here. Make sure you include the grave accent character at the end of the line to continue the command to the next line.

```
-MessageTrackingLogEnabled $true
```

11.   On the next line, use the MessageTrackingLogMaxAge argument to set the maximum age of the message tracking logs. Use the timespan data type to supply the value to the MessageTrackingLogMaxAge argument. To do this, use the value stored in the *$dteMaxAge* variable. This line of code is shown here. At the end of the line, use the grave accent character to continue the code to the next line.

```
-MessageTrackingLogMaxAge $dteMaxAge
```

12.   Now we need to configure the size of the logging directory. To do this, use the Message-TrackingLogMaxDirectorySize argument of the *Set-MailboxServer* cmdlet. When you specify a value for the directory size, you can tell it you want MB for megabytes, GB for gigabytes, KB for kilobytes, and even B for bytes and TB for terabytes. To make it easy to change later, we stored the max directory size value in a variable called *$intSize*. The code that sets this argument is shown here:

```
-MessageTrackingLogMaxDirectorySize $intSize
```

13.   The last parameter we need to configure for message tracking is the path for log storage. This needs to be a local path on the Exchange server. We used the following line of code to configure the MessageTrackingLogPath argument:

```
-MessageTrackingLogPath $strLogPath
```

14.   Save your script as *yourname*EnableMessageTracking.ps1. Run your script. If it does not produce the desired results, then compare it with EnableMessageTracking.ps1.

15.   This concludes this one step further exercise.

Chapter 9 Quick Reference

To	Do This
Create a new user in both Windows and in Exchange	Use the *New-Mailbox* cmdlet
Find mailboxes that do not have quota limits applied to them	Use the *Get-Mailbox* cmdlet
Disable a mailbox	Use the *Disable-Mailbox* cmdlet
Enable a mailbox for an existing user	Use the *Enable-Mailbox* cmdlet
Produce a listing of all storage groups on the Exchange server	Use the *Get-StorageGroup* cmdlet
Produce information about the Exchange Mailbox database	Use the *Get-MailboxDatabase* cmdlet
Produce a listing of all Exchange 2007–specific cmdlets	Use the *Get-ExCommand* cmdlet
Produce a listing of the logging level of all Exchange event logs	Use the *Get-EventLogLevel* cmdlet

Appendix A
Cmdlets Installed with Windows PowerShell

The following cmdlets are installed with Windows PowerShell. This list gives you an idea of the sort of things you can do "out of the box" with Windows PowerShell. Please note that the description field (returned from Windows PowerShell) is often truncated in this list. To obtain more specific information on Windows PowerShell cmdlets, you can use the *Get-Help* cmdlet, as shown here:

```
Get-Help Set-Location
```

Table A-1   Default PowerShell Cmdlets

Name	Definition
Add-Content	Add-Content [-Path] <String[...
Add-History	Add-History [[-InputObject] ...
Add-Member	Add-Member [-MemberType] <PS...
Add-PSSnapin	Add-PSSnapin [-Name] <String...
Clear-Content	Clear-Content [-Path] <Strin...
Clear-Item	Clear-Item [-Path] <String[]...
Clear-ItemProperty	Clear-ItemProperty [-Path] <...
Clear-Variable	Clear-Variable [-Name] <Stri...
Compare-Object	Compare-Object [-ReferenceOb...
ConvertFrom-SecureString	ConvertFrom-SecureString [-S...
Convert-Path	Convert-Path [-Path] <String...
ConvertTo-Html	ConvertTo-Html [[-Property] ...
ConvertTo-SecureString	ConvertTo-SecureString [-Str...
Copy-Item	Copy-Item [-Path] <String[]>...
Copy-ItemProperty	Copy-ItemProperty [-Path] <S...
Export-Alias	Export-Alias [-Path] <String...
Export-Clixml	Export-Clixml [-Path] <Strin...
Export-Console	Export-Console [[-Path] <Str...
Export-Csv	Export-Csv [-Path] <String> ...
ForEach-Object	ForEach-Object [-Process] <S...
Format-Custom	Format-Custom [[-Property] <...
Format-List	Format-List [[-Property] <Ob...
Format-Table	Format-Table [[-Property] <O...
Format-Wide	Format-Wide [[-Property] <Ob...

Table A-1   Default PowerShell Cmdlets

Name	Definition
Get-Acl	Get-Acl [[-Path] <String[]>]...
Get-Alias	Get-Alias [[-Name] <String[]...
Get-AuthenticodeSignature	Get-AuthenticodeSignature [-...
Get-ChildItem	Get-ChildItem [[-Path] <Stri...
Get-Command	Get-Command [[-ArgumentList]...
Get-Content	Get-Content [-Path] <String[...
Get-Credential	Get-Credential [-Credential]...
Get-Culture	Get-Culture [-Verbose] [-Deb...
Get-Date	Get-Date [[-Date] <DateTime>...
Get-EventLog	Get-EventLog [-LogName] <Str...
Get-ExecutionPolicy	Get-ExecutionPolicy [-Verbos...
Get-Help	Get-Help [[-Name] <String>] ...
Get-History	Get-History [[-Id] <Int64[]>...
Get-Host	Get-Host [-Verbose] [-Debug]...
Get-Item	Get-Item [-Path] <String[]> ...
Get-ItemProperty	Get-ItemProperty [-Path] <St...
Get-Location	Get-Location [-PSProvider <S...
Get-Member	Get-Member [[-Name] <String[...
Get-PfxCertificate	Get-PfxCertificate [-FilePat...
Get-Process	Get-Process [[-Name] <String...
Get-PSDrive	Get-PSDrive [[-Name] <String...
Get-PSProvider	Get-PSProvider [[-PSProvider...
Get-PSSnapin	Get-PSSnapin [[-Name] <Strin...
Get-Service	Get-Service [[-Name] <String...
Get-TraceSource	Get-TraceSource [[-Name] <St...
Get-UICulture	Get-UICulture [-Verbose] [-D...
Get-Unique	Get-Unique [-InputObject <PS...
Get-Variable	Get-Variable [[-Name] <Strin...
Get-WmiObject	Get-WmiObject [-Class] <Stri...
Group-Object	Group-Object [[-Property] <O...
Import-Alias	Import-Alias [-Path] <String...
Import-Clixml	Import-Clixml [-Path] <Strin...
Import-Csv	Import-Csv [-Path] <String[]...
Invoke-Expression	Invoke-Expression [-Command]...
Invoke-History	Invoke-History [[-Id] <Strin...
Invoke-Item	Invoke-Item [-Path] <String[...
Join-Path	Join-Path [-Path] <String[]>...

Table A-1   Default PowerShell Cmdlets

Name	Definition
Measure-Command	Measure-Command [-Expression...
Measure-Object	Measure-Object [[-Property] ...
Move-Item	Move-Item [-Path] <String[]>...
Move-ItemProperty	Move-ItemProperty [-Path] <S...
New-Alias	New-Alias [-Name] <String> [...
New-Item	New-Item [-Path] <String[]> ...
New-ItemProperty	New-ItemProperty [-Path] <St...
New-Object	New-Object [-TypeName] <Stri...
New-PSDrive	New-PSDrive [-Name] <String>...
New-Service	New-Service [-Name] <String>...
New-TimeSpan	New-TimeSpan [[-Start] <Date...
New-Variable	New-Variable [-Name] <String...
Out-Default	Out-Default [-InputObject <P...
Out-File	Out-File [-FilePath] <String...
Out-Host	Out-Host [-Paging] [-InputOb...
Out-Null	Out-Null [-InputObject <PSOb...
Out-Printer	Out-Printer [[-Name] <String...
Out-String	Out-String [-Stream] [-Width...
Pop-Location	Pop-Location [-PassThru] [-S...
Push-Location	Push-Location [[-Path] <Stri...
Read-Host	Read-Host [[-Prompt] <Object...
Remove-Item	Remove-Item [-Path] <String[...
Remove-ItemProperty	Remove-ItemProperty [-Path] ...
Remove-PSDrive	Remove-PSDrive [-Name] <Stri...
Remove-PSSnapin	Remove-PSSnapin [-Name] <Str...
Remove-Variable	Remove-Variable [-Name] <Str...
Rename-Item	Rename-Item [-Path] <String>...
Rename-ItemProperty	Rename-ItemProperty [-Path] ...
Resolve-Path	Resolve-Path [-Path] <String...
Restart-Service	Restart-Service [-Name] <Str...
Resume-Service	Resume-Service [-Name] <Stri...
Select-Object	Select-Object [[-Property] <...
Select-String	Select-String [-Pattern] <St...
Set-Acl	Set-Acl [-Path] <String[]> [...
Set-Alias	Set-Alias [-Name] <String> [...
Set-AuthenticodeSignature	Set-AuthenticodeSignature [-...
Set-Content	Set-Content [-Path] <String[...

Table A-1 Default PowerShell Cmdlets

Name	Definition
Set-Date	Set-Date [-Date] <DateTime> ...
Set-ExecutionPolicy	Set-ExecutionPolicy [-Execut...
Set-Item	Set-Item [-Path] <String[]> ...
Set-ItemProperty	Set-ItemProperty [-Path] <St...
Set-Location	Set-Location [[-Path] <Strin...
Set-PSDebug	Set-PSDebug [-Trace <Int32>]...
Set-Service	Set-Service [-Name] <String>...
Set-TraceSource	Set-TraceSource [-Name] <Str...
Set-Variable	Set-Variable [-Name] <String...
Sort-Object	Sort-Object [[-Property] <Ob...
Split-Path	Split-Path [-Path] <String[]...
Start-Service	Start-Service [-Name] <Strin...
Start-Sleep	Start-Sleep [-Seconds] <Int3...
Start-Transcript	Start-Transcript [[-Path] <S...
Stop-Process	Stop-Process [-Id] <Int32[]>...
Stop-Service	Stop-Service [-Name] <String...
Stop-Transcript	Stop-Transcript [-Verbose] [...
Suspend-Service	Suspend-Service [-Name] <Str...
Tee-Object	Tee-Object [-FilePath] <Stri...
Test-Path	Test-Path [-Path] <String[]>...
Trace-Command	Trace-Command [-Name] <Strin...
Update-FormatData	Update-FormatData [[-AppendP...
Update-TypeData	Update-TypeData [[-AppendPat...
Where-Object	Where-Object [-FilterScript]...
Write-Debug	Write-Debug [-Message] <Stri...
Write-Error	Write-Error [-Message] <Stri...
Write-Host	Write-Host [[-Object] <Objec...
Write-Output	Write-Output [-InputObject] ...
Write-Progress	Write-Progress [-Activity] <...
Write-Verbose	Write-Verbose [-Message] <St...
Write-Warning	Write-Warning [-Message] <St...

Appendix B
Cmdlet Naming

The cmdlets installed with Windows PowerShell all follow a standard naming convention. In general, they use a verb–noun pair. For example, there are four commands that start with the verb *add*. "Add what?" you may ask. This is where the noun comes into play: *Add-Content*, *Add-History*, *Add-Member*, and *Add-PSSnapin*. When creating cmdlets, you should endeavor to follow the same kind of naming convention. The recognition of this naming convention is helpful in learning the cmdlets that come with Windows PowerShell.

Table B-1 Cmdlet Naming

Count	Verb	Examples
4	Add	*Add-Content, Add-History, Add-Member*
4	Clear	*Clear-Content, Clear-Item*
1	Compare	*Compare-Object*
1	ConvertFrom	*ConvertFrom-SecureString*
1	Convert	*Convert-Path*
2	ConvertTo	*ConvertTo-Html, ConvertTo-SecureString*
2	Copy	*Copy-Item, Copy-ItemProperty*
4	Export	*Export-Alias, Export-Clixml, Export-Console*
1	ForEach	*ForEach-Object*
4	Format	*Format-Custom, Format-List, Format-Table*
29	Get	*Get-Acl, Get-Alias*
1	Group	*Group-Object*
3	Import	*Import-Clixml, Import-Csv*
3	Invoke	*Invoke-Expression, Invoke-History*
1	Join	*Join-Path*
2	Measure	*Measure-Command, Measure-Object*
2	Move	*Move-Item, Move-ItemProperty*
8	New	*New-Alias, New-Item, New-ItemProperty*
6	Out	*Out-Default, Out-File, Out-Host*
1	Pop	*Pop-Location*
1	Push	*Push-Location*
1	Read	*Read-Host*
5	Remove	*Remove-Item, Remove-ItemProperty*
2	Rename	*Rename-Item, Rename-ItemProperty*
1	Resolve	*Resolve-Path*
1	Restart	*Restart-Service*

Table B-1   Cmdlet Naming

Count	Verb	Examples
1	Resume	*Resume-Service*
2	Select	*Select-Object, Select-String*
13	Set	*Set-Acl, Set-Alias*
1	Sort	*Sort-Object*
1	Split	*Split-Path*
3	Start	*Start-Service, Start-Sleep, Start-Transcript*
3	Stop	*Stop-Process, Stop-Service, Stop-Transcript*
1	Suspend	*Suspend-Service*
1	Tee	*Tee-Object*
1	Test	*Test-Path*
1	Trace	*Trace-Command*
2	Update	*Update-FormatData, Update-TypeData*
1	Where	*Where-Object*
7	Write	*Write-Debug, Write-Error, Write-Host*

Appendix C
Translating VBScript to Windows PowerShell

 Note   Thanks to the Microsoft Scripting Guys for permission to include this reference. You can find this and other resources at their Web site: *http://www.microsoft.com/technet/ scriptcenter/resources/qanda/default.mspx*

One of the cornerstones of education is the concept of scaffolding, the idea that it is easier to learn something new if you relate your new knowledge to, and build upon, existing knowledge. For example, suppose you've spent your entire driving life behind the wheel of a car with an automatic transmission. Now, you'd like to learn how to drive a car that has a manual transmission. Should you forget everything you've ever learned about driving and start all over again from scratch?

Well, OK, maybe some people *would* be better off doing that. For most people, however, starting over from scratch makes no sense. Instead, by building on what you already know, you'll find it much easier to learn to drive a stick shift. For one thing, that enables you to focus solely on learning how to shift. There's no need to learn how to turn on the windshield wipers or signal for a left-hand turn; after all, you already know how to do those things.

The same is true when it comes to learning Windows PowerShell. Yes, Windows PowerShell is different from VBScript, sometimes dramatically different. However, the underlying concepts between the two are often exactly the same: An *if* statement allows you to take alternate routes depending on a specified condition; an uppercase a is still an A; a constant remains a value that cannot be changed during the running of a script. If you're familiar with VBScript, you actually have a head start over people who know nothing about scripting or programming. After all, you already understand many of the basic concepts. You don't have to learn the function of a *Do ... While* loop; you just have to learn the Windows PowerShell syntax for a *Do ... While* loop.

Hence this guide to translating VBScript to Windows PowerShell. We should point out, right from the start, that this is not intended to be a word-for-word translation guide; for better or worse, things don't quite work that way. Instead, it's designed to act as a reference guide as you begin writing your first Windows PowerShell scripts. After all, sooner or later you're bound to run into a situation in which you find yourself thinking, "OK, I need to use a *Select Case* statement here. I know how to do that in VBScript, but how do I do that in Windows PowerShell?" That's where this guide can come in handy; it takes all the

VBScript functions, statements, and operators and shows you, as much as possible, a Windows PowerShell equivalent.

> **Note**   Incidentally, we tried to find an equivalent for most of the commands in the VBScript Language Reference; however, we would never claim that we found the *best* equivalent for these commands. If you know of a better, faster, or easier way to, say, format a number as currency in Windows PowerShell, please let us know. We'll publish these alternate approaches as an addendum to this guide. The online version of this VBScript to Windows PowerShell conversion guide is located on the Microsoft Scripting Guys Web site at *http://www.microsoft.com/technet/scriptcenter/topics/winpsh/convert/default.mspx*

VBScript Function	Windows PowerShell Equivalent
Abs	*Definition:* Returns the absolute value of a number.
	For system administrators, VBScript's *Abs* function, which returns the absolute value of a number, is like having a spare house key hidden somewhere in the backyard: Most likely you'll never use it, but if you ever *do* need a spare key (or an absolute value function), well.... Although Windows PowerShell doesn't have a built-in method for returning the absolute value of a number, you can achieve that result by using the .NET Framework's System.Math class and the Abs method. This command assigns the absolute value of –15 to the variable *$a:*
	`$a = [math]::abs(-15)`
	When you run this command and then echo back the value of *$a* (something you can do simply by typing **$a**), you should get the following:
	`15`
Array	*Definition:* Returns a variant containing an array.
	In VBScript, it's pretty easy to create an array: All you have to do is dimension a variable as an array, or use the *Array* function to add multiple values to a variable. Believe it or not, in Windows PowerShell, it's even *easier* to create an array—all you have to do is assign multiple values to a variable; no special functions or methods are required. For example, this command assigns all the colors of the rainbow to a variable named *$a:*
	`$a = "red","orange","yellow","green","blue","indigo","violet"`
	When you run this command and then echo back the value of *$a*, you should get the following:

	`red`
	`orange`
	`yellow`
	`green`
	`blue`
	`indigo`
	`violet`

VBScript Function	Windows PowerShell Equivalent
Asc	*Definition:* Returns the ANSI character code corresponding to the first letter in a string.

	It's surprising how often scripters need to convert a character value (such as the letter A) to its ASCII equivalent (65). In Windows PowerShell, you can determine the ASCII value of a character by using this crazy-looking line of code (which takes the character value of the letter A and then converts the result to a byte value):
	
	```$a = [byte][char] "A"```
	
	When you run this command and then echo back the value of *$a*, you should get the following:
	
	```65```

Atn	*Definition:* Returns the arctangent of a number.

	Granted, this one doesn't come up terribly often in system administration scripts. Nevertheless, if you ever *do* need to calculate the arctangent of an angle, you can do so using the System.Math class and the Atan method. This command assigns the arctangent of a 90-degree angle to the variable *$a:*
	
	```$a = [math]::atan(90)```
	
	When you run this command and then echo back the value of *$a*, you should get the following:
	
	```1.55968567289729```

CBool	*Definition:* Returns an expression that has been converted to a variant of subtype Boolean.

	Sure, you can convert a string or numeric value to a Boolean value (True or False): All you have to do is convert the data type of the variable to a Boolean type. As far as we know, 0 will always be converted to False, and anything that isn't 0 (even something as nonsensical as the string value *cat*) will be converted to True. In the following example, we assign the value 0 to the variable *$a*, then convert *$a* to a Boolean value:
	
	```$a = 0```
	```$a = [bool] $a```
	
	When you run this command and then echo back the value of *$a*, you should get the following:
	
	```False```

VBScript Function	Windows PowerShell Equivalent
CByte	*Definition:* Returns an expression that has been converted to a variant of subtype Byte.
	What do you mean, "Windows PowerShell is great and all, but there's probably no way to convert a variable to the byte data type?" As it turns out, that's about as easy a conversion as you could hope to make. For example, the first of these two commands assigns a string value to the variable $a; the second command then converts $a to the byte data type (which, incidentally, consists of integers from 0 to 255):
	`$a = "11.45"` `$a = [byte] $a`
	When you run these two commands and then use the GetType() method to determine the data type of $a, you should get the following:

	`IsPublic IsSerial Name`
	`-------- -------- ----`
	`True     True     Byte`

	Incidentally, the value of $a will now be 11.
CCur	*Definition:* Returns an expression that has been converted to a variant of subtype Currency.
	Windows PowerShell uses the same data types as the .NET Framework; because the .NET Framework does not support the Currency data type, Windows PowerShell doesn't support this data type, either. However, although you cannot convert a variable to the Currency data type, you can at least format the value so that it looks like a currency value when displayed onscreen. The following command assigns the value 13 to the variable $a and formats the value so that it displays as currency:
	`$a = "{0:C}" -f 13`
	This command uses the .NET Framework currency formatting string "{0:C}" to format the value as currency (note that the value to be formatted is included as part of the -f parameter).
	When you run the command and then echo back the value of $a, you should get the following:
	`$13.00`

VBScript Function	Windows PowerShell Equivalent

CDate	*Definition:* Returns an expression that has been converted to a variant of subtype Date.
	
	Need to make sure that a value is treated as a date? Then do this. First, assign the value to a variable; here we're assigning the string 11/1/2006 to the variable *$a*:
	
	`$a = "11/1/2006"`
	
	In fact, if we now call the GetType() method, we'll see that *$a* is a string variable:
	
	`IsPublic IsSerial Name`
	`-------- -------- ----`
	`True     True     String`
	
	To convert *$a* to a date-time value, we can use this command:
	
	`$a = [datetime] $a`
	
	When you run this command and check the data type for *$a*, you should get the following:
	
	`IsPublic IsSerial Name`
	`-------- -------- ----`
	`True     True     DateTime`

CDbl	*Definition:* Returns an expression that has been converted to a variant of subtype Double.
	
	The double data type "contains a double-precision, floating-point number in the range −1.79769313486232E308 to −4.94065645841247E-324 for negative values; 4.94065645841247E-324 to 1.79769313486232E308 for positive values"
	
	Whew.
	
	If it turns out you need a double-precision, floating-point number like that, you can use Windows PowerShell to convert a variable to the double data type. The following two commands assign a string value to the variable *$a*, then convert *$a* to the double data type:
	
	`$a = "11.45"`
	`$a = [double] $a`
	
	If you run these two commands and then use the GetType() method against *$a*, you should get back the following information:
	
	`IsPublic IsSerial Name`
	`-------- -------- ----`
	`True     True     Double`

VBScript Function	Windows PowerShell Equivalent
Chr	*Definition:* Returns the character associated with the specified ANSI character code.
	Here's a question for you: Suppose you have an ASCII value and you need to convert that value to a real character—how are you supposed to do *that*?
	Well, one way is to simply take the integer value (ASCII values are always integer values) and convert its data type to character. This command converts ASCII 34 to a character value and then stores that value in the variable *$a*:
	`$a = [char]34`
	When you run this command and then echo back the value of *$a*, you should get the following:
	`"`
CInt	*Definition:* Returns an expression that has been converted to a variant of subtype Integer.
	Need to convert a value to the integer data type? No problem: Not only will Windows PowerShell make the conversion for you, but it will also round-off the value to the nearest whole number. (Some languages convert a value to an integer simply by stripping off the decimal point.) The following two commands assign a string value to the variable *$a*, then convert the data type of *$a* to integer:
	`$a = "11.57"` `$a = [int] $a`
	When you run these two commands and then echo back the value of *$a*, you should get the following:
	`12`
	And if you run the GetType() method against *$a*, you'll see it now has the following data type:
| | ```
IsPublic IsSerial Name
-------- -------- ----
True     True     Int32
``` |
CLng	*Definition:* Returns an expression that has been converted to a variant of subtype Long.
	"Long" values are integers in the range −2,147,483,648 to 2,147,483,647. The following two commands show how you can convert a value to the long data type. In command no. 1, we assign a value to the variable *$a*; in command no. 2, we then convert *$a* to a long value:
	`$a = "123456789.45"` `$a = [long] $a`
	When you run this command and then echo back the value of *$a*, you should get the following:
	`123456789`
	Note: What happened to the .45 on the end of our original value? Well, remember, long values must be *integers*. Therefore, Windows PowerShell rounds a value to the nearest whole number when converting that value to the long data type.
```

VBScript Function	Windows PowerShell Equivalent
Cos	*Definition:* Returns the cosine of an angle.
	In a million years, you'll never *once* have to calculate the cosine of an angle in one of your scripts. Still, better safe than sorry, right? In Windows PowerShell, you can determine the cosine of an angle using the System.Math class and the Cos method. This sample command returns the cosine of a 45-degree angle and then stores the value in a variable named *$a*:
	`$a = [math]::cos(45)`
	When you run this command and then echo back the value of *$a*, you should get the following:
	`0.52532198881773`
CreateObject	*Definition:* Creates and returns a reference to an Automation object.
	In Windows PowerShell, you create new COM objects by using the *New-Object* cmdlet. To do so, call *New-Object*, passing the cmdlet the -comobject parameter, which tells Windows PowerShell to create a new COM object rather than, say, a new .NET Framework object. The -comobject parameter is then followed by the ProgID of the COM object.
	For example, the following two commands create an instance of Microsoft Excel and then, just to prove that the first command *did* create an instance of Excel, the second command makes the application visible onscreen:
	`$a = new-object -comobject Excel.Application` `$a.visible = $True`
	Incidentally, when using the *New-Object* cmdlet, you might want to add the -strict parameter, like so:
	`$a = new-object -comobject Excel.Application -strict`
	That helps ensure that you are working with a true COM object and not a COM wrapper around a .NET object.
CSng	*Definition:* Returns an expression that has been converted to a variant of subtype Single.
	If you've read this conversion guide from the very beginning, then you already know way more about data types than you probably wanted to know. Nevertheless, here's yet another fact about data types: A single value is "a single-precision, floating-point number in the range −3.402823E38 to −1.401298E-45 for negative values; 1.401298E-45 to 3.402823E38 for positive values." Can you convert a variable to the single data type? The following two commands argue that you can. In the first command, we assign a value to the variable *$a*; in the second command, we convert *$a* to the single data type:
	`$a = "11.45"` `$a = [single] $a`
	When you run these commands and then use the GetType() method to return the data type for *$a*, you should get the following:

	`IsPublic IsSerial Name`
	`-------- -------- ----`
	`True     True     Single`

VBScript Function	Windows PowerShell Equivalent
CStr	*Definition:* Returns an expression that has been converted to a variant of subtype String.

There will be times (especially when you work with databases) when you'll have a numeric value that needs to be treated as a string. Can you convert a numeric value into a string value? Of course you can. To begin with, assign the numeric value to a variable (in this example, we assign 17 to $a):

```
$a = 17
```

If we want to verify that $a is really a numeric value, we can do this using the Get-Type() method:

```
IsPublic IsSerial Name
-------- -------- ----
True     True     Int32
```

Now, what about converting this to a string value? Here you go:

```
$a = [string] $a
```

When you run this command and then check the data type of $a, you should get the following:

```
IsPublic IsSerial Name
-------- -------- ----
True     True     String
```

VBScript Function	Windows PowerShell Equivalent
Date	*Definition:* Returns the current system date.

In VBScript, you can use the Date function to assign the current date (and only the current date, not the current time as well) to a variable. In Windows PowerShell, you can do the same thing by calling the *Get-Date* cmdlet and using the -format d (for date) parameter. For example, this command assigns the current date to the variable $a:

```
$a = get-date –format d
```

When you run this command and then echo back the value of $a, you should get back something similar to this:

2/8/2007

VBScript Function	Windows PowerShell Equivalent
DateAdd	*Definition:* Returns a date to which a specified time interval has been added.

No scripting language (or at least none that we know of) can predict the future. However, many of them at least enable you to predict when the future will occur. For example, suppose today is 2/8/2007. What will the date be 37 days from now? In Windows PowerShell, you can determine that by using the *Get-Date* cmdlet along with the appropriate method. For example, this command calculates the date 37 days from the current date (using the AddDays() method) and stores that value in the variable *$a*:

```
$a = (get-date).AddDays(37)
```

If this command is run on 2/8/2007, you should get the following when you echo back the value of *$a*:

```
Saturday, March 17, 2007 11:33:27 AM
```

Of course, you aren't limited to working only with the AddDays() method. Here are other date arithmetic methods available to you:

```
(get-date).AddHours(37)
(get-date).AddMilliseconds(37)
(get-date).AddMinutes(37)
(get-date).AddMonths(37)
(get-date).AddSeconds(37)
(get-date).AddTicks(37)
(get-date).AddYears(37)
```

You can also combine these methods in a single command. This command calculates the time 2 hours and 34 minutes from now. To do that, it first uses AddHours() to determine the time 2 hours from now, then takes the resulting value and uses the AddMinutes() method to determine the time 34 minutes from *then*. (Note the use of parentheses, which ensures that AddHours() is run first and AddMinutes() is run only when AddHours() is done.) Here's the command:

```
$a = ((get-date).AddHours(2)).AddMinutes(34)
```

VBScript Function	Windows PowerShell Equivalent
DateDiff	*Definition:* Returns the number of intervals between two dates.

The VBScript DateDiff function is used to determine the amount of time (months, weeks, days, hours, etc.) between two date-time values. In Windows PowerShell, you can perform this same kind of date arithmetic using the *New-TimeSpan* cmdlet.

For example, the following command calculates the amount of time between the current date and time and 11:30 P.M. on December 31, 2006. Note that the *Get-Date* cmdlet is used to create the two date-time values. Also note that a dollar sign ($) is used to preface each of the *Get-Date* commands, and each command is enclosed in parentheses. That ensures that Windows PowerShell first calculates the two date-time values, and only *then* uses *New-TimeSpan* to determine the time interval.

The command itself looks like this:

```
$a = New-TimeSpan $(Get-Date) $(Get-Date -month
12 -day 31 -year 2006 -hour 23 -minute 30)
```

When you run this command and then echo back the value of *$a*, you should get the following (depending, of course, on the current date and time):

```
Days               : 109
Hours              : 3
Minutes            : 55
Seconds            : 0
Milliseconds       : 0
Ticks              : 94317000000000
TotalDays          : 109.163194444444
TotalHours         : 2619.91666666667
TotalMinutes       : 157195
TotalSeconds       : 9431700
TotalMilliseconds  : 9431700000
```

Suppose all you really care about is the number of days between the two dates. In that case, just echo back the value of the Days property:

```
$a.Days
```

VBScript Function	Windows PowerShell Equivalent
DatePart	*Definition:* Returns the specified part of a given date.

Given a date-time value, the *DatePart* function can tease out just a portion of that value, such as the hour, minute, or second of the day. In Windows PowerShell, the *Get-Date* cmdlet provides the same capability: Just call *Get-Date* and take a peek at the desired property value. Here are some examples:

```
$a = (get-date).day
$a = (get-date).dayofweek
$a = (get-date).dayofyear
$a = (get-date).hour
$a = (get-date).millisecond
$a = (get-date).minute
$a = (get-date).month
$a = (get-date).second
$a = (get-date).timeofday
$a = (get-date).year
```

Suppose you *do* need to know just the hour of the day. No problem; first, use this command to grab the value of the Hour property and store it in the variable *$a*:

```
$a = (get-date).hour
```

And then simply echo back the value of *$a*. Depending on the time of day when you ran the command, you should get back something like this (based on a 24-hour clock):

```
15
```

DateSerial	*Definition:* Returns a variant of subtype Date for a specified year, month, and day.

OK, we're not sure how often (if ever) this one comes up, but the *DateSerial* function in VBScript enables you to create a date just by passing the appropriate values for the year, month, and day:

```
MyDate1 = DateSerial(2006, 12, 31)
```

(Hey, we said we didn't know how often this comes up.)

You can achieve roughly the same effect in Windows PowerShell by calling the *Get-Date* cmdlet and passing the appropriate values:

```
$a = get-date -y 2006 -mo 12 -day 31
```

Notice that, in Windows PowerShell, we need to include parameters for the year (-y), the month (-mo), and the day (-day). We can, however, abbreviate the year and the month to make the finished product more closely mimic the *DateSerial* function.

When you run this command and then echo back the value of *$a*, you should get something similar to the following:

```
Sunday, December 31, 2006 1:27:42 PM
```

VBScript Function	Windows PowerShell Equivalent
DateValue	*Definition:* Returns a variant of subtype Date.
	How can you make sure Windows PowerShell treats a value as a date and not as, say, a string? One way is to explicitly "cast" that value as a date-time value. For example, this command assigns the string 12/1/2006 to the variable *$a*, at the same time making *$a* a date-time value:
	`$a = [datetime] "12/1/2006"`
	When you run this command and then use the GetType() method to retrieve the data type for *$a*, you should get the following:

	`IsPublic IsSerial Name`
	`-------- -------- ----`
	`True     True     DateTime`

Day	*Definition:* Returns a whole number between 1 and 31, inclusive, representing the day of the month.
	So, in conclusion—yes, did you have a question? You say you have an automated procedure that's supposed to run only on the 10th and 25th of each month? You say you don't know how to use Windows PowerShell to determine the day portion of the month? Hey, no problem, this is an easy one to answer: All you have to do is call the *Get-Date* cmdlet, then grab the value of the Day property. For example, this command retrieves the value of the Day property for the current date and stores that value in the variable *$a*:
	`$a = (get-date).day`
	When you run this command and then echo back the value of *$a*, you should get the following, assuming you're running the command on, say, 9/17/2006:
	17

VBScript Function	Windows PowerShell Equivalent
Escape	*Definition:* Encodes a string so that it contains only ASCII characters.

Admittedly, this is another one of those functions you probably don't use on a daily basis. To quote from the VBScript Language reference:

"The Escape function returns a string (in Unicode format) that contains the contents of charString. All spaces, punctuation, accented characters, and other non-ASCII characters are replaced with %*xx* encoding, where xx is equivalent to the hexadecimal number representing the character. Unicode characters that have a value greater than 255 are stored using the %u*xxxx* format."

Hey, why not?

Shockingly, Windows PowerShell doesn't include a built-in method for encoding a string in this fashion. However, you can easily do this by loading the .NET Framework System.Web class and then using the Web.Utility class URLEncode method. In other words, by executing a pair of commands similar to this:

```
[Reflection.Assembly]::LoadWithPartialName("System.Web")
$a = [web.httputility]::urlencode
("http://www.microsoft.com/technet/scriptcenter/default.mspx")
```

When you run this command and then echo back the value of *$a*, you should get the following:

```
http%3a%2f%2fwww.microsoft.com%2ftechnet%2fscriptcenter%2fdefault.mspx
```

And yes, that's what it's *supposed* to look like.

Eval	*Definition:* Evaluates an expression and returns the result.

OK, we're not sure how often you need to evaluate an expression (such as a mathematical equation) and simply know whether that expression is true or false. If you *do* need to do this, however, you can do so simply by using the -eq comparison operator. For example, this command evaluates the expression $2 + 2 = 45$ and then stores the evaluation (true or false) in the variable *$a*:

```
$a = 2 + 2 -eq 45
```

When you run this command and then echo back the value of *$a*, you should get the following:

```
False
```

Exp	*Definition:* Returns *e* (the base of natural logarithms) raised to a power.

You say your company will go broke unless you can find a way to raise *e* to a specified power? Relax; in Windows PowerShell, you can do this by using the System.Math class and the Exp method. Here's an example that raises *e* to the second power and assigns the resulting value to the variable *$a*:

```
$a = [math]::exp(2)
```

When you run this command and then echo back the value of *$a*, you should get the following:

```
7.38905609893065
```

VBScript Function	Windows PowerShell Equivalent

Filter	*Definition:* Returns a zero-based array containing a subset of a string array based on specified filter criteria.
	
	To tell you the truth, we've never actually seen anyone use the *Filter* function; however, we can see where it *might* be useful. Given an array, *Filter* enables you to do a wild card search of items within that array. For example, suppose you have an array with the following items:
	
	`Monday`
	`Month`
	`Merry`
	`Mansion`
	`Modest`
	
	Using the *Filter* function and the wild card value *mon** would return a subarray containing all the values that start with the letters m-o-n:
	
	`Monday`
	`Month`
	
	In Windows PowerShell, you create a similar substring by using the *Where-Object* cmdlet and weeding out only those values that start with *mon* (note that you use the -like operator to do a wild card search like that). The first of the following two commands creates an array named *$a* and assigns five string values to that array. The second command takes *$a* and pipes the values to *Where-Object*, which selects all the values that start with *mon* and assigns them to the variable *$b*:
	
	`$a = "Monday","Month","Merry","Mansion","Modest"`
	`$b = ($a | where-object {$_ -like "Mon*"})`
	
	When you run this command and then echo back the value of *$b*, you should get the following:
	
	`Monday`
	`Month`

FormatCurrency	*Definition:* Returns an expression formatted as a currency value using the currency symbol defined in the system Control Panel.
	
	To format a Windows PowerShell value as currency, you simply use the .NET Framework formatting commands. The following two commands assign the value 1000 to the variable *$a*, then use the currency formatting string "{0:C}" to format the value as currency (note that the value to be formatted is included as part of the -f parameter):
	
	`$a = 1000`
	`$a = "{0:C}" -f $a`
	
	When you run this command and then echo back the value of *$a*, you should get the following:
	
	`$1,000.00`

VBScript Function	Windows PowerShell Equivalent
FormatDateTime	*Definition:* Returns an expression formatted as a date or time.

The .NET Framework enables you to create a vast array of custom date formats, far too many to cover in this introductory guide. Fortunately, you can create the four basic date-time formats without having to use any fancy (and sometimes confusing) custom formatting strings. Instead, just employ the four methods shown below:

```
$a = (get-date).tolongdatestring()
$a = (get-date).toshortdatestring()
$a = (get-date).tolongtimestring()
$a = (get-date).toshorttimestring()
```

When you run these commands and then echo back the values of *$a*, you should get something similar to the following, in order:

```
Wednesday, September 13, 2006
9/13/2006
7:57:25 PM
7:57 PM
```

FormatNumber	*Definition:* Returns an expression formatted as a number.

For most people, formatting a number simply means specifying the number of decimal points to be displayed. In Windows PowerShell, you can use .NET formatting strings to specify the number of decimal places. The following example assigns the value 11 to the variable *$a*, then uses the .NET formatting string "{0:N6}" to format *$a* so that it displays 6 digits beyond the decimal point (that's what the 6 in the formatting string is for):

```
$a = 11
$a = "{0:N6}" -f $a
```

When you run this command and then echo back the value of *$a*, you should get the following:

```
11.000000
```

Note: Windows PowerShell will round numbers up or down as needed to fit the new format. For example, suppose *$a* is equal to 11.54543 and you decide to format it with just a single decimal point. Windows PowerShell will assign the value 11.5 to *$a* (because the discarded decimal digits—4543—are rounded down to 5).

Incidentally, this formatting command will also insert the appropriate list separator. For example, try running these two commands and see what you get back:

```
$a = 11000000
$a = "{0:N6}" -f $a
```

When you echo back the value of *$a* (at least on a machine using the default setting for U.S. English), you'll get back the following value:

```
11,000,000.000000
```

VBScript Function	Windows PowerShell Equivalent
FormatPercent	*Definition:* Returns an expression formatted as a percentage (multiplied by 100) with a trailing % character.
	In Windows PowerShell, you can format a value as a percent by using the .NET formatting methods. For example, these two commands set the value of $a to .113, then use .NET formatting to format $a as a percentage:
	`$a = .113` `$a = "{0:P1}" -f $a`
	The formatting command is interpreted like this: You specify the format type in brackets—{}—with the entire method (brackets and all) enclosed in double quote marks. The 0 is the index number of the item to be formatted (in this case it's a 0 because we're dealing with a single string value). The P indicates that we want to format the value as a percentage, and the 1 represents the number of digits to display following the decimal point.
	Got all that? Excellent.
	The format method is then followed by the -f parameter and the value to be formatted ($a).
	When you run this command and then echo back the value of $a, you should get the following:
	`11.3 %`
GetLocale	*Definition:* Returns the current locale ID value.
	InVBScript you can identify the user's locale (which determines such things as keyboard layout and alphabetic sort order, as well as date, time, number, and currency formats) by calling the *GetLocale* function and then translating the returned ID number. You can get this same locale ID in Windows PowerShell by using the *Get-Culture* cmdlet and looking at the value of the LCID property:
	`$a = (get-culture).lcid`
	When you run this command and then echo back the value of $a, you should get the following, provided your computer has U.S. English configured for its language and regional settings:
	`1033`
	If you'd prefer to see the locale name (as opposed to the ID number) use this command instead:
	`$a = (get-culture).displayname`
	That will return information similar to this:
	`English (United States)`

VBScript Function	Windows PowerShell Equivalent
GetObject	*Definition:* Returns a reference to an Automation object from a file.
	OK, we'll level with you: We're taking the easy way out on this one. Although Windows PowerShell does not include a *GetObject* command, it *is* possible to load the Microsoft.VisualBasic assembly and then use the Interaction class and *its* GetObject method:

	`[reflection.assembly]::LoadWithPartialName("'Microsoft.VisualBasic")`
	`$a= [Microsoft.VisualBasic.Interaction]::GetObject("WinNT://atl-ws-01/`
	`Administrator")`

	That part's easy. To actually *use* this object reference is far more complicated, requiring the use of binding flags and the InvokeMember method, and, well, it goes way beyond what we can cover in this introductory manual. The best thing to do? Assume that there is no GetObject equivalent and forget about it. The second best thing to do: Check the following Web site for an example of using the Visual Basic .NET GetObject method from within Windows PowerShell: *http://mow001.blogspot.com/2006/04/access-adsi-winnt-provider-from-monad.html*
GetRef	*Definition:* Returns a reference to a procedure that can be bound to an event.
	Not applicable. As far as we know, this is a Web page–only command.
Hex	*Definition:* Returns a string representing the hexadecimal value of a number.
	How do you convert a decimal number to a hexadecimal value? Why, you use the .NET formatting methods, of course. (How else would you do it?) For example, these two commands assign the value 4517 to the variable *$a*, then use .NET formatting to return the hexadecimal equivalent of 4517:
	`$a = 4517` `$a = "{0:X}" -f $a`
	The formatting command is interpreted like this: You specify the format type in brackets—{}—with the entire method (brackets and all) enclosed in double quote marks. The 0 is the index number of the item to be formatted (in this case, 0 because we're dealing with a single string value). The X indicates that we want to format the value as a hexadecimal number.
	The format method is then followed by the -f parameter and the value to be formatted (*$a*).
	When you run this command and then echo back the value of *$a*, you should get the following:
	`11A5`

VBScript Function	Windows PowerShell Equivalent
Hour	*Definition:* Returns a whole number between 0 and 23, inclusive, representing the hour of the day.
	Not that days, months, and years aren't important, mind you, but sometimes all you really need to know is the hour. To return an integer value indicating the hour (based on a 24-hour clock), just use the *Get-Date* cmdlet and take a peek at the value of the Hour property:
	`$a = (get-date).hour`
	When you run this command at 4:00 P.M. and then echo back the value of *$a*, you should get the following:
	`16`
InputBox	*Definition:* Displays a prompt in a dialog box, waits for the user to input text or click a button, and returns the contents of the text box.
	OK, this was a tough one. At first we figured that the easiest way to create an input box would be to rely on the .NET Framework and Visual Basic .NET. That worked, but with one major problem: The input box always appeared behind all the other windows on the desktop. That meant that the input box would appear, but no one would ever see it. Not exactly what we were hoping for.
	At our wit's end, we did what anyone else would do in our situation: We started searching the Internet looking for sample code we could steal. And, sure enough, we found some, courtesy of /\/\o\/\/, a Windows PowerShell MVP. (Check out *http://mow001.blogspot.com/2006/04/access-adsi-winnt-provider-from-monad.html;* when it comes to Windows PowerShell, this guy knows what he's talking about.) Here's the solution /\/\o\/\/ came up with:

	`$a = new-object -comobject MSScriptControl.ScriptControl`
	`$a.language = "vbscript"`
	`$a.addcode("function getInput() getInput =`
	`inputbox(`"Message box prompt`",`"Message Box Title`") end function" )`
	`$b = $a.eval("getInput")`

	We won't bother trying to explain how this works; we'll simply note that it *does* work. We'll also point out that you have to type this exactly as shown; in particular, that means including all the little backticks (the grave accent character [`]) when assigning a message box prompt and title.
	By the way, thanks, /\/\o\/\/!

VBScript Function	Windows PowerShell Equivalent
InStr	*Definition:* Returns the position of the first occurrence of one string within another.

The *InStr* function is primarily used to determine whether a specific character or set of characters can be found in a string. In Windows PowerShell, you can test for the existence of a substring by using the Contains() method. For example, here we assign the word *wombat* to a variable named *$a*, then use Contains() to determine whether or not the letter m appears anywhere in that string. In turn, our True/False return value is stored in the variable *$b*:

```
$a = "wombat"
$b = $a.contains("m")
```

When you run this command and then echo back the value of *$b*, you should get the following:

```
True
```

What if we used *this* command:

```
$b = $a.contains("x")
```

That's right: Windows PowerShell would report back False because there is no x in wombat.

And no i in team.

Confession time: The *InStr* function is typically used to determine whether a specified substring exists in a parent string; most of the time, script writers only care whether or not the substring can be found. Technically, though, *InStr* doesn't return a Boolean value (that is, True or False); instead, it returns the character position of the first instance of the substring. If that's what you'd *really* like to do, you can use the IndexOf() method instead of the Contains()method. For example, consider these two lines of code:

```
$a = "wombat"
$b = $a.indexof("m")
```

If you run these two lines of code and then echo back the value of *$b*, you'll get back this:

```
2
```

Why? Because the letter m can first be found in the third character position in *wombat*. (Yes, we know. But the first character occupies position 0, meaning the second character occupies position 1 and the third character occupies position 2). If the letter m could *not* be found in the string, then a −1 would be returned.

VBScript Function	Windows PowerShell Equivalent
InStrRev	*Definition:* Returns the position of an occurrence of one string within another, from the end of string.
	To the best of our knowledge, no Scripting Guy has ever used the *InStrRev* function. (Or, if they have, they won't admit it.) What *InStrRev* does is examine a string value and then determine the *last* occurrence of a specified substring.
	We don't blame you. But here's an example. Suppose you run *InStrRev* against the string value *1234x6789x1234*, specifying the letter x as the substring you're searching for. In that case, *InStrRev* will return a 10, because the last x happens to be the 10th character in the string.
	OK. Now, what if you want to perform this same trick in Windows PowerShell? No problem, just use the LastIndexOfAny method, like so:
	```$a = "1234x6789x1234"``` ```$b = $a.lastindexofany("x")```
	When you run those two commands and then echo back the value of *$b*, you should get the following:
	9
	And, no, that's not a mistake. In .NET, the first character position in a string is actually position 0; that makes the 10th character (the character we're interested in) position 9. (A good thing to keep in mind if and when you start doing string manipulation in Windows PowerShell.)
Int/Fix	*Definition:* Returns the integer portion of a number.
	Friends, are you plagued by decimal points? Would you just as soon strip off those pesky little decimal values and leave yourself with a clean, pure integer value? Then have we got a deal for you. In Windows PowerShell, you can remove decimal places by using the System.Math class and the Truncate method. For example, here we assign the value 11.98 to *$a*, then use Truncate to remove the .98:
	```$a = 11.98``` ```$a = [math]::truncate($a)```
	When you run this command and then echo back the value of *$a*, you should get the following:
	11
	Note: Keep in mind that the truncate method simply removes all numbers following the decimal point; it does not round values to the nearest whole number. If you want to do that, use the Round method instead.

VBScript Function	Windows PowerShell Equivalent
IsArray	*Definition:* Returns a Boolean value indicating whether a variable is an array.

When it comes to working with arrays, Windows PowerShell is a bit more forgiving than VBScript. For example, VBScript will blow up with a "Type mismatch" error should you try to directly echo the value of an array; instead, you need to set up a *For … Each* loop to get at those values (or specify individual values one at a time). With Windows PowerShell, you don't have to worry about that; a simple command such as this will echo back all the values in the array *$a*, no *For … Each* loop required:

```
$a
```

That said, there will still be times when you'll find it useful to know, in advance, whether or not you are dealing with an array. In Windows PowerShell, that can be done by using the -is operator and then checking to see if the item has an array data type. In these two lines of code, we create an array named *$a*, then check to see whether or not we really *do* have an array. The return value (True or False) is then stored in the variable *$b*:

```
$a = 22,5,10,8,12,9,80
$b = $a -is [array]
```

When you run this command and then echo back the value of *$b*, you should get the following:

```
True
```

| IsDate | *Definition:* Returns a Boolean value indicating whether an expression can be converted to a date. |

Windows PowerShell makes it easy to format and manipulate date and time values … provided, of course, that you actually *have* date and time values. To verify that a value truly *is* a date-time value, all you have to do is use the -is operator and check to see whether the data type is datetime. For example, these two lines of code assign a value to the variable *$a* and then determine whether or not *$a* is a date-time value:

```
$a = 11/2/2006
$a -is [datetime]
```

When you run this command, you should get the following:

```
False
```

Note: Why is this False; why isn't 11/2/2006 a valid date? That's easy: To assign a date to a variable, you need to enclose that date in double quote marks and specify the [datetime] variable type:

```
$a = [datetime] "11/2/2006"
```

Without the double quote marks, Windows PowerShell believes that this is a mathematical expression: 11 divided by 2 divided by 2006. In fact, if you check the value of *$a*, you'll get back this:

```
0.00274177467597208
```

With the quotes but without the [datetime] specified, Windows PowerShell thinks this is a string and still returns False.

VBScript Function	Windows PowerShell Equivalent

IsEmpty	*Definition:* Returns a Boolean value indicating whether a variable has been initialized.
	
	Rather than get bogged down in a long discussion on metaphysics, let's go with a rudimentary explanation of the difference between an empty variable and a null variable. A null variable is a value we know nothing about; we can't even say for certain whether the variable *has* a value. By contrast, we know the value of an empty variable: It's nothing. An empty variable is a variable that has no value (for example, it's been assigned an empty string as its value). A null variable—well, like we said, we don't know anything at all about a null variable.
	
	So how do we know whether or not a variable is empty? Well, for now, about the only approach we've come up with is to check and see whether or not the variable has a length equal to 0. An empty variable has a length equal to 0; a null variable does not. (Because we don't know anything about a null variable, we have no idea what its length might be.) Confused? We don't blame you. But maybe this example will help. In our first command, we assign an empty string ("") to the variable $a; in the second command, we use the -eq operator to determine whether or not the length of $a is equal to 0. That value gets stored in the variable $b:
	
	`$a = ""`
	`$b = $a.length -eq 0`
	
	When you run this command and then echo back the value of $b, you should get the following:
	
	`True`
	
	We can't guarantee that this will always work, but it's a good place to start.

IsNull	*Definition:* Returns a Boolean value that indicates whether an expression contains no valid data (Null).
	
	It's often useful to know whether or not a value is Null; scripters who have worked with Active Directory have often run into problems when trying to do something as seemingly trivial as echo back the value of a property, at least if that property turns out not to *have* a value. In Windows PowerShell, you can check for a Null value simply by using the -eq comparison operator to compare a variable with the system variable $Null. For example, this command compares $b to $Null, and stores the results of that comparison in $a:
	
	`$a = $z -eq $null`
	
	When you run this command and then echo back the value of $a, you should get the following, assuming, of course, that $z really *is* Null:
	
	`True`
	
	If you then use a similar command to determine whether or not $a is Null (i.e., $a —eq $null) you should get back False; that's because $a *isn't* Null.

VBScript Function	Windows PowerShell Equivalent
IsNumeric	*Definition:* Returns a Boolean value indicating whether an expression can be evaluated as a number.
	OK, so this one turned out to be a bit more complicated than we anticipated; that's because neither Windows PowerShell nor the .NET Framework includes a "generic" method for testing whether or not a given value is a number. After toying with the notion of doing this using regular expressions, we finally decided to use Visual Basic .NET instead. In the following set of commands, we assign the value 44.5 to the variable *$a*, then load the Microsoft.VisualBasic assembly. With the assembly loaded, we can then use the Visual Basic IsNumeric function to determine whether or not 44.5 is a number:
	```\n$a = 44.5\n[reflection.assembly]::LoadWithPartialName("'Microsoft.VisualBasic")\n$b = [Microsoft.VisualBasic.Information]::isnumeric($a)\n```
	As you might expect, when we run these commands and then echo back the value of *$b*, we get the following:
	```\nTrue\n```
	If we change the value of *$a* to "44.5a" and re-run the commands, we'll get back this:
	```\nFalse\n```
IsObject	*Definition:* Returns a Boolean value indicating whether an expression references a valid Automation object.
	That's a good question: How *can* you tell whether or not a variable is an object reference; that is, how can you tell whether a variable is a pointer to a COM object or a .NET object? Well, one way is to invoke the -is parameter and see whether the variable really *is* an object. For example, in the following two commands, we create an object reference named *$a*. We then check to see whether or not *$a* is an object reference, with the resulting value (True or False) stored in the variable *$b*:
	```\n$a = new-object -comobject scripting.filesystemobject\n$b = $a -is [object]\n```
	When you run this command and then echo back the value of *$b*, you should get the following:
	```\nTrue\n```
	As we intimated, .NET objects will also be identified as objects using this command.

VBScript Function	Windows PowerShell Equivalent
Join	*Definition:* Returns a string created by joining a number of substrings contained in an array.
	There will be times (trust us, there will be) when you want to take all the values in an array and transform them into a single string. In Windows PowerShell, you can do that using the System.String class and the Join method. For example, in the first of the following two commands, we assign the letters h-e-l-l-o to an array variable named *$a*; in the second command, we use the Join method to combine those values into a string variable named *$b*. Notice that we pass Join two parameters: The separator (i.e., the character we want inserted between each array item) and the array to be joined. In this example, we don't want *any* character inserted between items, so we simply pass an empty string:
	`$a = "h","e","l","l","o"` `$b = [string]::join("", $a)`
	When you run this command and then echo back the value of *$b*, you should get the following:
	`hello`
	What if we wanted to place a backslash (\) between each item? Then we'd use this command:
	`$b = [string]::join("\", $a)`
	In turn, the value of *$b* would be equal to this:
	`h\e\l\l\o`
	Cool, huh?
LBound	*Definition:* Returns the smallest available subscript for the indicated dimension of an array.
	Typically, the lower bound of an array (i.e., the index number assigned to the first element in the array) is 0. In Windows PowerShell, you can verify that by using the GetLowerBound() method. For example, suppose we use the following command to create an array named *$a*:
	`$a = 1,2,3,4,5,6,7,8,9`
	We can then use this command to determine the lower bound of the array and store that value in the variable *$b*:
	`$b = $a.getlowerbound(0)`
	Note: The parameter 0 passed to GetLowerBound() simply means that we want to look at the first dimension in the array. If we were working with a multidimensional array, we could supply other values to GetLowerBound().
	When you run this command and then echo back the value of *$b*, you should get the following:
	`0`

VBScript Function	Windows PowerShell Equivalent
LCase	*Definition:* Returns a string that has been converted to lowercase.
	Using Windows PowerShell, can you convert all the characters in a string to their lowercase equivalent? Of course you can; all you have to do is call the ToLower() method. For example, here we assign 26 uppercase letters to the variable $a; we then use the ToLower() method to convert all the characters in the string to lowercase:
	```$a = "ABCDEFGHIJKLMNOPQRSTUVWXYZ"``` ```$a = $a.ToLower()```
	When you run this command and then echo back the value of *$a,* you should get the following:
	```abcdefghijklmnopqrstuvwxyz```
Left	*Definition:* Returns a specified number of characters from the left side of a string.
	What's that? You want to know if it's possible to use Windows PowerShell to return the first *x* characters in a string? Of course it is: All you have to do is call the Substring method, passing two parameters: The starting character (with 0 being the first character position) and the number of characters to return. For example, this command assigns the letters of the alphabet to a variable named *$a,* then uses Substring to reassign *$a* just the first three letters in the string:
	```$a="ABCDEFGHIJKLMNOPQRSTUVWXYZ"``` ```$a = $a.substring(0,3)```
	When you run this command and then echo back the value of *$a,* you should get the following:
	```ABC```
Len	*Definition:* Returns the number of characters in a string or the number of bytes required to store a variable.
	The "length" of a string is simply the number of characters contained in that string. In Windows PowerShell, you can determine the length of a string by retrieving the value of the aptly named Length property. In this example, we stored the 26 letters of the English alphabet in a variable named *$a,* then assign the length of that string to the variable *$b*:
	```$a = "abcdefghijklmnopqrstuvwxyz"``` ```$b = $a.length```
	When you run this command and then echo back the value of *$b,* you should get the following:
	```26```
LoadPicture	*Definition:* Returns a picture object.
	Not applicable. This command is designed for use with Web pages. And, to the best of our understanding, it doesn't work the way it's supposed to anyway.

VBScript Function	Windows PowerShell Equivalent
Log	*Definition:* Returns the natural logarithm of a number.
	Most people probably have the natural logarithms for all known numbers committed to memory. If you don't, and you need to know the log for a particular number, then use the System.Math class and the Log method. This command returns the log of 100 and assigns the value to the variable *$a*:
	`$a = [math]::log(100)`
	When you run this command and then echo back the value of *$a*, you should get the following:
	`4.60517018598809`
LTrim	*Definition:* Returns a copy of a string without leading spaces (LTrim), trailing spaces (RTrim), or both leading and trailing spaces (Trim).
	In VBScript, the LTrim function is used to remove any blank spaces that appear at the *beginning* of a string; in Windows PowerShell, you can carry out this same task by using the TrimStart() method. For example, these two commands assign a string value to the variable *$a*, then use the TrimStart() method to remove the blank spaces from the beginning of the string (note that, for illustration purposes, we've used dots to represent blank spaces):
	`$a = ".........123456789.........."` `$a = $a.TrimStart()`
	When you run this command and then echo back the value of *$a*, you should get the following:
	`123456789.........`
RTrim	*Definition:* Returns a copy of a string without leading spaces (LTrim), trailing spaces (RTrim), or both leading and trailing spaces (Trim).
	In VBScript, the *RTrim* function is used to remove any blank spaces that appear at the *end* of a string; in Windows PowerShell, you can carry out this same task by using the TrimEnd() method. For example, these two commands assign a string value to the variable *$a*, then use the TrimEnd() method to remove the blank spaces from the end of the string (note that, for illustration purposes, we've used dots to represent blank spaces):
	`$a = ".........123456789.........."` `$a = $a.TrimEnd()`
	When you run this command and then echo back the value of *$a*, you should get the following:
	`..........123456789`

VBScript Function	Windows PowerShell Equivalent
Trim	*Definition:* Returns a copy of a string without leading spaces (LTrim), trailing spaces (RTrim), or both leading and trailing spaces (Trim).
	You had to know that this one was coming: In VBScript, the Trim function is used to remove any blank spaces that appear at the beginning or the end of a string; in Windows PowerShell, you can carry out this same task by using the Trim() method. For example, these two commands assign a string value to the variable $a, then use the Trim() method to remove the blank spaces from both the beginning and the end of the string (note that, for illustration purposes, we've used dots to represent blank spaces):
	`$a = "..........123456789.........."` `$a = $a.Trim()`
	When you run this command and then echo back the value of $a, you should get the following:
	`123456789`
Mid	*Definition:* Returns a specified number of characters from a string.
	Sometimes the good stuff—at least when it comes to Oreo cookies and string values—is found in the middle. With Oreos, you can get to the stuff in the middle by unscrewing the cookie; with string values, you can get to the stuff in the middle by calling the Substring() method. In the following example, we assign a string value to the variable $a and then use the SubString() method to retrieve a portion of that string. And what portion are we retrieving? To answer that, let's first look at the two commands:
	`$a="ABCDEFG"` `$a = $a.substring(2,3)`
	Notice that we're passing Substring() two parameters, a 2 and a 3. The 2 represents the character position in the main string, where we want to start grabbing letters. We want to start with the third character, so we pass a 2. No, that's not a typo: We pass a 2 because the first character in the string is in position 0. That means the second character is found in position 1, and the third character—the one we're interested in—resides in position 2.
	The 3, meanwhile, indicates the number of characters we want to extract. In other words, we want to start at position 2 and grab the next three characters.
	Pretty simple when you think about it.
	When you run this command and then echo back the value of $a, you should get the following:
	`CDE`

VBScript Function	Windows PowerShell Equivalent
Minute	*Definition:* Returns a whole number between 0 and 59, inclusive, representing the minute of the hour.
	Wow, you need to know the exact *minute* for a specified date-time value? No problem, just use the *Get-Date* cmdlet and grab the value of the Minute property:
	`$a =(get-date).minute`
	When you run this command and then echo back the value of *$a*, you should get the following (depending on the actual time, of course):
	`24`
Month	*Definition:* Returns a whole number between 1 and 12, inclusive, representing the month of the year.
	Need to get the number representing the month for a specified date (e.g., 1 for January, 2 for February, etc.)? Then just use the *Get-Date* cmdlet, the -f parameter, and the MM .NET formatting command. This command returns a numeric value representing the month of the year for the current date:
	`$a = get-date -f "MM"`
	When you run this command (at least during the month of September) and then echo back the value of *$a*, you should get the following:
	`09`
	If you don't want the leading zero, then retrieve the month value and change it to an integer data type. How do you do that? Like this:
	`$a = [int] (get-date -f "MM")`
MonthName	*Definition:* Returns a string indicating the specified month.
	Sometimes, all you want to know is that we're in month number 9; at other times, you'd prefer to know the *name* of the month (e.g., September). In Windows PowerShell, you can determine the name of the month by using the *Get-Date* cmdlet and then using the -f formatting parameter and the value MMMM. In other words, this command will retrieve the name of the month for the current month and store that value in the variable *$a*:
	`$a = get-date -f "MMMM"`
	When you run this command and then echo back the value of *$a*, you should get the following (depending on the actual month):
	`September`

VBScript Function	Windows PowerShell Equivalent
MsgBox	*Definition:* Displays a message in a dialog box, waits for the user to click a button, and returns a value indicating which button the user clicked.
	Windows PowerShell does not posses built-in methods for displaying message boxes. However, it's very easy to use the *New-Object* cmdlet to create an instance of the Windows Script Host (WSH) Shell object; from there you can use the WSH Popup method to display a message box. The following example first uses *New-Object* (and the -comobject parameter) to create an instance of the Wscript.Shell object. In the second command, the WSH Popup method is used to display a message box, with the resulting action (i.e., the value of the button the user clicked to dismiss the message box) stored in the variable *$b*:
| | ```
$a = new-object -comobject wscript.shell
$b = $a.popup("This is a test",0,"Test Message Box",1)
``` |
	For more information on the parameters used when displaying the message box, visit the following Web site: *http://msdn2.microsoft.com/en-us/library/x83z1d9f.aspx*
Now	*Definition:* Returns the current date and time according to the setting of your computer's system date and time.
	If you're looking for easy one, then you came to the right place: Assigning the current date and time to a variable is no more difficult than using the *Get-Date* cmdlet. For example:
| | ```
$a = get-date
``` |
| | When you run this command and then echo back the value of *$a*, you should get something similar to the following: |
| | ```
Tuesday, September 05, 2006 10:24:04 AM
``` |
Oct	*Definition:* Returns a string representing the octal value of a number.
	As script writers, a question we always ask ourselves is this, "Where would we be without octal numbers?"
	Well, OK, good point. Still, you never know, maybe someday you *will* have to use Windows PowerShell to convert a decimal value to its octal equivalent. If and when that time comes, you can do this using the .NET Framework Convert class and the ToString() method. Just pass ToString() two parameters:
	The decimal value to be converted (in our sample command, 999).
	The value 8 (the second parameter tells .NET to convert the value to its octal equivalent).
	In other words, do something like this:
| | ```
$a = [Convert]::ToString(999,8)
``` |
| | When you run this command and then echo back the value of *$a*, you should get the following: |
| | ```
1747
``` |
```

VBScript Function	Windows PowerShell Equivalent

Replace	*Definition:* Returns a string in which a specified substring has been replaced with another substring a specified number of times.
	
	The world as we know it would come to a crashing halt if we didn't have search-and-replace commands. In Windows PowerShell, you can do a simple search-and-replace on any string value simply by using the -replace parameter and specifying two things: (1) the string value to search for, and (2) the replacement text.
	
	For example, the following two commands assign a value to the variable $a, then use -replace to replace all instances of the letter x with the letter a:
	
	`$a = "bxnxnx"`
	`$a = $a -replace("x","a")`
	
	When you run this command and then echo back the value of $a, you should get the following:
	
	`banana`

RGB	*Definition:* Returns a whole number representing an RGB color value.
	
	If you are a Web designer, you might very well find yourself needing to calculate RGB color values. Although Windows PowerShell doesn't include a built-in method or function for calculating RGB values, you can write a simple equation that will do the math for you. In the following example, we assign values to three different variables, representing the three color components: $blue, $green, $red. We then calculate the RGB value and store the result in the variable $a:
	
	`$blue = 10`
	`$green= 10`
	`$red = 10`
	`$a = [long] ($blue + ($green * 256) + ($red * 65536))`
	
	When you run these commands and then echo back the value of $a, you should get the following:
	
	`657930`

VBScript Function	Windows PowerShell Equivalent
Right	*Definition:* Returns a specified number of characters from the right side of a string.

You can use the Substring() method to retrieve a specified number of characters from the beginning of a string (see Left). That's great, but how do you return a specified number of characters from the *end* of a string?

Here's one sneaky way to do that. Use the Substring() method, specifying the following two parameters:

- The starting position, which should be the length of the string minus the number of characters you're after. If you want the last 4 characters in the string, then use the length minus 4.

- The number of characters you want returned

For example, these two commands assign a value to the variable $a, then use the Substring() method to retrieve the last 9 characters in the string:

```
$a = "ABCDEFGHIJKLMNOPQRSTUVWXYZ"
$a = $a.substring($a.length - 9, 9)
```

When you run this command and then echo back the value of *$a*, you should get the following:

```
RSTUVWXYZ
```

Rnd	*Definition:* Returns a random number.

Although VBScript doesn't require a lot of code to generate a random number, the code that *is* required is a bit cryptic, to say the least. In Windows PowerShell, the process is much easier: All you need to do is create an instance of the System. Random class and then call the Next method, passing this method the first and last numbers in the series. For example, these two commands create an instance of System.Random and then store a random number between 1 and 100 in the variable *$b*:

```
$a = new-object random
$b = $a.next(1,100)
```

When you run this command and then echo back the value of *$b*, you should get something like the following:

```
72
```

And, of course, the next time you run the command, you should get something different.

To generate a random integer (not necessarily an integer falling between a specified starting and ending number), just call the Next method without supplying any additional parameters:

```
$b = $a.next()
```

VBScript Function	Windows PowerShell Equivalent
Round	*Definition:* Returns a number rounded to a specified number of decimal places.
	When working with system administration scripts (and performing chores like returning free disk space on a drive), you'll often get back numbers similar to this: 45.987654321. More often than not, you don't really need all those decimal places; instead, you'd just as soon round the value up (or down).
	In Windows PowerShell, all you have to do is use the System.Math class and the Round method. This command rounds the number 45.987654321 to two decimal places (notice the value 2 passed as the second parameter to the method). The resulting value is then stored in the variable *$a*:
	`$a = [math]::round(45.987654321, 2)`
	When you run this command and then echo back the value of *$a*, you should get the following:
	`45.99`
ScriptEngine	*Definition:* Returns a string representing the scripting language in use.
	Not really applicable; after all, if you're running Windows PowerShell, you're using the Windows PowerShell script engine. Still, you can use the *Get-Host* cmdlet and the Version property to return information about *which* version of Windows PowerShell you're running:
	`$a = (get-host).version`
	When you run this command and then echo back the value of *$a*, you should get the following, depending on which build you are using:
| | ```
Major  Minor  Build  Revision
-----  -----  -----  --------
1      0      0      0
``` |
ScriptEngine-BuildVersion	*Definition:* Returns the build version number of the scripting engine in use.
	You're right about that, it *can* be useful to know which build of Windows PowerShell you happen to be running. Fortunately, you can determine that simply by calling the *Get-Host* cmdlet and then taking a peek at the value of the Version.Build property:
	`$a = (get-host).version.build`
	When you run this command and then echo back the value of *$a*, you should get the following, depending on which build you are using:
	`0`
ScriptEngine-MajorVersion	*Definition:* Returns the major version number of the scripting engine in use.
	Determining the major version of Windows PowerShell itself is a snap. All you have to do is call the *Get-Host* cmdlet and then grab the value of the Version.Major property. The following command determines the major version and then stores that value in the variable *$a*:
	`$a = (get-host).version.major`
	When you run this command and then echo back the value of *$a*, you should get the following, depending on which version of PowerShell you are running:
	`1`
```

VBScript Function	Windows PowerShell Equivalent
ScriptEngine-MinorVersion	*Definition:* Returns the minor version number of the scripting engine in use.
	As you might expect, if you can use Windows PowerShell to determine the major version of the product, you can also use it to determine the minor version. In fact, all you have to do is call the *Get-Host* cmdlet and take a look at the value of the Version.Minor property. This command returns the minor version and stores it in the variable *$a*:
	`$a = (get-host).version.minor`
	When you run this command and then echo back the value of *$a*, you should get the following, depending on which version of PowerShell you are running:
	`0`
Second	*Definition:* Returns a whole number between 0 and 59, inclusive, representing the second of the minute.
	Is it useful for you to be able to take a specified date and time and throw out everything but the seconds? In other words, if today is 12:29:16 on 9/30/2006, is it useful for you to be able to determine that the seconds are equal to 16?
	To tell you the truth, we don't know whether that's useful or not. If it *is* useful, however, you can do that in Windows PowerShell by using the *Get-Date* cmdlet and then examining the value of the Second property:
	`$a = (get-date).second`
	When you run this command (assuming it really *is* 12:29:16 on 9/30/2006) and then echo back the value of *$a*, you should get the following:
	`16`
SetLocale	*Definition:* Sets the global locale and returns the previous locale.
	To be honest, we didn't put much effort into this one; after all, SetLocale works only in Web pages, and Windows PowerShell is not designed for use in Web pages. So, we let this one slide.
Sgn	*Definition:* Returns an integer indicating the sign of a number.
	Quick: Is that a negative number or a positive number? An easy way to verify that in Windows PowerShell is to use the System.Math class and the Sign method. For example, this command uses the Sign method to determine the sign of –453:
	`$a = [math]::sign(-453)`
	When you run this command and then echo back the value of *$a*, you should get the following:
	`-1`
	If you check the sign of a positive number (e.g., 453), you should get back something like this (actually, you should get back something *exactly* like this):
	`1`

VBScript Function	Windows PowerShell Equivalent
Sin	*Definition:* Returns the sine of an angle.
	In mathematics, the sine of an angle is defined as ... well, it doesn't matter what the definition is. Instead, all that matters is that, in Windows PowerShell, you can use the System.Math class and the Sin method. For example, this command calculates the sine of a 45-degree angle and then stores the result in the variable *$a*:
	`$a = [math]::sin(45)`
	When you run this command and then echo back the value of *$a*, you should get the following:
	`0.850903524534118`
Space	*Definition:* Returns a string consisting of the specified number of spaces.
	Sometimes it's just enough that you can do something; it doesn't matter if you have to use some sort of crazy approach to do it. For example, in VBScript, you can use the *Space* function to create a string consisting of *x* number of consecutive blank spaces. Can you pull off this same feat in Windows PowerShell? You sure can, all you have to do is, well, take a blank space and multiply it by 25:
	`$a = " " * 25`
	Sure it's crazy. But, like we said, it works. Run the command, then use this command to add the letter *x* to the end of the string:
	`$a = $a + "x"`
	Guess what you'll get if you now echo back the value of *$a*? That's right, 25 blank spaces followed by the letter x:
	x

VBScript Function	Windows PowerShell Equivalent
Split	*Definition:* Returns a zero-based, one-dimensional array containing a specified number of substrings.
	"Returns a zero-based, one-dimensional array containing a specified number of substrings." Granted, that doesn't sound too terribly interesting. Nevertheless, the VBScript *Split* function (or the Windows PowerShell Split() method) can be incredibly useful. For example, suppose you have a comma-delimited list of computer names. As a single string value, that's of minimal use; as an *array*, however, that opens up a whole world of possibilities, including the opportunity to loop through each item in the array and perform a task against each of those items (i.e., each of those computers).
	So how do you turn a delimited string into an array? Here's how:
	`$a = "atl-ws-01,atl-ws-02,atl-ws-03,atl-ws-04"` `$b = $a.split(",")`
	In the first command, we simply assign a series of computer names (separated by commas) to the variable *$a*. In the second command, we use the Split method to separate the list of names and store them in an array named *$b*. Note the sole parameter passed to the Split() method: ",", which simply indicates that the comma is used as the delimiter (or, if you prefer, separator).
	When you run this command and then echo back the value of *$b*, you should get the following:

	`atl-ws-01`
	`atl-ws-02`
	`atl-ws-03`
	`atl-ws-04`

Sqr	*Definition:* Returns the square root of a number.
	Finally, a mathematical construct we all recognize! Granted, you probably need to calculate square roots about as often as you need to calculate arctangents. (On the other hand, and unlike arctangents, at least most of us know what square roots are.) Best of all, even if you *don't* know what square roots are, you can still calculate them by using the System.Math class and the Sqrt method. For example, this command determines the square root of 144 and stores the result in the variable *$a*:
	`$a = [math]::sqrt(144)`
	When you run this command and then echo back the value of *$a*, you should get the following:
	`12`

VBScript Function	Windows PowerShell Equivalent
StrComp	*Definition:* Returns a value indicating the result of a string comparison.
	Can we tell you whether two strings are identical? We can, provided you tell us one thing: Do you want a case-sensitive comparison or a case-insensitive comparison?
	Let's try a case-insensitive comparison for starters. In the following set of commands, we assign values to variables $a and $b. We then use the System.String class and the Compare() method to compare the two strings. Note that we pass the Compare() method three parameters: The two strings to be compared, and the value *$True*, which indicates that we want to do a case-insensitive comparison.

```
$a = "dog"
$b = "DOG"
$c = [String]::Compare($a,$b,$True)
```

When you run this command and then echo back the value of *$c*, you should get the following:

```
0
```

Note: A 0 means that the strings are identical. Any other value means that the strings are *not* identical.

Of course, these strings are identical because we did a case-insensitive comparison. Suppose we use *this* command, which does a case-sensitive comparison:

```
$c = [String]::Compare($a,$b,$False)
```

This time you get back –1, meaning that the strings are *not* identical (because the letter cases are not the same).

String	*Definition:* Returns a repeating character string of the length specified.

The String function provides a quick, reasonably fail-safe way to create a string consisting of a specified number of repeating characters. In other words, a string similar to this:

```
"===================="
```

(Yeah, we know. But this is sometimes useful when formatting data for display in a command window.)

If you ever *do* need to string together 20 equal signs or what-have-you in Windows PowerShell, you can accomplish this task by multiplying (yes, we said multiplying) an equals sign by 20 (strange, but true):

```
$a = "=" * 20
```

When you run this command and then echo back the value of *$a*, you should get the following:

```
====================
```

VBScript Function	Windows PowerShell Equivalent
StrReverse	*Definition:* Returns a string in which the character order of a specified string is reversed.
	How many times have you said to yourself, "Gosh, if only there was a way for me to reverse the character order of a specified string"? That's what we thought.
	Shockingly, Windows PowerShell has no equivalent to VBScript's *StrReverse* function; fortunately, though, we found at least one way to achieve the same effect. The following set of commands (which we won't bother explaining in any detail) assigns the value Scripting Guys to the variable *$a*, then uses a *For ... Next* loop to reverse the order of the characters in the string:
	`$a = "Scripting Guys"` `for ($i = $a.length - 1; $i -ge 0; $i--) {$b = $b + ($a.substring($i,1))}`
	When you run this command and then echo back the value of *$b*, you should get the following:
	`syuG gnitpircS`
	Note: Believe it or not, that's what you're *supposed* to get back!
Tan	*Definition:* Returns the tangent of an angle.
	Windows PowerShell wouldn't be much of a scripting language if it allowed you to calculate arctangents but *didn't* allow you to calculate tangents. Fortunately, that's not the case: You can determine the tangent of an angle by using the System.Math class and calling the Tan method. Here's a command that calculates the tangent of a 45-degree angle and then stores that value in the variable *$a*:
	`$a = [math]::tan(45)`
	When you run this command and then echo back the value of *$a*, you should get the following:
	`1.61977519054386`
Time	*Definition:* Returns a variant of subtype Date indicating the current system time.
	OK, give us a hard one. What's that? You'd like to store just the current time—and only the current time—in a variable? Fortunately, that's not very hard; for example, one way we can do that is to call the *Get-Date* cmdlet, then use the -displayhint parameter to assign just the current time to a variable. Sort of like this command, in which we store the current time to the variable *$a*:
	`$a = get-date -displayhint time`
	When you run this command and then echo back the value of *$a*, you should get the following (assuming you run it at 11:22:37 A.M.):
	`11:22:37 AM`

VBScript Function	Windows PowerShell Equivalent

Timer	*Definition:* Returns the number of seconds that have elapsed since 12:00 A.M. (midnight).
	
	In VBScript, the Timer function is typically used to determine how long it takes a script, function, or subroutine to execute. If that's what you want to do, then you can use the Windows PowerShell *Measure-Command* cmdlet to calculate elapsed time. The following command creates a *For ... Next* loop that runs from 1 to 100,000, writing each value of *$a* to the screen as it goes. Along the way, the *Measure-Command* cmdlet is used to keep track of how long it takes for the command to finish:
	
	``measure-command {
	    for ($a = 1; $a -le 100000; $a++)
	        {write-host $a}
	            }```
	
	When you run this command, you should get back information similar to the following:
	
	``Days : 0
	Hours : 0
	Minutes : 1
	Seconds : 9
	Milliseconds : 365
	Ticks : 693655925
	TotalDays : 0.000802842505787037
	TotalHours : 0.0192682201388889
	TotalMinutes : 1.15609320833333
	TotalSeconds : 69.3655925
	TotalMilliseconds : 69365.5925```

TimeSerial	*Definition:* Returns a variant of subtype Date containing the time for a specific hour, minute, and second.
	
	Like *DateSerial*, this is a function that is in no danger of being overused. However, if you want to pass in values for the hours, minutes, and seconds and get back a *time* value (as opposed to a date-time value), the following command will do the trick:
	
	```$a = get-date -h 17 -mi 10 -s 45 -displayhint time```
	
	Note: As you probably figured out for yourself, the -h parameter represents the hours, the -mi parameter represents the minutes, and the -s parameter represents the seconds. Values for the hours are based on a 24-hour clock.
	
	When you run this command and then echo back the value of *$a*, you should get the following:
	
	```5:10:45 PM```

VBScript Function	Windows PowerShell Equivalent

TimeValue	*Definition:* Returns a variant of subtype Date containing the time.
	
	OK, so you have a string value (say, 1:45 A.M.) and you'd like to convert that to a date-time value, is that right? No problem; Windows PowerShell can do that for you. In this command, we not only assign the string *1:45 AM* to the variable *$a*, but we also explicitly give *$a* a datetime data type:
	
	`$a = [datetime] "1:45 AM"`
	
	When you run this command (assuming it was run on 9/21/2006) and then echo back the value of *$a*, you should get the following:
	
	`Thursday, September 21, 2006 1:45:00 AM`

TypeName	*Definition:* Returns a string that provides variant subtype information about a variable.
	
	In system administration scripting, it's often useful to know what type of a variable you're working with; for example, databases don't like it if you try to save string data into a field reserved for numeric data. In Windows PowerShell, you can use the GetType() method to determine the variable type of any variable. For example, the following set of commands assigns the value 55.86768 to the variable *$a*, then uses GetType() to retrieve the Name of the *$a* variable type. The resulting type name is assigned to the variable *$b*:
	
	`$a = 55.86768`
	`$b = $a.gettype().name`
	
	When you run this command and then echo back the value of *$b*, you should get the following:
	
	`Double`

UBound	*Definition:* Returns the largest available subscript for the indicated dimension of an array.
	
	There are at least two ways to determine the index number of the last item in a Windows PowerShell array. For example, suppose we have the following array:
	
	`$a = "a","b","c","d","e"`
	
	With a 5-item array, the last item has an index number of 4 (because the first item in the array is actually item 0). But how do we *know* that? One way is to use the GetUpperBound() method. This command returns the upper bound for the first dimension (i.e., dimension 0) in the array *$a*:
	
	`$a.getupperbound(0)`
	
	You can also get the same results by subtracting 1 from the array's Length property:
	
	`$a.length-1`
	
	When you run either command you should get the following:
	
	`4`

VBScript Function	Windows PowerShell Equivalent

UCase	*Definition:* Returns a string that has been converted to uppercase.
	
	Sometimes, bigger truly *is* better, which is one reason you might want to convert all the characters in a string to their uppercase equivalent. How do you pull off such a feat in Windows PowerShell? That's easy, you just call the ToUpper() method. For example, these two commands assign the letters of the alphabet to the variable $a, then use the ToUpper() method to convert each of those letters to uppercase:
	
	`$a = "abcdefghijklmnopqrstuvwxyz"`
	`$a = $a.ToUpper()`
	
	When you run this command and then echo back the value of $a, you should get the following:
	
	`ABCDEFGHIJKLMNOPQRSTUVWXYZ`

Unescape	*Definition:* Decodes a string encoded with the *Escape* function.
	
	Suppose someone hands you a string value like this one, a value that has been encoded using the VBScript *Escape* function (or its equivalent):
	
	`http%3a%2f%2fwww.microsoft.com%2ftechnet%2fscriptcenter%2fdefault.mspx`
	
	Can you use Windows PowerShell to decode this value (i.e., turn it back into a regular string value)? You can if you use the .NET Framework's System.Web.HTTPUtility class and the URLDecode() method. Assuming that the string value is stored in the variable $a, these two commands should do the trick:
	
	`[Reflection.Assembly]::LoadWithPartialName("System.Web")`
	`$a = [web.httputility]::urldecode($a)`
	
	When you run the commands and then echo back the value of $a, you should get the following:
	
	`http://www.microsoft.com/technet/scriptcenter/default.mspx`

VBScript Function	**Windows PowerShell Equivalent**
VarType	*Definition:* Returns a value indicating the subtype of a variable.

In VBScript, you can use the *VarType* function to return an integer value that represents a particular data type (for example, a 9 represents an object). To be honest, we don't know how to do this in Windows PowerShell (i.e., return an integer value as opposed to the actual data type name). And, to be equally honest, we don't think it matters much.

Technical Note: VBScript uses a data type known as a variant. That means that its types are composed of two things: A chunk of memory where the type value is stored, and a description of the type. If you have a set of bits stored in memory somewhere, that's not enough to tell where it's a number 32 or the space character or a certain object with certain values. Because of that, VBScript's *VarType* function returns an integer that tells you the type bit for the variant.

PowerShell variables are strongly typed. That means there is no exact equivalent for the *VarType* function. To determine the data type in a PowerShell variable, you pipe the contents of the variable to *Get-Member* and rely on the cmdlet to tell you the type. There's no way to have an enumeration that maps to each possible data type; because you can construct new data types on the fly, that enumeration would have to account for an infinite number of data types. Needless to say, that would be a pretty tough job.

VBScript Function	Windows PowerShell Equivalent
Weekday	*Definition:* Returns a whole number representing the day of the week.

Definition: Returns a whole number representing the day of the week.

If you want to return an integer value representing a day of the week (for instance, getting back a *6* as opposed to getting back *Friday*), well, that's really none of our business, is it? To tell you the truth, we don't know of any way built into Windows PowerShell to do this; however, you *can* do this by using the .NET Framework's Microsoft.VisualBasic.DateAndTime class and the DatePart function. The following three commands assign the current date and time to the variable *$a*, load the Microsoft.VisualBasic assembly, then use the *DatePart* function to return an integer representing the day of the week. Note that *DatePart* requires two parameters:

- w, which tells the function we want the day of the week
- *$a*, the date we want to check

Here are the commands:

```
$a = get-date
[reflection.assembly]::LoadWithPartialName("'Microsoft.VisualBasic")
[Microsoft.VisualBasic.DateAndTime]::DatePart("w",$a)
```

Or, if you're really gung-ho, here's another approach:

The *Get-Date* cmdlet returns a System.DateTime object that has a DayOfWeek property. This property is an enumeration (a sequence of numbers that each represents something), with 0 representing Sunday, 1 representing Monday, and so on. If you type *(Get-Date).DayOfWeek*, you will see the text representation of the day. To get at the underlying numeric value, you need to type this:

```
(Get-Date).DayOfWeek.value__
```

Note: The value is followed by two underscores.

Of course, because the DayOfWeek enumeration starts by numbering Sunday at 0 rather than 1, you need to add 1 at the end of this last command to get the same result as the VBScript function.

```
(Get-Date).DayOfWeek.value__ + 1
```

Assuming you run these commands on a Friday, you should get back the following:

6

VBScript Function	Windows PowerShell Equivalent
WeekdayName	*Definition:* Returns a string indicating the specified day of the week.
	Determining the day of the week (Monday, Tuesday, Wednesday, etc.) is a tad bit convoluted in VBScript; you have to first call the Weekday function (which returns an integer value representing the day of the week) and then call the *WeekdayName* function to translate that integer into a string value. In Windows PowerShell, this is actually much easier; you simply get the desired date and then get the value of the DayOfWeek property. For example, this command assigns the DayOfWeek for the current date to the variable *$a*:
	`$a = (get-date).dayofweek`
	When you run this command and then echo back the value of *$a*, you should get something similar the following:
	`Friday`
	What if you wanted to determine the day of the week for a date other than the current one? No problem; this command returns the day of the week for 12/25/ 2007:
	`$a = (get-date "12/25/2007").dayofweek`
	And here's what you get back after running that command:
	`Tuesday`
Year	*Definition:* Returns a whole number representing the year.
	Don't feel bad, sometimes the Scripting Guys forget what year it is, too. Or at least we used to, until we realized we could use Windows PowerShell to determine the year for us. All we have to do is call the *Get-Date* cmdlet and then grab the value of the Year property. For example, this command retrieves the current year and stores that value in the variable *$a*:
	`$a = (get-date).year`
	When you run this command and then echo back the value of *$a*, you should get the following (assuming the command was run during the year 2006):
	`2006`
	Of course, you can determine the year for *any* date; all you have to do is ask *Get-Date* to work with that date instead. For example, this command returns the year for the date 9/15/2005:
	`$a = (get-date "9/15/2005").year`
	When you run this command and then echo back the value of *$a*, you should get the following:
	`2005`

VBScript Statement	Windows PowerShell Equivalent
Call	*Definition:* Transfers control to a Sub or Function procedure. The *Call* statement is optional in VBScript: You can call a subroutine or function either by using the *Call* statement followed by the procedure name or by simply specifying the procedure name. The *Call* statement is not used at all in Windows PowerShell; instead, you call a function simply by specifying the function name followed by any function parameters. For example, this command calls the function *MultiplyNumbers*, supplying a pair of parameters (25 and 67): `multiplynumbers 25 67`
Class	*Definition:* Declares the name of a class, as well as a definition of the variables, properties, and methods that make up the class. Although it *is* possible to create a class in Windows PowerShell, it's not a very straightforward process and definitely goes beyond the scope of this introductory manual. So, for the time being, forget we even mentioned it.

Const	*Definition:* Declares constants for use in place of literal values.
	
	A constant is nothing more than a variable whose value cannot be changed while a script is running. In Windows PowerShell, you can define a constant by using the *Set-Variable* cmdlet and specifying three parameters:
	
	■ -name, the name of the constant (don't include the $)
	
	■ -value, the value of the constant
	
	■ -option constant, to create a constant as opposed to a standard variable
	
	For example, this command creates a constant named $ForReading, with a value of 1:
	
	`set-variable -name ForReading -value 1 -option constant`
	
	If you try to assign a new value to this constant, you'll get an error message similar to this:
	
	`Cannot overwrite variable ForReading because it is read-only or constant.`

Dim	*Definition:* Declares variables and allocates storage space. In VBScript, the *Dim* statement is used to declare a variable, typically without assigning that variable a value of any kind. To declare a variable in Windows PowerShell, but without assigning a value to the variable, use a command similar to this: `$a = [string]` This command creates a new, empty string variable named *$a*. In order to declare a variable without assigning it a value, you must specify a data type (although this data type can later be changed).

VBScript Statement	Windows PowerShell Equivalent
Do ... Loop	*Definition:* Repeats a block of statements while a condition is True or until a condition becomes True.

The preceding definition pretty much says it all: A *Do ... While* loop enables you to repeat a block of code over and over again, at least as long as a specified condition is true. By comparison, a *Do ... Until* loop enables you to repeat a block of code over and over again, at least *until* a specified condition becomes true. As you might have guessed, you can create either type of loop using Windows PowerShell.

To begin with, let's take a look at the *Do ... While* loop. To create a *Do ... While* loop, you need the following items:

- The *Do* keyword

- The action (or actions) you want to perform. These actions must be contained within curly braces.

- The *While* keyword

- The condition that will spell the end of the loop. (In other words, when this condition is met then the loop should end.)

The following example assigns the value 1 to the variable $a, then uses that variable as part of a *Do ... While* loop. The action to be performed is fairly simple, we just echo back the value of $a, then use the ++ operator to increment $a by 1. That's what this portion of the code does:

```
{$a; $a++}
```

Meanwhile, we'll keep the loop running as long as $a is less than (-lt) 10:

```
($a -lt 10)
```

Here's the complete example:

```
$a = 1
do {$a; $a++} while ($a -lt 10)
```

And here's what you'll get back if you execute those two lines of code:

```
1
2
3
4
5
6
7
8
9
```

The *Do ... Until* loop is constructed the same way, except that we use the *Until* keyword instead of the *While* keyword. In this example, the loop is designed to run until $a is equal to (-eq) 10:

```
$a = 1
do {$a; $a++} until ($a -eq 10)
```

And here's what you'll get back if you execute these two lines of code:

```
1
2
3
4
5
6
7
8
9
```

VBScript Statement	Windows PowerShell Equivalent
Erase	*Definition:* Reinitializes the elements of fixed-size arrays and deallocates dynamic-array storage space.
	The *Erase* statement is similar to a check for a million dollars: Although we have no doubt that these items exist, the Scripting Guys have little experience with either one. Suppose you have an array with 9 items. When you run the *Erase* statement against that array, you'll still have an array with 9 items; however, none of those items will have a value (string values will now be empty, whereas numeric values will be set to 0).
	Got that? Like we said, we run across the *Erase* statement about as often as we run across a million dollars. However, if you need to set all the values in an array to 0, well, here's a command that can do that for you:
	`for ($i = 0; $i -lt $a.length; $i++) {$a[$i] = 0}`
	Let's assume that *$a* started off life as an array with the following values:
	1 2 3 4 5 6
	Here's what *$a* looks like after running the preceding command:
	0 0 0 0 0 0
Execute	*Definition:* Executes one or more specified statements.
	The VBScript *Execute* statement enables you to assign an expression (typically lines of VBScript code) to a variable; you can then "execute" that variable as though it were code hard-coded into the script itself (as opposed to code existing only in memory).
	Don't worry about it; we'll just show you what we mean. In the following example, the string value "get-date" is assigned to the variable *$a*. The *Invoke-Expression* cmdlet is then used to execute *$a* as though the value had been typed from the command prompt:
	`$a = "get-date"` `invoke-expression $a`
	When you run these two commands, you'll get back the current date and time (because the string value "get-date" will be executed as a command).

VBScript Statement	Windows PowerShell Equivalent
ExecuteGlobal	*Definition:* Executes one or more specified statements in the global namespace of a script.
	Is there a difference between Execute and ExecuteGlobal? Yes, but we decided it wasn't all that important, at least not for now. In turn, that meant we could simply use the same example for both statements. In the following example, the string value "get-date" is assigned to the variable *$a*. The *Invoke-Expression* cmdlet is then used to execute *$a* as though the value had been typed from the command prompt:

	<pre>$a = "get-date"
	invoke-expression $a</pre>

	When you run these two commands, you'll get back the current date and time (because the string value "get-date" will be executed as a command).
Exit	*Definition:* Exits a block of *Do ... Loop, For ... Next, Function,* or *Sub* code.
	In Windows PowerShell, you can "prematurely" break out of a loop by using the break command; this is equivalent to using the *Exit Do* or *Exit For* statement in VBScript. For example, the following Windows PowerShell script creates an array (*$a*) containing 9 values. The script then uses a *For ... Each* loop to enumerate all the items in that array; however, if any of those items is equal to 3—if ($i -eq 3)—then the break command is used to exit the loop right then and there. The script itself looks like this:

	<pre>$a = 1,2,3,4,5,6,7,8,9
	foreach ($i in $a)
	{
	    if ($i -eq 3)
	    {
	        break
	    }
	    else
	    {
	        $i
	    }
	}</pre>

	And here's what you get back when you run the script:

	<pre>1
	2</pre>

VBScript Statement	Windows PowerShell Equivalent
For Each ... Next	*Definition:* Repeats a group of statements for each element in an array or collection.

A *For ... Each* loop is designed to automatically run through all the items in a collection or array. In Windows PowerShell, you can iterate all the items in a collection by using the ForEach-Object collection (or its more commonly used alias, *foreach*). To set up a *For ... Each* loop in Windows PowerShell, call *foreach* followed by two parameters:

- The collection you want to iterate. This value must be enclosed in parentheses.

- The action you want to perform on each item in that collection. This value must be enclosed in curly braces: {}.

For example, the following command sets up a *For ... Each* loop that uses the *Get-ChildItem* cmdlet to return a collection of all the files found in the folder C:\Scripts. Note the syntax that must be used: ($i in get-childitem c:\scripts). Obviously, this is different from what you are used to. After all, in VBScript, you "kick off" a *For ... Each* loop using code similar to this:

```
For Each i in colItems
```

However, in Windows PowerShell, you call *foreach* and then kick things off using code like this:

```
($i in $colItems)
```

After specifying the loop condition, the command then indicates the behavior to be performed:

```
{$i.extension}
```

This simply says, "For each item ($i) in the collection, echo back the value of the Extension property."

Here's the actual command:

```
foreach ($i in get-childitem c:\scripts) {$i.extension}
```

You should get back something similar to this, depending on the files found in C:\Scripts:

```
.gif
.xls
.xls
.txt
.txt
.xls
.ps1
.ps1
.zip
.vbs
.txt
.ppt
```

VBScript Statement	Windows PowerShell Equivalent
For ... Next	*Definition:* Repeats a group of statements a specified number of times.

For ... Next   A *For ... Each* loop is designed to run a block of code against each and every item in a collection; by contrast, a *For ... Next* loop is typically designed to run a specific number of times. For example, to run a code block 10 times, you might set up a loop that begins with a counter-variable set to 1. Each time through the loop, the counter-variable is incremented by 1, and the loop ends only after that counter-variable is equal to 10.

In other words, something similar to this:

```
for ($a = 1; $a -le 10; $a++) {$a}
```

In this command, we use the *For* keyword followed by two items: The loop condition (enclosed in parentheses) and the code we want to execute each time we run through the loop (enclosed in curly braces). The loop condition requires three values:

- The starting value. We want our loop to run from 1 to 10, so we set a counter-variable named *$a* equal to 1.

- The ending value. We want the loop to run 10 times, so we specify that the loop should continue as long as *$a* is less than or equal to 10. If and when the value of *$a* becomes greater than 10, the loop automatically ends.

- The "incrementer." Each time through the loop we want the value of *$a* to increase by 1; therefore, we use the ++ operator. Suppose we wanted to increment *$a* by 2 each time through the loop (equivalent to Step 2 in a VBScript loop). In that case, we would use this syntax: $a+=2, which adds 2 to the current value of *$a*.

As to the code we want to run each time through the loop, well, here we're keeping it pretty simple; we're just echoing back the current value of *$a*:

```
{$a}
```

Here's what we'll get back when we execute this command:

```
1
2
3
4
5
6
7
8
9
10
```

VBScript Statement	Windows PowerShell Equivalent
Function	*Definition:* Declares the name, arguments, and code that form the body of a Function procedure.

You can define a function in Windows PowerShell by using the *function* statement followed by:

- The name of the function

- The task to be performed by the function (enclosed in curly braces)

For example, the following command defines a function named *MultiplyNumbers*. This function will take two arguments ($args[0] and $args[1]) and multiply those two values. Here's the command itself:

```
function multiplynumbers { $args[0] * $args[1] }
```

After a function has been defined, you can call that function simply by specifying its name and (in this case) the two values you want multiplied:

```
multiplynumbers 38 99
```

When you run the preceding command, you should get back the following:

```
3762
```

VBScript Statement	Windows PowerShell Equivalent
If … Then … Else	*Definition:* Conditionally executes a group of statements, depending on the value of an expression.

If you know how to use *If … Then* statements in VBScript, then you have a nice head start using *If … Then* statements in Windows PowerShell. After all, the underlying philosophy is exactly the same; all you have to do is learn the Windows PowerShell syntax.

With that in mind, let's take a look at a simple *If … Then* statement in Windows PowerShell. Before we go much further, we should note that we could have typed the entire statement on a single line. We *could* have, but we didn't, mainly because we wanted to keep things as simple and easy-to-follow as possible.

But we could have.

Here's our example that, after assigning the value 5 to the variable $a, uses an *If … Then* statement to determine whether or not $a is less then 10, and then echoes back the appropriate message:

```
$a = 5
if ($a -gt 10)
    {"The value is greater than 10."}
else
    {"The value is less than 10."}
```

Right off the bat, you should notice two things. First, although we refer to this as an *If … Then* statement, we never actually use the word *Then*. Instead, all we need is the keyword *If* followed by the condition we are checking for, enclosed in parentheses:

```
if ($a -gt 10)
```

The second thing to notice? There's no *Endif* keyword (or its equivalent). In Windows PowerShell, you typically don't need to using "ending" statement like *Endif, Loop, Next,* etc.

Immediately following the condition, we have the action we want to take if the condition is true, that is, if $a really *is* greater than 10. These actions must be enclosed in curly braces, like so:

```
{"The value is greater than 10."}
```

So far, what we've looked at is equivalent to the following VBScript code:

```
If a > 10 Then    Wscript.Echo "The value is greater than 10."
```

All we have to do now is add the *Else* statement. We do that simply by typing in the keyword *Else* followed by the action to be taken should the condition *not* be true. In other words:

```
else
    {"The value is less than 10."}
```

And, yes, we could include an *Elseif* (or two or three or …) in here as well. In fact, here's a revised *If … Then* statement that includes an *Elseif*. If the value of $a is red, a message to that effect will be echoed to the screen; if the value of $a is white—elseif ($a -eq "white")—a message to *that* effect is echoed to the screen. (Note that the Elseif condition must be enclosed in parentheses, and the Elseif action must be enclosed in curly braces.) Otherwise (else) a message saying that the color is blue is echoed back to the screen.

Here's what our new example looks like:

```
$a = "white"
if ($a -eq "red")
    {"The color is red."}
elseif ($a -eq "white")
    {"The color is white."}
else
    {"The color is blue."}
```

VBScript Statement	Windows PowerShell Equivalent
On Error	*Definition:* Enables or disables error handling.

By default, Windows PowerShell issues an error message the moment an error occurs. If you prefer that processing continue without displaying an error message, then set the value of the Windows PowerShell automatic variable *$ErrorAction-Preference* to SilentlyContinue. You know, like this:

```
$erroractionpreference = "SilentlyContinue"
```

Incidentally, your choices for this variable include:

- SilentlyContinue
- Continue (the default value)
- Inquire
- Stop

To illustrate the differences between these error-handling states, suppose we have the following script, a script that features a syntax error on the very first line:

```
bob
$a = 2
$b = 2
$c = 2 + 2
$c
```

If you run this script and error handling is set to Continue, you'll get back the following:

```
The term 'bob' is not recognized as a Cmdlet, function,
operable program, or script file. Verify the term and try again

At C:\scripts\test.ps1:1 char:4
+ bob <<<<
4
```

As you can see, the script ended up running, and the value 4 is echoed back to the screen, but only after a detailed error message has been displayed.

By contrast, here's what you get when error handling has been set to SilentlyContinue:

```
4
```

The script continued to process, and no error was reported.

If error handling is set to Inquire, Windows PowerShell will suspend operations and ask you how you wish to proceed:

```
Action to take for this exception:
The term 'bob' is not recognized as a Cmdlet, function,
operable program, or script file. Verify the term and try again.
[C] Continue  [I] Silent Continue  [B] Break  [S] Suspend  [?] Help
(default is "C"):
```

Finally, here's what happens if error,handling is set to Stop:

```
The term 'bob' is not recognized as a Cmdlet, function,
operable program, or script file. Verify the term and try again
.
At C:\scripts\test.ps1:1 char:4
+ bob <<<<
```

In this case, the error message is displayed, and the script terminates; the value 4 is not displayed because once the error occurred, no additional lines of code were executed.

VBScript Statement	Windows PowerShell Equivalent
Option Explicit	*Definition:* Forces explicit declaration of all variables in a script.
	In VBScript, the *Option Explicit* statement forces you to declare all variables before using them in a script. To do the same thing in Windows PowerShell, use the *Set-PSDebug* cmdlet and the -strict parameter, like so:
	`set-psdebug -strict`
	What will that do for you? Well, suppose you now try to execute a command similar to this, using the uninitialized variable *$z*:
	`$a = 2 + $z`
	You will not get an answer; instead, you will get the following error message:
	`The variable $z cannot be retrieved because it has not been set yet.`
	To turn off this behavior, use this command:
	`set-psdebug -off`
Private	*Definition:* Declares private variables and allocates storage space. Declares, in a Class block, a private variable.
	The *Private* statement in VBScript is concerned with classes; we're going to take the liberty of extending the definition of Private here, primarily because we aren't going to talk about classes. Instead of discussing private variables in terms of classes, we are going to discuss private variables in terms of scope.
	In Windows PowerShell, all you have to do is set the scope to Private. For example, this command creates a variable named *$a* with the scope set to private. Note that, when specifying a scope, you do not preface the variable name with a $; however, in your commands, you will still refer to this variable as *$a*.
	Here's the command:
	`$Private:a = 5`
	Because this is a private variable, it will be available only in the scope in which it was created. If you type $a from the command prompt, you'll get back the value of *$a*. However, if you run a script that simply echoes back the value of *$a*, you won't get back anything; that's because, as a private variable, *$a* is not available outside the command shell scope.
Property Get	*Definition:* Declares, in a Class block, the name, arguments, and code that form the body of a Property procedure that gets (returns) the value of a property.
	The VBScript *Get* statement is used when working with VBScript classes. Custom classes are theoretically possible in Windows PowerShell, but lie far beyond the scope of this introductory document. Therefore, we'll take the easy way out and simply say that there is no Windows PowerShell equivalent to the *Get* statement.
Property Let	*Definition:* Declares, in a Class block, the name, arguments, and code that form the body of a Property procedure that assigns (sets) the value of a property.
	The VBScript *Let* statement is used when working with VBScript classes. Custom classes are theoretically possible in Windows PowerShell, but lie far beyond the scope of this introductory document. Therefore, we'll take the easy way out and simply say that there is no Windows PowerShell equivalent to the *Let* statement.

VBScript Statement	Windows PowerShell Equivalent
Property Set	*Definition:* Declares, in a Class block, the name, arguments, and code that form the body of a Property procedure that sets a reference to an object.
	The VBScript *Set* statement is used when working with VBScript classes. Custom classes are theoretically possible in Windows PowerShell, but lie far beyond the scope of this introductory document. Therefore, we'll take the easy way out and simply say that there is no Windows PowerShell equivalent to the *Set* statement.
Public	*Definition:* Declares public variables and allocates storage space. Declares, in a Class block, a private variable.
	Windows PowerShell enables you to create a global (public) variable simply by specifying the scope when you create the variable. For example, this command creates a variable named *$a* with the scope set to Global. Note that, when specifying a scope, you do not preface the variable name with a $; however, the variable will, in fact, be named *$a*.
	`$Global:a = 199`
	Here's an interesting use for global variables. Start up Windows PowerShell, but do *not* declare the variable *$a*. Instead, put the preceding line of code in a script (e.g., test.ps1), run the script, and *then* type **$a** from the command prompt. You should get back the following:
	`199`
	Because this is a global variable, it's available in scripts, in the command shell, and in any other scope. Cool, huh?
	Note: Admittedly, this isn't quite the same as what the *Public* statement does in VBScript; that's because the VBScript statement is concerned with classes, and we aren't discussing Windows PowerShell classes in this introductory series. Therefore, we've extended the definition of public to include Windows PowerShell scopes. That gives us a chance to talk about the Windows PowerShell global variables, which we find very cool.
Randomize	*Definition:* Initializes the random-number generator.
	The *Randomize* statement (or its equivalent) is not required in Windows PowerShell. Instead, you can generate a random number using code similar to this:
	`$a = new-object random` `$b = $a.next()`
	When you run this command and then echo back the value of *$b*, you should get back something similar to the following:
	`1558696419`

VBScript Statement	Windows PowerShell Equivalent
ReDim	*Definition:* Declares dynamic-array variables, and allocates or reallocates storage space at procedure level.

ReDim

Definition: Declares dynamic-array variables, and allocates or reallocates storage space at procedure level.

In general, there's no need for a *ReDim* statement in Windows PowerShell; arrays can be resized without having to explicitly call ReDim (and without having to explicitly preserve the existing contents of the array). For example, suppose the following 5 items are assigned to the array *$a*:

```
$a = 1,2,3,4,5
```

Want to add a new value—100—to the array? This is all you have to do:

```
$a = $a + 100
```

If you echo back the value of *$a*, you'll get the following:

```
1
2
3
4
5
100
```

Likewise, you can truncate an array without explicitly redimensioning anything. Suppose you want only the first three values in *$a*. This code assigns just those first three values (using the syntax 0..2, which means start with item 0 in the array, end with item 2, and take all the values in between) and assigns them to *$a*:

```
$a = $a[0..2]
```

What do you get back when you execute this command? This is what you get back:

```
1
2
3
```

Rem

Definition: Includes explanatory remarks in a program.

To add a comment to a Windows PowerShell script (or a Windows PowerShell command, for that matter), simply preface that comment with the pound sign (#); anything following the pound sign will be treated as a comment and ignored by the script processor. For example, this command calls the *Get-Date* cmdlet and then tacks on a comment explaining what the cmdlet does:

```
get-date # This Cmdlet retrieves the current date and time
```

When you execute this command, you'll simply get back the current date and time; the comment will be ignored. That's also true with this command:

```
get-date # get-help
```

The *Get-Date* cmdlet will be executed; the *Get-Help* cmdlet will not. That's because, in this example, Get-Help is a comment, not a command.

VBScript Statement	Windows PowerShell Equivalent
Select Case	*Definition:* Executes one of several groups of statements, depending on the value of an expression.

In VBScript, you can test for multiple possibilities by using a long and sometimes complicated series of *If ... Then ... ElseIf* statements. Alternatively, you can achieve the same effect—with far less typing—by using a *Select Case* statement.

In Windows PowerShell, you can emulate (and, in some ways, improve upon) the *Select Case* statement by using the *Switch* statement. To explain how the *Switch* statement works, let's take a look at some sample code:

```
$a = 5
switch ($a)
    {
        1 {"The color is red."}
        2 {"The color is blue."}
        3 {"The color is green."}
        4 {"The color is yellow."}
        5 {"The color is orange."}
        6 {"The color is purple."}
        7 {"The color is pink."}
        8 {"The color is brown."}
        default {"The color could not be determined."}
    }
```

In the preceding code, we assign the value 5 to the variable *$a*. We then create a Switch block that assesses the value of *$a* and takes the appropriate action based on that value:

```
switch ($a)
```

As you can see, all we have to do is insert the *Switch* keyword followed by the value to be tested (which must be enclosed in parentheses).

Next, we list the possible values for *$a* along with the corresponding action (this entire block, incidentally, must be enclosed in curly braces). For example, if *$a* is equal to 1, we want to echo back a message saying that the color is red. Therefore, we use this line of code, with the action to be taken enclosed in curly braces:

```
1 {"The color is red."}
```

See how that works? (It's actually pretty easy.) We can also specify an action to be taken if none of the preceding *Case* statements are true (the same thing you do with *Case Else* in VBScript). To do that, we simply use the default condition followed by the desired action:

```
default {"The color could not be determined."}
```

VBScript Statement	Windows PowerShell Equivalent

Set	*Definition:* Assigns an object reference to a variable or property, or associates a procedure reference with an event.
	
	You do not need to use the *Set* statement (or any sort of equivalent keyword/command) in order to create an object reference in Windows PowerShell. Instead, you simply use the *New-Object* cmdlet, followed by (in the case of COM objects) the -comobject parameter and the ProgID of the object to be created.
	
	For example, the following two commands create an instance of Microsoft Excel and then, just to prove that the instance of Excel *was* created, make the application visible onscreen:
	
	`$a = new-object -comobject Excel.Application`
	`$a.visible = $True`

Stop	*Definition:* Suspends execution.
	
	If you have the Microsoft Scripting Debugger installed, you can insert *Stop* statements that temporarily suspend the script each and every time they are encountered. Windows PowerShell does not have a similar feature (in part because it does not have a script debugger). However, you *can* run Windows PowerShell in step-by-step mode, which is roughly akin to putting a *Stop* statement after each and every line of code. That can be done by using the *Set-PSDebug* cmdlet and using the -step parameter:
	
	`set-psdebug -step`
	
	To exit the step-by-step mode, simply use this command:
	
	`set-psdebug -off`

Sub	*Definition:* Declares the name, arguments, and code that form the body of a Sub procedure.
	
	Windows PowerShell supports only functions, as opposed to functions and subroutines. You can define a function in Windows PowerShell by using the *function* statement followed by:
	
	■ The name of the function
	
	■ The task to be performed by the function (enclosed in curly braces)
	
	For example, the following command defines a function named *MultiplyNumbers*. This function will take two arguments ($args[0] and $args[1]) and then multiply those two values. Here's the command:
	
	`function multiplynumbers { $args[0] * $args[1] }`
	
	From then on, you can call the function simply by specifying the function name and the two values you want multiplied:
	
	`multiplynumbers 38 99`
	
	When you run the preceding command, you should get back the following:
	
	`3762`

VBScript Statement	Windows PowerShell Equivalent
While ... Wend	*Definition:* Executes a series of statements as long as a given condition is True.

The VBScript *While ... Wend* loop is just another way of creating a *Do ... While* loop. (You can never have too many ways to create loops, at least not in VBScript.) You can create a *While* loop in Windows PowerShell by using the *-surprise -while* statement. *While* takes two parameters:

■ The loop conditions (in other words, how long do you intend to keep looping)

■ The action to be performed in each iteration of the loop

In the following example, the value 1 is assigned to the variable *$a*. A *While* loop is then established that does two things:

■ Continues to loop as long as the value of *$a* is less than (-lt) 10

■ On each iteration of the loop, displays the current value of *$a*, and then increments that value by 1. In Windows PowerShell, the ++ operator increments a value by 1; the syntax $a++ is equivalent to VBScript's a = a + 1.

Here's the sample code:

```
$a = 1
while ($a -lt 10) {$a; $a++}
```

And here's what you should get back after running the preceding commands:

```
1
2
3
4
5
6
7
8
9
```

With	*Definition:* Executes a series of statements on a single object.

As far as we know, there is no Windows PowerShell equivalent to the *With* statement.

VBScript Err Object	Windows PowerShell Equivalent
Description Property	*Definition:* Returns or sets a descriptive string associated with an error.
	So what *was* the last error that occurred? If you need to know that, just get the value of error number 0 and then call the ToString() method. The following command retrieves information from the most recent error and uses the ToString() method to assign the value to the variable *$a*:
	`$a = $error[0].ToString()`
	When you run this command and then echo back the value of *$a*, you should get back something similar to the following:

	`The term 'error[0]' is not recognized as a Cmdlet, function,`
	`operable program, or script file. Verify the term and try`
	`again.`

HelpContext Property	*Definition:* Sets or returns a context ID for a topic in a Help file.
	If an error is associated with a topic in a Help file, you can retrieve that information using the HelpLink property. This command assigns the HelpLink property for the most recent error in the error collection to the variable *$a*:
	`$a = $error[0].helplink`
HelpFile Property	*Definition:* Sets or returns a fully qualified path to a Help file.
	If an error is associated with a topic in a Help file, you can retrieve that information using the HelpLink property; the first part of the link will be the fully qualified path to the Help file itself. This command assigns the HelpLink property for the most recent error in the error collection to the variable *$a*:
	`$a = $error[0].helplink`
Number Property	*Definition:* Returns or sets a numeric value specifying an error. Number is the Err object's default property.
	We're just guessing here, but we assume that the ErrorRecord property is designed to return the error number. However, we've never actually encountered a numbered error in Windows PowerShell; in our experience, ErrorRecord usually returns a string value such as this:
	`ScriptHalted`
	Still, you can always give this command a try and see what happens:
	`$error[0].errorrecord`
Source Property	*Definition:* Returns or sets the name of the object or application that originally generated the error.
	To determine which object or component was responsible for an error, you can check the value of the Source property. This command assigns the Source property for the most recent error in the error collection to the variable *$a*:
	`$a = $error[0].source`
	When you run this command and then echo back the value of *$a*, you should get back something similar to the following:
	`System.Management.Automation`

VBScript Err Object	Windows PowerShell Equivalent
Clear Method	*Definition:* Clears all property settings of the Err object.
	The VBScript Err object keeps track of only the last error that occurred; in contrast, and by default, Windows PowerShell keeps track of the last 256 errors that occurred. Among other things, that changes the definition of "clearing" an error in Windows PowerShell. If you want to mimic VBScript, you can clear the last error—and only the last error—by setting the last error to an empty string (the zero in square brackets represents the last error in the collection):
	`$error[0] = ""`
	Alternatively, you can clear out the entire error collection by using the Clear() method:
	`$error.clear()`
Raise Method	*Definition:* Generates a run-time error.
	When testing scripts, script writers need to ensure that their scripts can respond appropriately to specific errors. One way to do that is to simulate those errors programmatically. In VBScript, this can be done using the *Raise* function; in Windows PowerShell, this same thing can be done using the Throw method. In the following command, an error message is assigned to the variable *$b*; the Throw method is then used to "throw" the error associated with *$b*:
	`$b = "The file could not be found."; throw $b`
	If you now check the value of the most recent error (i.e., $error[0]) you'll get back the following:
	`The file could not be found.`

VBScript Operator	Windows PowerShell Equivalent
Addition operator (+)	*Definition:* Sums two numbers.
	Here's a shocker: In Windows PowerShell, you add two numbers by using the plus sign. In other words:
	`$a = 2 + 2`
	We'll let you figure out for yourself what the value of *$a* will be equal to.
And operator (AND)	*Definition:* Performs a logical conjunction on two expressions.
	The AND operator evaluates two arguments and returns True only if both arguments are actually true. For example, suppose we want to evaluate the following two statements, then store the verdict in the variable *$a*:
	■ 23 is greater than 12
	■ 12 is greater than 40
	Here's the command we'd use:
	`$a = 23 -gt 12 -and 12 -gt 40`
	As you might expect, if you run the command and then echo back the value of *$a*, you'll get the following:
	`False`

VBScript Operator	Windows PowerShell Equivalent
Assignment operator (=)	*Definition:* Assigns a value to a variable or property.
	Assigning a value to a variable is no big deal in Windows PowerShell: You put the variable on the left side of the equation, the value to be assigned on the right side, and an equals sign (=) smack dab in the middle. For example, this command assigns the string value *test* to the variable *$a*:
	`$a = "test"`
	And this command assigns the sum of the numbers 1, 2, and 3 to *$a*:
	`$a = 1 + 2 + 3`
Concatenation operator (&)	*Definition:* Forces string concatenation of two expressions.
	In VBScript, you can join two or more strings by using either the plus sign (+) or the ampersand (&).
	Note: Or, if you want to sound fancy: In VBScript you can *concatenate* two or more strings by using either the plus sign (+) or the ampersand (&).
	In Windows PowerShell, you can concatenate two or more strings by using the plus sign (don't even bother trying to use the ampersand). For example, this command combines the word *test*, a blank space, and the word *value* and stores the resulting string in a variable named *$a*:
	`$a = "test" + " " + "value"`
	When you run this command and then echo back the value of *$a*, you should get the following:
	`test value`
Division operator (/)	*Definition:* Divides two numbers and returns a floating-point result.
	Divide and conquer. We can't make any promises regarding the conquer part of that statement, but in Windows PowerShell, you can divide a pair of numbers by using backslash (/) as the division operator. For example, this commands divides 761 by 11 and stores the value in the variable *$a*:
	`$a = 761 / 11`
	When you run this command and then echo back the value of *$a*, you should get the following:
	`69.1818181818182`
Eqv operator (Eqv)	*Definition:* Performs a logical equivalence on two expressions.
	No doubt Eqv has its uses; we're just not sure if it has any *practical* uses. Although there might be a Windows PowerShell equivalent, we have to be honest: We didn't look real hard for one.

VBScript Operator	Windows PowerShell Equivalent
Exponentiation operator (^)	*Definition:* Raises a number to the power of an exponent.
	Interestingly enough, Windows PowerShell doesn't have a built-in exponentiation operator. So does that mean you're out of luck if you need to raise 8 to the third power? Of course not; all you need to do is use the System.Math class and the Pow method:
	`$a = [math]::pow(8,3)`
	When you run this command and then echo back the value of *$a*, you should get the following:
	512
Imp operator (Imp)	*Definition:* Performs a logical implication on two expressions.
	What do we know about the Imp operator? Two things: (1) It's not supported in Visual Basic .NET, and (2) We have never heard of anyone actually using it. Therefore, we're going to say that it doesn't really matter whether or not there's a Windows PowerShell equivalent.
Integer division operator (\)	*Definition:* Divides two numbers and returns an integer result.
	In VBScript, the integer division operator returns only the integer portion of an answer, stripping off decimal points without rounding the number either up or down. For example, 100 / 26 is equal to 3.84615384615385; however, 100 \ 26 is equal to 3 (just the integer portion of the answer).
	Note: OK, so that's not 100% true; that's only true for whole numbers. Given a fractional value, that value will be rounded up or down before division takes place. But that's all right; we've accounted for that by converting the values in the equation to integers before we divide them.
	You can perform integer division in Windows PowerShell by using the .NET Framework class System.Math and the Floor method. The following command divides 100 by 26 and then stores the integer portion of the answer in the variable *$a*:
	`$a = [math]::floor([int] 100 / [int] 26)`
	When you run this command and then echo back the value of *$a*, you should get the following:
	3

VBScript Operator	Windows PowerShell Equivalent

Is operator (IS)	*Definition:* Compares two object reference variables.
	
	In VBScript, the IS operator is used to determine whether two object references refer to the same object. This differs from Windows PowerShell, in which the IS operator is used to determine whether a variable has a specified data type. (In other words, it all depends on what the definition of "is" is.) That doesn't mean that you can't compare objects in Windows PowerShell; you can. It just means that you need to use the *Compare-Object* cmdlet to carry out this task. In the following example, we create two instances of the Scripting.Dictionary object. We then use *Compare-Object* to compare the two object references, tacking on the -includeequal parameter to ensure that we'll get back an answer even if the two objects *are* identical:
	
	`$a = new-object -comobject scripting.dictionary`
	`$b = new-object -comobject scripting.dictionary`
	`$c = compare-object $a $b –includeequal`
	
	When you run this command and then echo back the value of $c, you should get the following:
	
	`InputObject                                    SideIndicator`
	`-----------                                    -------------`
	`{}                                                  ==`
	
	The == SideIndicator means that the two objects are equal.
	
	Here's a modified example in which the two objects are *not* equal: One references the Scripting.Dictionary object, whereas the other references the Scripting.File-System object. Here are the commands:
	
	`$a = new-object -comobject scripting.dictionary`
	`$b = new-object -comobject scripting.filesystemobject`
	`$c = compare-object $a $b –includeequal`
	
	And here's what we get back when we run these commands and then echo the value of $c:
	
	`InputObject                                    SideIndicator`
	`-----------                                    -------------`
	`System.__ComObject                                  =>`
	`{}                                                  <=`
	
	Although it is somewhat meaningless when working with COM objects, the => and <= symbols indicate which of the two objects contain a given item (such as an individual line in a text file).

Mod operator (Mod)	*Definition:* Divides two numbers and returns only the remainder. The Mod operator is a bit of an odd duck (although it *does* have its uses): It divides two numbers and then returns the remainder. In Windows PowerShell, you can achieve the same effect by using the % operator. For example, this command divides 28 by 5, then stores the remainder in the variable *$a*: `$a = 28 % 5` When you run this command and then echo back the value of *$a*, you should get the following:

3

VBScript Operator	Windows PowerShell Equivalent
Multiplication operator (*)	*Definition:* Multiplies two numbers.
	If you need to multiply two numbers in Windows PowerShell, you can do what pretty much everyone who needs to multiply two numbers does: Just use the asterisk (*) as the multiplication symbol. For example, this command multiplies 45 by 334 and stores the result in the variable *$a*:
	`$a = 45 * 334`
	For those few of you who didn't bother to do this equation in your head, *$a* should be equal to this:
	`15030`
Not operator (NOT)	*Definition:* Performs logical negation on an expression.
	Before you go any further, remember, the Scripting Guys don't make up these operators; we just report back what they do. The NOT operator is designed to test whether an expression is false. If an expression *is* false, then the NOT operator reports back True. If an expression is true, then the NOT operator reports back False.
	Like we said, we don't make these things up, although, now that we think about it, this one *does* sound like something the Scripting Guys would come up with, doesn't it?
	For example, this command uses the NOT operator to evaluate the following expression 10 * 7.7. = 77:
	`$a = -not (10 * 7.7 -eq 77)`
	Because this expression is true, if you run this command and echo back the value of *$a*, you'll get the following:
	`False`
Or operator (OR)	*Definition:* Performs a logical disjunction on two expressions.
	The OR operator evaluates two expressions and returns True if either of the expressions are true; you will get back the value False only if both parts are False. For example, suppose we want to evaluate the following two statements, then store the verdict in the variable *$a*:
	■ 23 is less than 12
	■ 12 is greater than 40
	Here's the command we'd use:
	`$a = 23 -lt 12 -or 12 -gt 40`
	As you might expect, if you run the command and then echo back the value of *$a*, you'll get the following, seeing as how both expressions are False:
	`False`

VBScript Operator	Windows PowerShell Equivalent
Subtraction operator (-)	*Definition:* Finds the difference between two numbers or indicates the negative value of a numeric expression. Actually, no, we *don't* know what 22,018 minus 1,915 is. But Windows PowerShell can determine that difference for us; just use the minus sign (–) as the subtraction operator. `$a = 22018 - 1915` Well, what do you know? We were right: The answer is *20,103.*

Xor operator (XOR)	*Definition:* Performs a logical exclusion on two expressions.
	
	The XOR operator is a crazy one. XOR evaluates two expressions and returns True if the two are different; that is, if one expression is True and the other expression is False. If both expression are true (or false), then XOR returns False.
	
	We told you it was crazy.
	
	Here's an example. This command evaluates the following two statements, then stores its verdict in the variable *$a*:
	
	■ 23 is less than 12
	■ 12 is greater than 40
	
	Here's the command
	
	`$a = 23 -gt 12 -xor 12 -lt 40`
	
	Because both expressions are true, if you run the command and then echo back the value of *$a*, you'll get the following:
	
	`False`

Index

Note: Page references in italics refer to figures; those followed by *t* refer to tables.

About the Author

Ed Wilson is a senior consultant at Microsoft Corporation and a scripting expert. He is a Microsoft Certified Trainer who delivers immensely popular workshops world-wide on VBScript, WMI, and Windows Power-Shell. He's written more than a dozen books, including four on scripting, such as *Microsoft VBScript Step by Step* (Microsoft Press, 2006), and *Microsoft Windows Scripting with WMI: Self-Paced Learning Guide* (Microsoft Press, 2005). Ed holds more than 20 industry certifications, including the MCSE and CISSP.

Windows Vista™ Resources for Administrators

Windows Vista Administrator's Pocket Consultant
William Stanek
ISBN 9780735622968

Portable and precise, this pocket-sized guide delivers immediate answers for the day-to-day administration of Windows Vista. Featuring easy-to-scan tables, step-by-step instructions, and handy lists, this book offers the straightforward information you need to solve problems and get the job done—whether you're at your desk or in the field!

Windows Vista Resource Kit
Mitch Tulloch, Tony Northrup, Jerry Honeycutt, Ed Wilson, Ralph Ramos, and the Windows Vista Team
ISBN 9780735622838

Get the definitive reference for deploying, configuring, and supporting Windows Vista—from the experts who know the technology best. This guide offers in-depth, comprehensive technical guidance on automating deployment; implementing security enhancements; administering group policy, files folders, and programs; and troubleshooting. Includes an essential toolkit of resources on DVD.

MCTS Self-Paced Training Kit (Exam 70-620): Configuring Windows Vista Client
Ian McLean and Orin Thomas
ISBN 9780735623903

Get in-depth preparation plus practice for Exam 70-620, the required exam for the new Microsoft Certified Technology Specialist (MCTS): Windows Vista Client certification. This 2-in-1 kit focuses on installing client software and configuring system settings, security features, network connectivity, media applications, and mobile devices. Ace your exam prep—and build real-world job skills—with lessons, practice tests, evaluation software, and more.

MCITP Self-Paced Training Kit (Exam 70-622): Installing, Maintaining, Supporting, and Troubleshooting Applications on the Windows Vista Client – Enterprise
Tony Northrup and J.C. Mackin
ISBN 9780735624085

Maximize your performance on Exam 70-622, the required exam for the new Microsoft® Certified IT Professional (MCITP): Enterprise Support Technician certification. Comprehensive and in-depth, this 2-in-1 kit covers managing security, configuring networking, and optimizing performance for Windows Vista clients in an enterprise environment. Ace your exam prep— and build real-world job skills—with lessons, practice tests, evaluation software, and more.

MCITP Self-Paced Training Kit (Exam 70-623): Installing, Maintaining, Supporting, and Troubleshooting Applications on the Windows Vista Client – Consumer
Anil Desai with Chris McCain of GrandMasters
ISBN 9780735624238

Get the 2-in-1 training kit for Exam 70-623, the required exam for the new Microsoft Certified IT Professional (MCITP): Consumer Support Technician certification. This comprehensive kit focuses on supporting Windows Vista clients for consumer PCs and devices, including configuring security settings, networking, troubleshooting, and removing malware. Ace your exam prep—and build real-world job skills—with lessons, practice tests, evaluation software, and more.

See more resources at **microsoft.com/mspress**
and **microsoft.com/learning**

Microsoft Press® products are available worldwide wherever quality computer books are sold. For more information, contact your bookseller, computer retailer, software reseller, or local Microsoft Sales Office, or visit our Web site at **microsoft.com/mspress**. To locate a source near you, or to order directly, call 1-800-MSPRESS in the United States. (In Canada, call **1-800-268-2222**.)

2007 Microsoft® Office System Resources for Developers and Administrators

Microsoft Office SharePoint® Server 2007 Administrator's Companion

Bill English with the Microsoft SharePoint Community Experts
ISBN 9780735622821

Get your mission-critical collaboration and information management systems up and running. This comprehensive, single-volume reference details features and capabilities of SharePoint Server 2007. It delivers easy-to-follow procedures, practical workarounds, and key troubleshooting tactics—for on-the-job results.

Microsoft Windows SharePoint Services Version 3.0 Inside Out

Jim Buyens
ISBN 9780735623231

Conquer Microsoft Windows SharePoint Services—from the inside out! This ultimate, in-depth reference packs hundreds of time-saving solutions, troubleshooting tips, and workarounds. You're beyond the basics, so now learn how the experts tackle information sharing and team collaboration—and challenge yourself to new levels of mastery!

Microsoft SharePoint Products and Technologies Administrator's Pocket Consultant

Ben Curry
ISBN 9780735623828

Portable and precise, this pocket-sized guide delivers immediate answers for the day-to-day administration of Sharepoint Products and Technologies. Featuring easy-to-scan tables, step-by-step instructions, and handy lists, this book offers the straightforward information you need to get the job done—whether you're at your desk or in the field!

Inside Microsoft Windows® SharePoint Services Version 3

Ted Pattison and Daniel Larson
ISBN 9780735623200

Get in-depth insights on Microsoft Windows SharePoint Services with this hands-on guide. You get a bottom-up view of the platform architecture, code samples, and task-oriented guidance for developing custom applications with Microsoft Visual Studio® 2005 and Collaborative Application Markup Language (CAML).

Inside Microsoft Office SharePoint Server 2007

Patrick Tisseghem
ISBN 9780735623682

Dig deep—and master the intricacies of Office SharePoint Server 2007. A bottom-up view of the platform architecture shows you how to manage and customize key components and how to integrate with Office programs—helping you create custom enterprise content management solutions.

Microsoft Office Communications Server 2007 Resource Kit

Microsoft Office Communications Server Team
ISBN 9780735624061

Your definitive reference to Office Communications Server 2007—direct from the experts who know the technology best. This comprehensive guide offers in-depth technical information and best practices for planning, designing, deploying, managing, and optimizing your systems. Includes a toolkit of valuable resources on CD.

Programming Applications for Microsoft Office Outlook® 2007

Randy Byrne and Ryan Gregg
ISBN 9780735622494

Microsoft Office Visio® 2007 Programming Step by Step

David A. Edson
ISBN 9780735623798

See more resources at **microsoft.com/mspress** *and* **microsoft.com/learning**

Microsoft Press® products are available worldwide wherever quality computer books are sold. For more information, contact your bookseller, computer retailer, software reseller, or local Microsoft Sales Office, or visit our Web site at **microsoft.com/mspress**. To locate a source near you, or to order directly, call 1-800-MSPRESS in the United States. (In Canada, call **1-800-268-2222**.)

Additional SQL Server Resources for Administrators
Published and Forthcoming Titles from Microsoft Press

Microsoft® SQL Server™ 2005 Reporting Services *Step by Step*
Hitachi Consulting Services • ISBN 0-7356-2250-7

SQL Server Reporting Services (SRS) is Microsoft's customizable reporting solution for business data analysis. It is one of the key value features of SQL Server 2005: functionality more advanced and much less expensive than its competition. SRS is powerful, so an understanding of how to architect a report, as well as how to install and program SRS, is key to harnessing the full functionality of SQL Server. This procedural tutorial shows how to use the Report Project Wizard, how to think about and access data, and how to build queries. It also walks the reader through the creation of charts and visual layouts to enable maximum visual understanding of the data analysis. Interactivity (enhanced in SQL Server 2005) and security are also covered in detail.

Microsoft SQL Server 2005 Administrator's Pocket Consultant
William R. Stanek • ISBN 0-7356-2107-1

Here's the utterly practical, pocket-sized reference for IT professionals who need to administer, optimize, and maintain SQL Server 2005 in their organizations. This unique guide provides essential details for using SQL Server 2005 to help protect and manage your company's data—whether automating tasks; creating indexes and views; performing backups and recovery; replicating transactions; tuning performance; managing server activity; importing and exporting data; or performing other key tasks. Featuring quick-reference tables, lists, and step-by-step instructions, this handy, one-stop guide provides fast, accurate answers on the spot, whether you're at your desk or in the field!

Microsoft SQL Server 2005 Administrator's Companion
Marci Frohock Garcia, Edward Whalen, and Mitchell Schroeter • ISBN 0-7356-2198-5

Microsoft SQL Server 2005 Administrator's Companion is the comprehensive, in-depth guide that saves time by providing all the technical information you need to deploy, administer, optimize, and support SQL Server 2005. Using a hands-on, example-rich approach, this authoritative, one-volume reference book provides expert advice, product information, detailed solutions, procedures, and real-world troubleshooting tips from experienced SQL Server 2005 professionals. This expert guide shows you how to design high-availability database systems, prepare for installation, install and configure SQL Server 2005, administer services and features, and maintain and troubleshoot your database system. It covers how to configure your system for your I/O system and model and optimize system capacity. The expert authors provide details on how to create and use defaults, constraints, rules, indexes, views, functions, stored procedures, and triggers. This guide shows you how to administer reporting services, analysis services, notification services, and integration services. It also provides a wealth of information on replication and the specifics of snapshot, transactional, and merge replication. Finally, there is expansive coverage of how to manage and tune your SQL Server system, including automating tasks, backup and restoration of databases, and management of users and security.

Microsoft SQL Server 2005 Analysis Services *Step by Step*
Hitachi Consulting Services • ISBN 0-7356-2199-3

One of the key features of SQL Server 2005 is SQL Server Analysis Services—Microsoft's customizable analysis solution for business data modeling and interpretation. Just compare SQL Server Analysis Services to its competition to understand/grasp the great value of its enhanced features. One of the keys to harnessing the full functionality of SQL Server will be leveraging Analysis Services for the powerful tool that it is—including creating a cube, and deploying, customizing, and extending the basic calculations. This step-by-step tutorial discusses how to get started, how to build scalable analytical applications, and how to use and administer advanced features. Interactivity (which is enhanced in SQL Server 2005), data translation, and security are also covered in detail.

Microsoft SQL Server 2005 Express Edition *Step by Step*
Jackie Goldstein • ISBN 0-7356-2184-5

Inside Microsoft SQL Server 2005: The Storage Engine
Kalen Delaney • ISBN 0-7356-2105-5

Inside Microsoft SQL Server 2005: T-SQL Programming
Itzik Ben-Gan • ISBN 0-7356-2197-7

Inside Microsoft SQL Server 2005: Query Processing and Optimization
Kalen Delaney • ISBN 0-7356-2196-9

For more information about Microsoft Press® books and other learning products,
visit: **www.microsoft.com/mspress** *and* **www.microsoft.com/learning**

Microsoft Press products are available worldwide wherever quality computer books are sold. For more information, contact your book or computer retailer, software reseller, or local Microsoft Sales Office, or visit our Web site at **www.microsoft.com/mspress**. To locate your nearest source for Microsoft Press products, or to order directly, call 1-800-MSPRESS in the United States. (In Canada, call **1-800-268-2222**.)

What do you think of this book?

We want to hear from you!

Do you have a few minutes to participate in a brief online survey?

Microsoft is interested in hearing your feedback so we can continually improve our books and learning resources for you.

To participate in our survey, please visit:

www.microsoft.com/learning/booksurvey/

...and enter this book's ISBN-10 number (appears above barcode on back cover*).
As a thank-you to survey participants in the United States and Canada, each month we'll randomly select five respondents to win one of five $100 gift certificates from a leading online merchant. At the conclusion of the survey, you can enter the drawing by providing your e-mail address, which will be used for prize notification only.

Thanks in advance for your input. Your opinion counts!

*Where to find the ISBN-10 on back cover

Example only. Each book has unique ISBN.

No purchase necessary. Void where prohibited. Open only to residents of the 50 United States (includes District of Columbia) and Canada (void in Quebec). For official rules and entry dates see:

www.microsoft.com/learning/booksurvey/